The Nature of the Common Law

The Nature of the Common Law

Melvin Aron
EISENBERG

Harvard University Press
Cambridge, Massachusetts
London, England
1988

Library of Congress Cataloging in Publication Data

Eisenberg, Melvin Aron.
  The nature of the common law.

  Bibliography: p.
  Includes index.
  1. Common law. 2. Judicial process. 3. Law—
Philosophy. I. Title.
K588.E37 1988   340'.1   87-31886
ISBN 0-674-60480-6 (alk. paper)

To Helen

Preface

Much of our law is based on authoritative texts, such as constitutions and statutes. The common law is that part of the law that is not based on such texts, but instead is within the province of the courts themselves to establish. This book concerns the manner in which common law rules should be and are established. To put it differently, this book frames a theory of common law adjudication.

An important question in framing a theory of adjudication is whether the same set of principles governs the interpretation of constitutions, the interpretation of statutes, and the establishment of common law rules. The position taken in this book is that the answer to this question is no. To paraphrase a comment by a reader of an earlier draft, although statutory and constitutional cases must be worked into any comprehensive analysis of adjudication, in the long run greater understanding will be gained if common law, statutory, and constitutional adjudication are analyzed separately. The principles that govern the role of the courts in each area differ in important respects, and each area is so complex that it requires an examination uncluttered by consideration of the special problems raised by the others. Historically, the first role of the courts in Anglo-American law was deciding common law cases. If we address this role first, what we learn about courts and law will help when we turn to the problems of statutory and constitutional interpretation.

Another issue in framing a theory of adjudication is whether to analyze adjudication as a universal phenomenon abstracted from particular societies, or in terms of the practices of particular legal systems. Again I have chosen the more particularized course: my focus in this book is almost exclusively on the United States. I believe, however, that much of the analysis in this book is directly applicable to the common law in other countries and that, as to the balance, the difference is a matter of degree rather than kind. To the extent that this is not so, the title of the book takes perhaps too much liberty, for which I hope I may be forgiven.

A significant portion of this book formed the basis of the Cooley Lectures, which I gave at the University of Michigan Law School in 1985. I am grateful to the Michigan faculty both for its invitation to give those lectures and for many useful comments offered during my stay; Donald Regan and Philip Soper made comments that were particularly enlightening. I also presented parts of the book at workshops at Columbia, UCLA, and Virginia; at a seminar and various faculty colloquia at Berkeley; and at faculty seminars at the University of Adelaide and Monash University in Australia. I gained much from these workshops, seminars, and colloquia, and thank all those who participated. Parts of the book were also presented at a meeting of the American Philosophical Association, at which I received a number of valuable suggestions from the commentators, Martin Golding and Tom Grey.

Outside these organized forums, Stephen Barnett, Stephen Bundy, Meir Dan-Cohen, Joseph Grodin, Lewis Kornhauser, Paul Mishkin, Robert Mnookin, Andrea Peterson, Joseph Raz, Edward Rubin, Philip Selznick, Gary Simson, Stephen Sugarman, Joseph Tussman, Jeremy Waldron, Harry Wellington, Kenneth Winston, and Jan Vetter read portions—in many cases, very large portions—of the manuscript and made extremely useful suggestions. Leah Hammett, Marina Hsieh, Harry Litman, Megan Wagner, and Margaret Meriwether did valuable work as research assistants. Marina Hsieh also reviewed the text and footnotes with an outstanding law-review editor's eye. My secretary, Vickie Parker, executed numerous revisions of hard-to-decipher drafts with her usual accuracy, incredible speed, and composure, tactfully corrected many errors in the preparation of the manuscript, and generally enabled me to go about my work by taking this side of things off my mind.

I am most indebted to Steven Burton, Robert Cooter, Kenneth Kress, Rod MacDonald, Robert Post, Judith Thomson, and Peter Westen, all of whom read drafts of the entire manuscript and made penetrating and detailed comments that went beyond any reasonable call of colleagueship or friendship.

Contents

The Nature of the Common Law

Chapter 1

Introduction

My purpose here is to develop the institutional principles that govern the way in which the common law is established in our society. Much of our law derives from rules laid down in constitutions, statutes, or other authoritative texts that the courts must interpret but may not reformulate. The common law, in contrast, is that part of the law that is within the province of the courts themselves to establish. In some areas of law, like torts and contracts, common law rules predominate. In other areas, like corporations, they are extremely important. In all areas, even those that are basically constitutional or statutory, they figure at least interstitially.

In developing the institutional principles that govern the establishment of the common law, it is essential at the outset to distinguish between two types of propositions that figure in common law adjudication: doctrinal propositions and social propositions. By doctrinal propositions, I mean propositions that purport to state legal rules and are found in or easily derived from textual sources that are generally taken to express legal doctrine. The most obvious group of doctrinal sources consists of official texts that are generally regarded as binding on a deciding court—principally, the so-called primary legal sources, such as statutes and precedents of the deciding court's jurisdiction. A second group of doctrinal sources consists of official texts that are not regarded as binding on a deciding court, such as precedents of other jurisdictions. A third group consists of texts that are the product of analyses by members and students of the profession who replicate the process of judicial reasoning and publish their analyses in forums that are conventionally regarded as secondary legal sources, such as treatises and law reviews.

By social propositions, I mean all propositions concerning the world other than doctrinal propositions, such as propositions of morality, policy, and experience.

Most modern analyses of law and adjudication can be largely defined in terms of their treatment of the interplay between doctrinal and social propositions, and the criteria that social propositions must satisfy if they are to be employed in establishing legal rules.

One leading line of analysis distinguishes, in effect, between cases that can be decided solely on the basis of binding doctrinal propositions and cases whose decision requires the employment of social propositions. The law, under this line of analysis, consists of the doctrinal propositions found in binding official texts. Cases that can be decided solely on the basis of such propositions, without the employment of social propositions (except insofar as a doctrine by its terms requires social propositions for its application), are put into one category, sometimes called "easy," "clear," or "regulated" cases. Here the judge is said to act as a law-finder. Cases in which the employment of social propositions figures in establishing (rather than merely applying) the deciding rule are put into another category, sometimes called "hard," "indeterminate," or "unregulated" cases. Here the judge is said to act with the power of a legislator, and to make new law by employing those social propositions he thinks best to adopt the rule he thinks best.[1]

Another line of analysis takes the position that the judge always acts as a law-finder. This analysis also draws a distinction between hard and easy cases, but the distinction is different. Easy cases are those controlled by relatively specific doctrinal rules. Hard cases are those that can only be decided by the application of relatively general doctrinal rules. The judge is said to decide hard cases by determining what general rule best fits prior institutional decisions and applying that rule to the case before him.[2]

Still a third line of analysis takes the position that the judge decides hard cases by determining what rules would satisfy some threshold test of fit with prior institutional decisions and then selecting, from among these, the rule he thinks best on the basis of his own moral and political convictions. In so deciding, the judge determines rather than makes law.[3]

I will show that none of these analyses properly accounts for common law adjudication. Under the institutional principles that govern the common law, social propositions are relevant in all cases. To put this differently, all common law cases are decided under a unified methodology, and under this methodology social propositions always figure in determining the rules the courts establish and the way in which those rules are extended, restricted, and applied. Easy cases are not cases that are controlled by relatively specific doctrinal rules, but cases in which a relevant doctrinal rule is supported by applicable social propositions. The common law does not consist of the doctrinal propositions found in binding official texts. Rather, it consists of the rules that would be generated at the present moment by application of the institutional principles that govern common law adjudication.

Although the judge is not limited to doctrines found in past official texts, neither is he free, as would be a legislator, to employ those social propositions he thinks best, or to establish those rules he thinks best, on the basis of his own moral and political convictions. Rather, the judge is under an obligation to employ only those social propositions that satisfy certain criteria, and to establish only those rules that are generated by the application of the institutional principles of adjudication. This obligation, like the obligation to faithfully employ constitutional and statutory texts, follows from the voluntary assumption of judicial office. That office, like all others, is held in trust. The rules of the trust are the institutional principles of adjudication, which are rooted in the social functions of the courts and justified by considerations of fairness and social welfare. Like a conventional trustee, the judge is morally bound by his acceptance of office to obey the rules that govern the conduct of his office.[4] Thus adjudication is driven not (or not only) by the rights of the parties, but by the duty of the judge, which runs both to the parties and to the larger society.

Chapter 2

The Social Functions
of Courts

The institutional principles of common law adjudication are rooted in the social functions of courts. Like other complex institutions, courts serve several functions, but two of these are paramount.

The first concerns the resolution of disputes. Complex societies characteristically need an institution that can conclusively resolve disputes deriving from a claim of right based on the application, meaning, and implications of the society's existing standards. In our society that institution is the courts, and the resolution of such disputes is accordingly a central function of our courts.[1]

This centrality is manifested in a variety of ways. To begin with, courts in our society are structured to be fundamentally passive. Unlike a legislature, a court may not properly initiate action on its own motion but may act only when set in motion by a party with a claim.[2] Correspondingly, a court is limited to action that is responsive to the claim made.[3] The kinds of claims a court may properly act upon are also limited. The claim normally must be contested—that is, the subject of a dispute.[4] The claimant normally must assert that the respondent has either infringed (or threatens to infringe) upon his rights, or is otherwise at fault in a manner that sufficiently involves the claimant's interests to render it appropriate for him to make a claim whose disposition turns on that fault.[5] The claim must be based on a standard that relates to social conduct rather than, say, on an artistic standard.[6] The standard on which the claim is based must rise to a certain level of significance, in terms of either the seriousness of the injury that typically results from its violation or the importance of the norm or policy that it reflects.

The second paramount function of the courts is the enrichment of the supply of legal rules.[7] Our society has an enormous demand for legal rules that private actors can live, plan, and settle by. The legislature cannot adequately satisfy this demand. The capacity of a legislature to generate legal rules is limited, and much of that capacity must be allocated to the production of rules concerning governmental matters, such as spending, taxes, and administration; rules that are regarded as beyond the courts' competence, such as the definition of crimes; and rules that are best administered by a bureaucratic machinery, such as the principles for setting the rates charged by regulated industries. Furthermore, our legislatures are normally not staffed in a manner that would enable them to perform comprehensively the function of establishing law to govern action in the private sector.[8] Finally, in many areas the flexible form of a judicial rule is preferable to the canonical form of a legislative rule. Accordingly, it is socially desirable that the courts should act to enrich the supply of legal rules that govern social conduct—not by taking on lawmaking as a free-standing function, but by attaching much greater emphasis to the establishment of legal rules than would be necessary if the courts' sole function was the resolution of disputes.[9]

Of course, the judicial establishment of legal rules would occur even if the sole function of the courts was to resolve disputes. If the courts are to explicate the application, meaning, and implications of the society's existing standards in new situations, they cannot simultaneously be prohibited from formulating rules that have not been previously announced. To begin with, modern society is in a state of continual change, creating a continual need for new legal rules to resolve new issues. Indeed, because of the inevitability of change, even the application of an old rule to a new case may constitute a new rule. For example, prior to the development of broadcasting the law of defamation drew a sharp distinction between written defamation, or libel, and oral defamation, or slander. Normally, slander required proof of actual damage, but libel did not.[10] With the advent of radio broadcasting, some cases held that defamation by broadcast was slander, because it was not written, while others held it was libel, because of its great potential for harmful effects.[11] Clearly the rule adopted in the former cases was as new as that adopted in the latter.[12] Moreover, even when social conditions have not changed, previously adopted legal rules must often be discarded because they were wrongly established. Finally, whether a previously adopted legal rule covers a given dispute may often depend on the degree of generality with which the rule was formulated in earlier cases, and that degree is often somewhat adventitious.[13]

Since the judicial establishment of legal rules would occur even if the sole function of the courts was to resolve disputes, it is difficult to show conclusively that courts also regard the enrichment of the supply of legal rules as desirable in itself. Consider, for this purpose, two possible models of the courts' role in establishing legal rules, which might be called the by-product model and the enrichment model. Under the by-product model, courts establish legal rules only as an incidental by-product of resolving disputes. To resolve disputes, courts must formulate and apply general propositions. Since the courts are official agencies, these propositions, once formulated, have some sort of legal status and effect. A court is justified in formulating such propositions, however, only insofar as is necessary to resolve the dispute before it, and no further. Under the enrichment model, in contrast, the establishment of legal rules to govern social conduct is treated as desirable in itself—although subordinated in a variety of important ways to the function of dispute-resolution—so that the courts consciously take on the function of developing certain bodies of law, albeit on a case-by-case basis.

It might be thought that the by-product model governs adjudication, since this is the model the courts often profess to follow, but observation of several important elements of judicial practice suggests that the enrichment model has greater descriptive power. For example, if the courts followed the by-product model we would expect to find that the rules adopted in judicial decisions were accorded weight (because officials, including courts, can be expected to be reasonably consistent over time), but not that they were treated as binding.[14] In contrast, if the courts followed the enrichment model we would expect to find that these rules were treated as binding. Under the principle of stare decisis, the latter is the case.[15]

Similarly, if courts followed the by-product model we would expect to find that opinions announced only those legal rules strictly necessary for the disposition of the dispute at hand. In contrast, if courts followed the enrichment model we would expect to find that opinions frequently announced more legal rules than were strictly necessary for that purpose. Inspection of judicial opinions shows that the latter is the case. Courts often announce rules to govern issues that are at best tangential to a resolution of the dispute before them. For example, in *Hamberger v. Eastman*[16] the question was whether the surreptitious installation of a listening device in an individual's bedroom constituted a tortious act. The court used the occasion to embrace the broad rule that individuals have a right of privacy that is infringed by intrusion into their physical and mental solitude, by public disclosure of private facts, by publicity that places them in a false light, and by appropriation of their name or likeness for the defendant's benefit. Similarly, in *Rowland v. Christian*[17] a social guest alleged that he had been injured as a result of his host's negligence. The court used the occasion to abolish the complex common law system governing a property owner's duty of care, which imposed different duties on trespassers, licensees, and invitees, and to replace that system with a general reasonableness standard.

Finally, if the courts followed the by-product model we would expect to find that judicial opinions would often explicitly split the stakes in a dispute, when the courts found the arguments in support of competing propositions equally persuasive.[18] Because that approach would often fail to produce clear legal rules, however, if courts followed the enrichment model we would expect to find that opinions would never or almost never explicitly split the stakes, no matter how well balanced the arguments. The latter is just the case. Of course, it is sometimes suggested that the resolution of disputes by the courts often embody covert compromises. That suggestion only serves to provide further support for the enrichment model. If the courts did not regard the establishment of legal rules as an end in itself, compromise would be explicit, not covert: a major purpose of covertness in such cases is to avoid the injection of doubt about the dispute into doubt about the rule.

In short, policy suggests that the courts should regard the enrichment of the supply of legal rules as desirable in itself, and observation suggests that they do so.

The function of resolving disputes faces toward the parties and the past. The function of enriching the supply of legal rules faces toward the general society and the future. As I will show, a major objective of the institutional principles of common law adjudication is to reconcile the tensions that may arise out of the difference in orientation between these two functions.

Chapter 3

Foundational Principles

In this chapter I will examine four foundational principles that govern the manner in which law is established and changed by the courts. I shall call these the principles of objectivity, support, replicability, and responsiveness. These principles are rooted in the social functions of the courts, as well as in considerations of structure and fairness which themselves reflect those social functions. The foundational principles, and the considerations of function, structure, and fairness that underlie them, provide the basis for determining the criteria that social propositions must satisfy if they are to figure in common law reasoning (Chapter 4). Together with the standards that the common law should satisfy (Chapter 5), the foundational principles also provide the basis for the more specific institutional principles that govern the basic modes of common law reasoning (Chapters 6 and 7).

Objectivity

Just as the courts are limited in the kinds of claims they may consider, so too are they limited in the manner in which they may decide claims. The power of a third party to conclusively resolve disputes may be legitimated on various bases, such as his access to supernatural forces, his charismatic attributes, or his reputation as a Solomonic figure with a special ability to discern justice. In a society like ours, which is complex, impersonal, and not officially religious, courts derive their legitimacy in substantial part from another source—objectivity.

The principle of objectivity entails several related ideas. One is the concept of impartiality, which requires the courts to be free of ties to the parties. Another is the concept of universality, which requires the courts to resolve disputes by establishing and applying rules that are applicable not merely to the parties to the immediate dispute but to all those who are similarly situated.[1] Accordingly, under the principle of objectivity a court should reason by articulating and applying rules that it is ready to apply in the future to all persons who are situated like the disputants.

Support

It is not enough that the rules that a court establishes and applies are objective in the sense that they are universal. These rules should also be supported by the general standards of the society or the special standards of the legal system. In this respect a court differs from a legislature, which can appropriately adopt legal rules that do not have such support.

This distinction between courts and legislatures rests on considerations of social function, structure, and fairness.

In terms of social function, the courts are the institution to which a person is entitled to go to resolve a dispute deriving from a claim of right based on the existing standards of the society or its legal system. Therefore, it is those standards from which the courts should reason when they resolve disputes. To put this differently, if the courts resolved disputes by reasoning from other types of standards, there would be no institution to which a member of the society could go to vindicate a claim of right based on existing standards. In contrast, the primary function of the legislature is to make rules to govern the future, and for the future the best course may be to alter existing standards.

In terms of structure, legislatures are conceived as representative institutions and are composed of a large number of members with diverse training and experience. In contrast, courts are conceived as nonrepresentative institutions, whose duties include faithfulness to a central tradition, and are usually made up of a handful of members with relatively homogeneous training and experience. Legislatures are designed to be directly responsive to the citizenry as a whole, which participates in the legislative process through elections, lobbying, and public hearings. In contrast, courts are designed to be directly responsive only to the disputants, who participate in the adjudicative process through proof of facts and reasoned argument, and to the profession, which engages in ongoing discourse with the courts through briefs, commentary, and other means. Legislatures must account to the citizenry on an ongoing basis, through frequent elections in which their records are at issue and through day-to-day scrutiny by the popular media. The accountability of courts, on the other hand, is deliberately limited: judges seldom stand for re-election in a meaningful way, nonprofessional criticism of judges and their decisions is usually frowned upon, and far from being subjected to the day-to-day scrutiny of the popular media, judges normally decline to defend a decision that is brought into public question. The combination of a representative conception, highly diverse training and experience, and responsiveness and accountability to the whole citizenry on an ongoing basis provides legitimacy to legislative rules even when they involve substantial departures from existing standards. In contrast, the rooting of common law rules in existing standards provides an added and needed source of legitimacy to the establishment of legal rules by an institution that is not conceived as representative, has a narrow base of experience, and is deliberately structured in a fashion that limits its accountability and responsiveness to the citizenry as a whole.[2]

Finally, in terms of fairness, a court, to a much greater degree than a legislature, acts by applying rules in a retroactive manner. This in turn gives rise to what might be called the retroactivity dilemma: how can it be fair to resolve a dispute concerning a past transaction by applying a legal rule that is articulated after the transaction occurred?[3] Requiring courts to reason from existing standards alleviates (although it does not eliminate) this dilemma, by ensuring that decisions are rooted in standards that the disputants either knew or had reason to know at the time of their transaction, albeit standards that had perhaps not previously been officially recognized as legal rules.

Replicability

Private actors who want to resolve disputes or make plans on the basis of the law must normally consult a lawyer. In a complex society in which many legal rules are established in judicial opinions, the law is not readily determinable by laymen. Thus in the vast majority of cases where law becomes important to private actors, as a practical matter the institution that determines the law is not the courts, but the legal profession. This is desirable, because determination by a private actor's lawyer is almost invariably less expensive, less time-

consuming, and less threatening than judicial proceedings, and because the very mass of the profession enables much more law to be
determined for purposes of planning and dispute-settlement than
would the relatively small cadre of judges.

Granted that it is desirable for lawyers as well as judges to be
able to determine the law, it becomes critical that lawyers should
be able to replicate the process of judicial reasoning and, therefore,
that the courts utilize a process of reasoning that is replicable by
lawyers. Planning and dispute-settlement on the basis of law depends on a determination of what the law presently is, not what the
law has been. Since the courts remain the final arbiters of law, if
courts did not use a replicable process of reasoning the profession
could not give reliable legal advice in planning and dispute-settlement, and planning and dispute-settlement on the basis of law would
be frustrated. Furthermore, planning and dispute-settlement on the
basis of law characteristically involve more than one lawyer. Therefore, it is important that all members of the profession should be
able to go about determining the law in the same way. The principle
of replicability serves as a coordinating device that creates a channel
through which the reasoning of the profession can flow, allowing
private actors to make individual and joint plans and settle disputes
on the basis of law without the need for official intervention.

The courts' use of a replicable process of reasoning also alleviates
the retroactivity dilemma, by enabling private actors, within limits,
to determine before they enter into a transaction the legal rules—
including the "new" legal rules—that will govern the transaction
if a dispute should arise. Through the use of a replicable process
of reasoning, the courts can resolve a dispute on the basis of a proposition whose official recognition as a legal rule may have been
predictable by the profession at the time of the transaction, even
though the proposition had not yet received such recognition at that
time.

Finally, replicability allows the parties to a dispute to become
active participants in the adjudicative process through proofs and
reasoned arguments. Such participation would be difficult or impossible if the parties did not know the kinds of proofs and arguments to which courts will attend in reaching their decisions.

An important aspect of the principle of replicability is that the
courts employ a consistent methodology across cases. For example,
if the courts employed one set of criteria for selecting relevant social
propositions in some cases and a wholly different set of criteria in

others, judicial reasoning would become nonreplicable unless there were clear principles that controlled which criteria were used in which cases.

While replicability serves the end of predictability, it does not assure predictability. Judicial decisionmaking involves judgments of various sorts, and since the judgments of any two persons may differ, complete predictability cannot be attained. Furthermore, the importance of predictability in any given area partly depends on the weight placed in that area on the value of planning as against the value of flexible response to new conditions, and on the value of channeling the behavior of private actors as against the value of responding to their fair expectations. The principle of replicability does not itself determine how much weight to give to these sometimes clashing values in any given area.

Responsiveness

Those who think about the theory of adjudication often focus on the court as an isolated actor.[4] To a certain extent this is understandable, because the courts are not structured to be directly responsive to the citizenry as a whole. There is, however, a social institution, intermediate between the courts and the larger society, to which the courts are structured to be directly responsive—the legal profession. The courts are not obliged to follow the profession, but they are obliged to be responsive to what the profession has to say. This obligation entails that the courts attend to the professional discourse and stand ready either to modify their views when that discourse is convincing or to give good reason showing why it is not convincing.[5] The principle of responsiveness thereby both serves as the basis of a critical feedback mechanism and enhances the courts' legitimacy by providing a measure of judicial accountability.

The discourse to which the courts are obliged to be responsive largely occurs in two basic arenas. The first is the arena of the particular case, in which discourse with the profession is effected through briefs and oral argument, and through lawyers' decisions whether to raise conceivable claims or defenses. The second arena is that of the profession as a whole. This wider arena is entered after final decision in the particular case is rendered. Discourse in this arena is effected primarily through the profession's critical evaluation of published opinions. The discourse takes its most obvious form in law reviews, treatises, and monographs, but it also occurs through other means, as in the opinions of sister courts, addresses by lawyers at judicial conferences, meetings of professional organizations at which both judges and lawyers are in attendance, and casual interchange among members of the bench and bar. Such discourse heavily shapes both the acceptability and interpretation of prior cases, and puts into a larger and critical perspective the social propositions relied on in prior cases and relevant to a case at bar. To put the matter sharply, while in form judicial opinions are published to the parties, who must accept them, in substance opinions are published to the profession, which may attempt to remold or reject them.

The narrower and wider arenas are intimately connected. The courts cannot be expected to keep abreast of all the literature of the law. Instead, it lies with counsel in a given case to bring the relevant literature to the court's attention.

In some cases, of course, persons other than members of the profession may evaluate common law opinions in a public forum, as through articles, books, editorials, or the like. A court should also be responsive to responsible evaluations of this type, when brought to its attention in the narrower arena, particularly insofar as the evaluations concern the social propositions employed in earlier opinions. The general community also communicates with the courts in very direct fashion through the jury: one function the modern jury serves is to give the courts a reading on what social propositions are accepted by the community at large.

The profession and the general community can also enter into the development of the common law through the legislature. This concept may seem paradoxical. After all, if the legislature has entered the picture a statutory rather than a common law rule must be in question. As a practical matter, however, the legislature often intervenes partially, by way of correction, in areas that it generally leaves to development by common law techniques. This corrective function is linked to discourse in the wider arena. Legislative correction is most likely to occur when the profession believes that a common law rule is unsound but cannot practicably or quickly be changed in the courts, or when wide criticism of a decision is expressed outside the profession. Legislative correction is therefore important not only in itself, but because it reflects and represents criticism to which the courts should be responsive.

Chapter 4

Social Propositions

In this chapter I examine the criteria that social propositions must satisfy if they are to figure in common law reasoning. Three types of social propositions will be considered: moral norms, policies, and experiential propositions. The relevant criteria, and the methodology for determining whether these criteria are satisfied, reflect both the social functions of the courts examined in Chapter 2 and the foundational principles examined in Chapter 3.

Moral Norms

Social propositions may figure in judicial reasoning at a variety of levels. At one extreme, they may play a role in the application of established legal rules to the facts of given cases. At the other, they may play a role in the establishment of entirely new legal rules. Between these extremes, they may enter into such intermediate processes as modifying established legal rules and making relatively general rules effective through the elaboration of more specific rules.

Moral norms—propositions that characterize conduct as right or wrong—provide a ready illustration of the different ways in which social propositions figure in judicial reasoning. In some cases, an established legal rule makes specific reference to morality, so that moral norms must be employed to apply the rule to the facts of a given case. Under the legal-duty rule in the law of contracts, for example, a bargain in which one party's performance consists only of an act he had already contracted to perform is unenforceable, subject to certain exceptions. Under one of these exceptions the bargain is enforceable if it consists of a modification of the prior contract that is fair and equitable in view of circumstances that were not anticipated when the prior contract was made.[1] Similarly, a promise to pay for a benefit conferred upon the promisor in the past is normally enforceable only if there was already a moral obligation to make compensation for the benefit.[2]

In other cases, the full meaning of a highly general legal rule can be developed only by employing moral norms to fashion more specific rules. For example, over the last thirty years the rule has emerged that a contract is unenforceable if it is unconscionable.[3] Since the concept of unconscionability is heavily based on fairness, its development must take account of moral norms.[4]

In still other cases, moral norms figure in the establishment of entirely new legal rules. For example, the three rules just discussed—that a bargain to perform a preexisting contractual duty is enforceable if it consists of a modification that is fair and equitable in view of unanticipated circumstances, that a promise to pay for a past benefit is enforceable if there was already a moral obligation to make compensation, and that unconscionability is a contract defense—undoubtedly sprang in significant part from an effort to keep contract law congruent with morality.

That moral norms should figure with particular weight in common law reasoning is not surprising. The common law is heavily concerned with the intertwined concepts of injuries and rights, and it is morality that largely shapes our perceptions of what constitutes injuries and rights. In large part, the task of the common law is not to determine what constitutes an injury or a right but to explore, on an ongoing basis, the extent to which actions that are perceived by the community as inflicting wrongful injuries should give rise to remedies at law.[5]

The question then arises, what criteria should a moral norm satisfy if it is to figure in common law reasoning? The answer is that when moral norms are relevant to establishing, applying, or changing common law rules, the courts should employ social morality, by which I mean moral standards that claim to be rooted in aspirations for the community as a whole, and that, on the basis of an appropriate methodology, can fairly be said to have substantial support in the community, can be derived from norms that have such support, or appear as if they would have such support.[6]

This institutional principle is based on the foundational principles of support and replicability and on the considerations of function, fairness, and structure that underlie those principles. To begin with, if the courts were not required to employ social morality, when moral norms are relevant in establishing the law, there would be no institution to which a member of the society could go to vindicate a claim of right based on the society's existing standards. Furthermore, given the manner in which courts are structured, the legitimacy of the judicial establishment of legal rules depends in large part on the employment of a process of reasoning that begins with social morality rather than with those moral standards the court thinks best. Requiring courts to employ social morality also alleviates (although it does not eliminate) the retroactivity dilemma, by ensuring that decisions are rooted in standards that the disputants either knew or had reason to know at the time of their transaction, albeit standards that had perhaps not been officially recognized as legal rules. Moreover, since moral norms and policies are relevant to the decision of all common law cases, if courts were free to employ whatever norms and policies they think best the profession would be unable to replicate the adjudicative process in cases where norms and policies were relevant, and could not reliably determine the law for purposes of planning and dispute-settlement. And since social morality is based on observable criteria, a process that requires the courts to draw on social morality is replicable by the profession, and thereby helps enrich the supply of legal rules and facilitates planning and dispute-settlement. (Different institutional principles may apply to areas of law based on a constitution, statute, or other canonical text. Such a text may embrace or subsume certain moral values. If it does, the court normally must account for those values in cases to which the text is relevant, even if those values are not embodied in social morality at the time of the decision.)

To what sources may a court look in determining social morality? Often, perhaps typically, the court can look to official sources, such as prior decisions. In many cases a relevant moral norm will have been explicitly articulated in these sources.[7] If this articulation has provoked no significant dissent in the professional discourse, or elsewhere in the wider arena, the court may usually assume that the norm has the requisite social support. In other cases a moral norm can be inferred on the ground that it best explains the doctrine found in these sources. Here too, in the absence of significant dissent the court may usually assume that the explanatory norm has the requisite support.

Nevertheless, official sources are not necessarily reliable and are certainly not exclusive on the issue of what constitutes social morality. Official sources are not necessarily reliable because they may reflect past morality, doctrine, or policy, rather than present morality. Official sources are not exclusive, because to the question, what constitutes social morality, the norms articulated or reflected in official sources are not an answer but only a powerful clue. Accordingly, the court may also look to unofficial sources. The court may, for example, attempt to determine what moral values justify existing social structures and institutions, and are therefore values to which citizens "are already in some way committed."[8] Or it may look to moral norms that are asserted as aspirations in popular sources, like newspapers and everyday conversation. The court may utilize moral norms found in such sources even if the norms are not universally practiced. No moral norm is practiced by all members of the community, and even those members of the community who usually practice a given moral norm typically don't practice it all the time. What counts is the asserted norm, provided only that it is efficacious (that is, not widely disregarded), because morality that is asserted and efficacious embodies a community view of right conduct.[9] Correspondingly, even a wide practice is not part of social morality unless it reflects a moral aspiration.

Where the moral norms to be derived from official or unofficial sources are insufficiently specific or not directly applicable, a judge may rely on his own judgment, as a participant-observer, concerning what norms appear as if they would have the requisite social support, provided he believes—or has no reason not to believe—that his judgment would be widely shared.[10] Suppose, for example, the judge concludes that it would be widely perceived as unfair for one party to a bargain knowingly to exploit the other party's lack of sophistication.[11] The judge could then properly conclude that there is a norm of social morality that it is wrong to engage in such exploitation, even though there is relatively little explicit expression of that moral norm in official or unofficial sources and it cannot be shown that the norm explains existing doctrine or justifies existing social structures or institutions. Correspondingly, in some cases the judge may properly employ a norm that is still emerging in the society, if he believes that the norm will soon attract substantial social support, and he is ready to pull back if that belief proves incorrect.

Finally, a court can determine social morality by extending other norms that have the requisite support. Extension may proceed by elaboration or development, or in other ways. To quote Rawls, "One of the aims of moral philosophy is to look for possible bases of agreement where none seem to exist. [Moral philosophy] must attempt to extend the range of some existing consensus."[12] Often, such extensions proceed either by beginning with specific moral judgments and fashioning a general moral principle that best summarizes, supports, and explains those judgments, or by beginning with general moral principles and developing specific moral judgments that are consistent with the principles. This approach, which is sometimes called coherence methodology, is often associated with coherence theories of morality. A coherence theory of morality may require an individual to use his personal moral principles and judgments as starting points to arrive at right morality. Coherence methodology, however, can be used equally well with shared moral principles and judgments.[13] The moral principles and judgments to which a court should apply this methodology are those principles and judgments that have the requisite social support.

Admittedly, as a practical matter it usually cannot be determined whether a moral norm truly has the requisite social support. Nevertheless, that determination is an empirical, albeit not normally a testable, judgment. This empirical judgment is subject to the check of discourse with counsel in oral argument and briefs; to the check of discourse among judges in a multijudge court; and to the check of professional and other discourse in the wider arena. If the court's empirical judgment appears mistaken the mistake is likely to be brought out by criticism in the wider arena, to which the court is obliged to be responsive.[14]

In short, the court is not obliged to establish empirically that a moral norm has the requisite social support in fact, which it cannot do, but to use appropriate methodology to make a judgment on that issue. In substance the court makes a claim that in its best judgment, on the basis of appropriate methodology, a norm has the requisite social support, and then opens the validity of that claim to discussion in the wider arena. If discourse in that arena then suggests that the court's judgment is mistaken, it is obliged to respond appropriately.

Suppose that in a case where morality seems relevant, two norms of social morality collide. If in such a case the issue is whether to preserve or abandon an established legal rule, the preferred solution would usually be to maintain the rule. For reasons of stability that will be discussed in Chapter 6, an established legal rule should not be discarded simply because another rule would be marginally more attractive.[15] The same result should usually prevail if there is both substantial social support for and opposition to a moral norm that underlies an established rule. So too, if a court is asked to establish a new legal rule under these circumstances, it would normally do well to follow Holmes:

> As law embodies beliefs that have triumphed in the battle of ideas and then have translated themselves into action, while there still is doubt, while opposite convictions still keep a battle front against each other, the time for law has not come; the notion destined to prevail is not yet entitled to the field.[16]

Nevertheless, the court may employ moral norms even in such cases. The court may, for example, believe that one colliding norm is regarded by the community as significantly more weighty than the other; or that one norm is waxing while the other is waning; or that one norm is more congruent with applicable policy and more consistent with the body of the law than the other; or that one norm is better connected to the community's fundamental concepts of justice. Similarly, where there is a collision between a relatively general principle and a relatively specific judgment, each of which appear to have substantial social support, the court may attempt to reconcile the two by reformulating either the general principle or the specific judgment so that they are in equilibrium.

The requirement that when moral norms are relevant in establishing common law rules the courts must employ only social morality does not mean that in establishing common law rules the courts can play no leadership role. A court may lead by identifying and clarifying social morality, putting its weight behind that morality, and reminding the community what its moral standards are. A court may lead by basing legal rules on moral norms that are waxing, although they conflict with norms that have more support but are waning. Most important, a court may lead by overturning legal rules that have lost their social support, and establishing in their place rules based on existing social standards. The landmark cases of the common law do not involve an attempt by the courts to change existing social standards, but a decision by the courts to bring legal rules into congruence with existing social standards.

Two basic kinds of objections can be made to the institutional principle that when a court employs moral norms in developing the common law, the norms it should employ are those of social morality. The first is that social morality is not a meaningful concept. People who make this objection are apt to point to an analysis of conventional morality by John Ely in his book *Democracy and Distrust*.

Ely's analysis turns in significant part on three arguments: (1) "Consensus or conventional morality is postulated as something 'out there' that can be discovered," but in fact there is no consensus to be discovered. (2) To the extent that conventional morality may seem to exist, it is likely to reflect only the morality of a dominant group. (3) If you press someone who claims that conventional morality means something, "you're likely to be given [either] some jejune maxim like 'no one should profit from his own wrong' " or moral opinions that are so abstract that they admit of almost any interpretation.[17]

Democracy and Distrust does not concern adjudication as such, but the power of the judiciary to nullify legislative enactments on constitutional grounds. Accordingly, the real thrust of Ely's arguments is only that conventional morality should not be used as a standard for the judicial review of statutes. Indeed, Ely explicitly recognizes that it may make sense to draw on conventional morality in deciding common law cases.[18] Nevertheless, the arguments are stated; they are not unique to Ely; if accurate, they would apply to common law adjudication despite Ely's disclaimer; and the vigor of the attack is such that Ely's analysis is frequently invoked by those who argue that the concept of social morality is empty.[19] Let us therefore examine the arguments.

The first argument begins by equating conventional and consensus morality. It then claims there is no consensus on moral norms, and therefore, by implication, no conventional morality. The argument is misleading, partly because it employs two ambiguous terms, *conventional morality* and *consensus*. The term *conventional morality* might refer narrowly to moral norms asserted in popular sources, or more broadly to what I have called social morality, which is a stream fed by numerous channels. To the extent that Ely's arguments are addressed to the narrower conception they do not necessarily bear on the broader. For purposes of advancing the discussion, I will treat Ely's arguments as if they are addressed to what I call social morality. The term *consensus* may mean either unanimity or majority of opinion.[20] If by consensus Ely means unanimity, his first argument is true, but not very significant, insofar as it asserts there is no unanimity on morality. If, on the other hand, by consensus Ely means majority of opinion, he is setting too limited a standard for determining social morality, and even under that standard his argument is contradicted by the common experience that we can often reach a pretty firm sense of what most people would regard as fair in a given case.

Ely's second argument is that if there is a social morality, it is likely to reflect only the morality of a dominant group. But there's nothing necessarily wrong with that, if it means only that in fashioning the common law rules that govern the general community, norms that have wide support will be favored over those that have little support. Of course, a community may be stratified through groups defined by such elements as class, ethnicity, religion, or occupation. As to any given issue, some groups may hold moral norms that vary from those that have substantial support in the general community. The presence of such variations, however, should not be a barrier to using the norms of the general community in fashioning common law rules, as long as the community is not exceptionally pluralistic and the norms claim to be rooted in aspirations for the community as a whole.[21]

Ely's third argument is that if a person who believes in social morality is asked what it means, he is likely to come up only with statements that are either vacuous or so abstract as to admit of any interpretation. Again, this argument is contradicted by experience. Moral norms such as "promises should be kept" and "lying is wrong" are neither vacuous nor susceptible to any interpretation. Furthermore, this argument confuses the definition of a concept and the instances that fall under it. People who are not expert at systematization often cannot give a satisfactory definition of a concept even though they can easily identify cases falling under it. As David Richards has pointed out, "When it comes to formulating principles, one has the phenomenon of the reasonable person, the person of sound moral convictions and practical wisdom, who is thrown into confusion and puzzlement when he or she tries to articulate the principles that underlie his or her judgments. . . . Here, often, a special kind of theoretical enterprise, calling on special kinds of intellectual talent, may be needed to articulate such principles."[22]

A second objection to the principle that in developing the common law the courts should employ social morality is that when moral norms are relevant in establishing legal rules, a judge may properly employ the moral norms he personally believes to be right even if he does not believe those norms are a part of social morality. I shall refer to the body of any given judge's private convictions concerning right and wrong conduct as personal morality. Kent Greenawalt, for example, has argued:

> [I]f the judge's convictions are very firm and if the issue involved is of great moral or social significance, I think a judge may follow these convictions even if he does not think they are shared by most members of the community. A judge is an agent for change in the law in marginal cases and, just as a legislator, he sometimes may rely on his own strongly held views in preference to those of the community.[23]

An initial difficulty raised by this kind of approach is that the principle it suggests for determining when a judge may properly establish the law by relying on his own moral views in preference to those of the community is very unclear in its contours: the judge's convictions must be "very firm" and the case must be "marginal." Presumably, a marginal case is not one in which an established doctrine by its terms requires a determination of moral norms for its application. For example, it seems unlikely that proponents of this approach would argue that the application of the rule that a promise to pay for a past benefit is enforceable, if there was already a moral obligation to make compensation, should depend on how the transaction happens to match up with the personal morality of the particular judge who decides the case. Presumably too, a marginal case is not one in which moral norms figure in the establishment of entirely new doctrines. For example, if there was neither doctrinal nor social support for the concept of a right to privacy, surely it would be improper for a court to determine that such a right should exist on the ground that society would, in the court's view, be the better for it.

Perhaps, therefore, marginal cases, in this context, are those that are intermediate between the application of an established doctrine to a given case and the establishment of an entirely new doctrine— such as cases that involve modifying an established doctrine or making a highly general doctrine effective through the elaboration of more specific rules. Assume the following facts: The right of privacy has been recognized as a general doctrinal principle, but its implications have not been fully worked out. Amateur and professional photographers commonly take pictures of people they see in the street, in shops, in airports, and in other public places. Often such pictures are displayed in galleries, sold to collectors, and published in photography magazines and books. Releases are never obtained in such cases, and objections are never made. It is clear that the community at large does not regard the practice as in any way improper. One day, however, a subject who sees his photograph in a gallery does object, and sues the photographer for invasion of his right of privacy. The judge accepts the fact that in the eyes of the community at large the defendant did not act improperly. According to the judge's personal morality, however, the photographer has acted wrongly. It is morally improper, the judge believes, to use another's face for private gain without that person's explicit consent, or to publicize, without consent, a gesture, a look, or a situation that most people would not deem embarrassing, but that the subject, for whatever reason, may want to keep from the eyes of the world at large.

Certainly the judge's moral view is appealing, and might well form the basis of a statute enacted by a like-minded legislature. Nevertheless, application of the judge's personal morality to this case (or of any norm of personal morality to any case) would conflict with the principles of support and replicability—or perhaps more cogently, the considerations in which those principles are rooted. A judge may arrive at his personal morality through a number of different techniques, including considered or unconsidered intuition, coherence methodology, the elaboration or application of first principles that are taken as self-evident, or the acceptance of a moral tradition. Those who think it proper for a judge to employ personal morality in establishing the law must be prepared to accept the application of whatever moral norms the judge holds: We cannot restrict the content of the judge's personal morality without departing from the very concept that in establishing legal rules the judge may properly employ the moral norms he personally believes to be right. If, however, judges were free to establish the law, in cases where moral norms were relevant, by application of whatever moral norms they hold, there would be no institution to which a member of the society could go to conclusively resolve disputes involving a claim of right based on the society's existing standards. Furthermore, serious problems of fairness would be raised by the imposition of liability on someone who, like the photographer, has played by all the prevailing social and legal rules as far as either he or a lawyer could determine them, but whose behavior did not conform to the court's personal morality.[24] Finally, if judges were free to establish the law through the application of their personal morality, the profession would be unable to replicate the adjudicative process in cases where moral norms were relevant, and therefore could not reliably determine the law for purposes of planning and dispute-settlement.

The case for the application of the judge's personal morality often seems to be bottomed in part on a notion of sincerity—a notion that it is somehow improper to require a judge to employ a moral norm that he does not personally believe to be right or to refrain from employing a moral norm that he does personally believe to be right. However, as a sensitive judge recently pointed out in an analogous connection, "The ordinary business of judges is to apply the law as they understand it to reach results with which they do not necessarily agree."[25] The moral obligation of the judge in common law cases, as regards social morality, is comparable to the moral obligation of the judge in constitutional or statutory cases, as regards the constitutional or statutory text. Just as the judge is under a moral obligation to faithfully employ constitutional or statutory texts in cases where they are relevant, whether or not he privately agrees with those texts, so is he under a moral obligation to faithfully employ the norms of social morality, when morality is relevant to establishing common law rules, whether or not he privately agrees with those norms. This obligation does not itself derive from, or solely from, social morality. By accepting and retaining office the judge undertakes an ongoing commitment to carry out the rules of the office, and moral reasons independent of social support lead to the conclusion that such a commitment imposes an obligation. Moreover, these rules of office—the institutional principles of the common law—are themselves supported not only by social morality but by independent considerations of fairness and social welfare.

This is not to say that a judge is never morally justified in deciding a case by the application of his own moral views. Take, for example, the following hypothetical, put by David Lyons in *Ethics and the Rule of Law:*

> Suppose that a legal system enforces severely discriminatory laws against blacks. As a way of trying to insure the stability of the system, the law provides that a white may claim damages from any black who publicly challenges his racial superiority. Suppose that a case has arisen in which there is ample evidence, admissible in law, to support a particular white man's claim for damages against a particular black man under this law. The decision that would seem to be required by law would vindicate this white man's claim and require the black man to pay him compensation for the supposed injury. Let us assume, finally, that this law cannot be nullified on constitutional grounds.[26]

Illustrative cases designed to show that a judge can refuse to enforce a legal rule on the ground that he believes it to be immoral are almost invariably set in a time or place other than our own. Lyons's hypothetical is no exception. The apparent inability to identify contemporary legal rules in our own culture that a judge could properly refuse to apply on the basis of his own moral convictions suggests that in the real life of the common law the issue is not apt to be pressing. It is also striking that most such illustrative cases involve, as does that of Lyons, a rule designed to oppress a genetically defined minority group. It is not clear how sharp the problem would be in other contexts. Nevertheless, the hypothetical touches a powerful chord and needs to be dealt with on the merits.

Lyons does not make clear in his hypothetical what view society takes toward the law in question. Let us assume that society favors the law. (If it doesn't, the case is not that interesting.) Lyons also does not make clear whether the issue is that the law is truly immoral or that the judge believes it to be truly immoral. However, it is not very useful to examine these problems unless we do so from the judge's perspective, and from that perspective only the judge's belief that a law is truly immoral can be relevant.

Lyons earlier points out that

> even if an official has a general obligation of fidelity to law, we can assume it has moral bounds. If the law he is called on to enforce is sufficiently immoral, there may be no moral argument for his adherence to it—not even if he has sincerely undertaken to apply the law as he finds it. A misguided or naive official under the Third Reich, who initially believes that the law he shall be called on to administer will not be outrageously immoral, may find that it requires him to verify the eligibility of persons for extermination in the gas chambers because they are Jews. He may in good conscience have undertaken to apply the law as he finds it, but I see no reason to suppose that his resulting obligation of fidelity to law extends this far. Such an obligation has moral limits.[27]

So, on comparable grounds, Lyons suggests that the judge in the black-challenge hypothetical might refuse to apply the law. Presumably, Lyons would also argue that a state governor who believed that abortion was truly murder would not be obliged to implement a statute that provided funds for indigent pregnant women seeking abortion, and that a judge who held the same belief would be free to deny injunctive relief against the governor. Perhaps so. At most, however, such scenarios do not demonstrate that personal morality should enter into the judge's determination of the law, but only that in very extreme cases all bets may be off and the judge's moral obligation to fulfill his office may be capsized by the moral horror of an action he is asked to take. In such extreme cases, Lyons's judge may be morally justified in following his own conscience, as by refusing to grant damages against blacks who challenge racial superiority, despite the law, just as Lyons's Third Reich official may follow his own conscience and refuse to verify the eligibility of Jews for extermination, despite the law.[28] But just as Lyons's Third Reich official would not by his act change the verification procedure, Lyons's judge would not by his act change the law against black challenge, which by hypothesis is clear, constitutional, and favored by the society.

It must also be kept in mind, in considering the problem of very extreme cases, that in our society the highly charged and divisive issues raised by such cases are normally allocated either to a legislature or to decision under a constitution. Highly charged and divisive issues are appropriate for the legislature by virtue of that body's popular mandate, the diversity of its membership, and the locus it provides for the fullest possible expression of clashing views in lobbying, in the press, in demonstrations, in hearings, and on the floor. Highly charged and divisive issues are appropriate for decision under a constitution because a constitution gives expression to values a community has committed itself to adhere to even during periods when a majority may not want to do so, as Odysseus had himself tied to the mast before his vessel passed the Sirens. The task of the judge in deciding a common law case is usually more mundane, in part just because of the availability of alternative forums that are much better suited to dealing with very extreme cases. Dealing with the issues of everyday life is normally adventure enough for the common law.

Policies

Policies characterize states of affairs as conducive or adverse to the general welfare. In contrast to moral norms, which characterize conduct as right or wrong, policies characterize states of affairs as good or bad.[29]

Like moral norms, policies figure in judicial reasoning at a variety of levels. In some cases, an established legal rule makes specific reference to policy, so that policy must be employed to apply the rule to the facts of given cases. For example, a person who causes injury through conduct that is negligent is ordinarily liable for damages. Whether conduct is negligent depends in part on whether the magnitude of the risk entailed in the conduct outweighs the social value attached to the interest the conduct advances.[30] Similarly, a person who engages in conduct that unreasonably invades another's interest in the use and enjoyment of his land is guilty of a nuisance. Whether conduct that invades the use and enjoyment of land is unreasonable depends in part on whether the gravity of the harm caused by the conduct outweighs the social value attached to its primary purpose.[31]

In other cases, the full meaning of a relatively general legal rule can be developed only by employing policies to fashion more specific rules. For example, there is a general rule that damages for breach of a bargain contract are measured by the injured party's expectation. The full meaning of this rule has been developed in part by fashioning more specific rules on such issues as foreseeability of damage and mitigation of loss.[32] Since the general rule is partly rooted in the policy of efficiency, these more specific rules have taken that policy into account.[33]

In still other cases, policies figure in the establishment of entirely new legal rules. For example, among the rules of contract law are that a donative promise—a promise to make a gift—is unenforceable unless relied upon; that a person who makes an enforceable promise will not be compelled to actually perform the promise unless damages are an inadequate remedy; that an unreasonable restraint on the alienation of property is invalid; and that the acceptance of an offer is normally effective when it is dispatched rather than when it is received. All these rules are based on policies rather than on moral norms. Under the first three rules the law does not make a person perform his promise, and the fourth rule certainly does not stem from any moral imperative.[34]

A special group of policies state desirable characteristics of legal rules. Among these are what might be called the administrability, informational-asymmetry, and opportunism policies.

The administrability policy is that the applicability of a legal rule should not depend on information of a kind that cannot be reliably determined by courts. For example, under the objective theory of interpretation in contract law the meaning of an expression usually depends on the interpretation that would be given to the expression by a reasonable person in the addressee's position, rather than on the addressor's subjective intention. This theory rests in part on the administrability policy.[35] So does the rule that liability for negligence depends on whether the actor's conduct conformed to that of a reasonable person, rather than on whether the actor did as well as he knew how.[36] Also under this policy, if a factual predicate F of a right or duty is difficult to establish by direct proof, but F is usually coupled with a surrogate fact S that is readily susceptible to such proof, the courts may appropriately establish a rule that liability will attach if S is shown, even though F and S are not invariably coupled. At their most modest, rules of this character take the form of presumptions. Often, however, they take the form of rules of substantive law. For example, the legal-duty rule, that if the performance of one party to a bargain consists of an act he had already contracted to perform the bargain is unenforceable, is justified in *Restatement (Second) of Contracts* on the ground that most such bargains are subject to some independent defect, such as unconscionability.[37]

The closely related informational-asymmetry policy is that the applicability of a legal rule should not depend on information that will characteristically be in the hands of only one of the parties. The doctrine of strict product liability, under which the supplier of a product is liable without fault for injuries caused by defects in the product that make it unreasonably dangerous, seems to rest partly on this policy. A supplier has relatively complete information concerning its production process, whereas the consumer has almost none.[38] This policy also supports the rule that common carriers are strictly liable for injury to goods in their possession.[39] Accidents to such goods characteristically occur far away from the shipper and at a site where the only witnesses are the carrier's employees, so that shippers would typically find it difficult to acquire information that would show the loss was due to the carrier's fault.[40]

The opportunism policy is that legal rules should not encourage exploitive conduct. For example, a contract in which a public official agrees to perform an act that is within the scope of his official duties is not enforceable even if the official was not legally obliged to perform the act. If such contracts were enforceable, citizens might come under pressure to tip public officials, and officials might allocate their energies according to who tipped them rather than on the basis of sound discretion.[41]

Closely related to policies that state desirable characteristics of legal rules are policies that concern the conditions under which moral wrongs should be recognized as legal wrongs. Among these are what might be called the policies of social gravity and private autonomy.

The policy of social gravity is that morally wrongful conduct should not give rise to liability unless its consequences are normally of sufficient importance, in terms of either the social interests implicated or the injury likely to result, to justify the social cost of official intervention. For example, the rule that unrelied-upon donative promises are unenforceable seems to rest in part on the proposition that although breaking a promise is wrong, failure to enforce donative promises will not have serious social effects and the defeat of a donative promisee's expectation is not a very serious injury.[42] Often the operation of the policy of social gravity is hidden, because it is reflected in common but unspoken assumptions about what does and does not constitute a legal wrong. For example, most lawyers would probably believe that cutting in line, although a moral wrong, is not in itself a legal wrong. A tacit application of the policy of social gravity is a major reason for this belief.

The policy of private autonomy is that morally wrongful conduct should not be made the basis of liability if doing so would unduly inject officials into intimate spheres of social conduct. For example, although the general rule is that bargains are enforceable, an exception is made for bargains concerning the allocation of responsibilities in the ongoing conduct of a marriage. This exception is based on the policy of private autonomy.[43] Similarly, the rule that unrelied-upon donative promises are unenforceable may rest in part on the proposition that it is desirable to leave gift relationships to personal trust and confidence.[44]

What criteria should a policy satisfy if it is to figure in common law reasoning? For the reasons applicable to the employment of moral norms, in establishing, applying, or changing common law rules the courts should employ policies that claim to characterize a state of affairs as good for the community as a whole, and that, on the basis of an appropriate methodology, can fairly be said to have substantial support in the community, can be derived from policies that have such support, or appear as if they would have such support. (As in the case of moral norms, different principles may apply to areas of law based on a canonical text, like a constitution or a statute. Such a text may embrace or subsume certain policy values. If it does, the court must account for those values in cases to which the text is relevant even if the values do not have the requisite social support at the time of the decision.)

The sources to which a court may look in determining what policies have the requisite social support parallel the sources to which a court may look in determining what moral norms have the requisite support. Often, perhaps typically, the relevant policies will be found in official sources. Sometimes policies will have been explicitly articulated in official sources. For example, a New York statute concerning directors' and officers' liability insurance declares that it "is the public policy of this state to spread the risk of corporate management."[45] An Oklahoma statute declares that it is "the policy of this state to provide for the reclamation and conservation of land subjected to surface disturbance by mining."[46] Similarly, under the business-judgment rule a corporate director is not liable for the loss resulting from a negligent business judgment if the judgment was made in good faith and on due inquiry and had a rational basis. Some precedents that adopt or apply this rule explicitly state the policy rationale that directors' liability should not be so extensive that able persons will not want to serve on boards.[47] If such a statement has provoked no significant dissent in the professional discourse or elsewhere, a court may normally assume that the policy has the requisite social support.

In other cases, a policy can be inferred from official sources on the ground that an established doctrine is best explained as a reflection of the policy. Here too, in the absence of significant dissent the courts may normally assume that the explanatory policy has the requisite social support. For example, the Minnesota case of *Sherlock v. Stillwater Clinic*[48] concerned the issue whether a physician who had negligently reported that a vasectomy had been successful was liable to the parents for expenses resulting from the consequent birth of a healthy but undesired child. In holding the physician liable, the court drew on a public policy to encourage family planning that it inferred from Minnesota statutes that subsidized family-planning services by local governments and legalized the sale, distribution, and advertisement of articles for preventing conception.[49]

A court may also look to unofficial sources. It may attempt to determine what policies justify existing social structures and institutions: for example, the court may conclude that since our economy is capitalistic, there is substantial social support for the policy that (all other things being equal) commerce should be facilitated. Alternatively, the court may attempt to determine if a state of affairs is characterized as good or bad in popular sources. Or, the court may rely on its own judgment of what policies would have substantial social support, provided it believes—or has no reason not to believe—that its judgment would be widely shared. As in the case of moral norms, although it usually cannot be determined whether a policy truly has the requisite support, that determination is empirical and is subject to the check of discourse in the wider arena. If that discourse suggests that the court's determination was mistaken, the court is obliged to respond appropriately.

Because of certain differences between moral norms and policies, several criteria in addition to requisite support should be satisfied if a court is to take a policy into account.

To begin with, while moral norms are usually long-lasting, policies may relate to conditions that are temporary or even fleeting, such as undue inflation or high unemployment. The rules made by courts should be durable—generalizable over time as well as over persons—and therefore should not be based on policies that seem transitory.[50]

This criterion spills over into another. Moral norms are almost invariably implemented with universal rules, but policies often need not be. Under the foundational principle of objectivity, the courts may implement policies only through rules that are universal. A legislature may properly grant special benefits to Chrysler Corporation to save it from bankruptcy on the ground that saving Chrysler from bankruptcy will be conducive to achieving the policy objective of full employment. A court, however, could not properly make a rule to benefit one failing company unless it was willing to apply the same rule to all failing companies.

Another criterion a policy should meet, if it is to figure in common law adjudication, is that it can fairly be implemented by remedies within the power of courts, such as the imposition of damages or the grant of injunctive relief. This criterion is usually not relevant in the case of moral norms. Violation of a moral norm usually entails a special injury to a given individual. Judicial remedies are tailored to redress just such injuries. In contrast, adequate implementation of a policy may require much more than damages or injunctive relief—may require, for example, government subsidies, taxation, or the creation of bureaucracies with expert skills, administrative resources, or both. In some cases, the difficulty of implementing a policy judicially may mean only that the policy will not be pervasively reflected in judicial decisions. In other cases, however, the courts should refrain from implementing any part of a policy because all aspects of the policy are interdependent, and piecemeal implementation would be undesirable. For example, suppose that before collective bargaining legislation had been adopted it became apparent that a policy in favor of collective bargaining had substantial social support. A court might nevertheless conclude that full implementation of the policy required a bureaucratic apparatus, and that the various elements of collective bargaining—such as free and fair ability to organize and to resist organization, bargaining in good faith, and free and fair union elections—were so interdependent that judicial implementation of only one or two elements would be more undesirable than total abstention.

Finally, policies, more often than moral norms, may rest on experiential propositions that can fairly be called into question. Accordingly, cases may arise where the court believes that a policy has substantial social support only because a relevant experiential proposition is not correctly perceived. In such cases the court may be justified in not employing the policy, provided it is willing to reverse its stand if, after publishing an opinion in which it explained the matter, its view was rejected in the wider arena.

Because policies figure so pervasively in legal reasoning, it might plausibly be argued that the policies employed by the courts are themselves law. David Lyons has suggested such a view:

> The judicial duty to decide cases responsibly does not end with easy cases, and a theory of hard cases tells judges what they must do to decide cases responsibly when they run out of legal rules. Though the relevant . . . policies are assumed to be drawn from outside the law, a theory of hard cases implies that courts are dutybound to appeal to them. If courts are dutybound to appeal to them, then those . . . policies are, for present purposes, indistinguishable from established rules of law. That is, they are the standards that must be used to guide decisions in hard cases.[51]

It is true that in some cases a policy is explicitly adopted in doctrinal form in such a manner as to be binding. The New York and Oklahoma statutes quoted above provide statutory examples; the cases on the business-judgment rule provide a common law example. However, with the exception of policies that are laid down in canonical texts, such as statutes, or made binding by the courts in a relatively explicit way, the view that policies employed by the courts are themselves law—a view that would extend as well to moral norms—confuses raw material and finished product. A metallurgist who wants to make steel is obliged to begin with iron and carbon, but neither iron nor carbon is steel. Any given legal rule will reflect an interplay between moral norms, policies, experiential propositions, and doctrinal propositions, but seldom are moral norms or policies translated into legal rules on a one-to-one basis. For example, the legal rule that a bargain promise is enforceable reflects the moral norm that promises should be kept. That moral norm, however, is not a legal rule. On the contrary, the legal rule is that a promise is unenforceable unless it is part of a bargain or meets some other independent criterion.

Furthermore, an institutional principle that policies or moral norms employed by the courts are themselves law would be dysfunctional, because it would imply that social propositions that figure in the establishment of legal rules remain binding even though they did not command the requisite social support when employed or lost that support thereafter.

That policies, like moral norms, should figure in common law reasoning is not surprising. Consideration of policies is an important element in the courts' function of enriching the supply of legal rules. If the courts are to establish legal rules to govern social conduct, it is desirable for them to consider whether those rules will be conducive to a good or a bad state of affairs.[52] Moreover, the relationship between morality and policy is itself disputed. Many believe that rightness reasons ultimately depend on general-welfare considerations, and even those who deny that dependence would usually agree that in judging whether conduct is right or wrong it is not irrelevant whether the conduct is conducive to the good or the bad.

Nevertheless, two different arguments are sometimes made against the employment of policies in common law reasoning. The first is that it is unsuitable for a nonrepresentative institution to be concerned with policy questions. The second is that in resolving a dispute growing out of a past transaction between two parties, it is unfair to take the general welfare into account.

These arguments were put into sharp form by Ronald Dworkin in his article, "Hard Cases."[53] Dworkin there put forward what he called "the rights thesis," that "judicial decisions in civil cases . . . characteristically are and should be generated by principle not policy."[54] The major underpinning for this thesis lay in what Dworkin called two objections to judicial originality, which might be thought of as an argument from democracy and an argument from fairness.

Dworkin begins by stating the argument from democracy in a relatively simple form:

> [A] community should be governed by men and women who are
> elected by and responsible to the majority. Since judges are, for
> the most part, not elected, and since they are not, in practice, re-
> sponsible to the electorate in the way legislators are, it seems to
> compromise that proposition when judges make law.[55]

He then elaborates the argument: Decisions concerning policies
require comparisons of the nature and intensity of different demands
distributed throughout the community. Such comparisons are appropriate for a legislature, but not for a judge.[56]

The argument in its simple form—judges should not make law
because they are not elected by and responsible to the majority—
does little more than assume its own conclusion. The legitimacy of
a social institution in general, and of the establishment of legal rules
by an official institution in particular, need not depend on whether
the institution satisfies the definitional test that it is democratic,
elected, and responsible to the majority, but instead may be based
on utility and social acceptance. The establishment of legal rules
by the courts, including the establishment of legal rules that take
policies into consideration, meets the latter tests and is constitu-
tionally sanctioned as well. The constitutions of the states create
judicial as well as legislative organs. The framers of these constitutions must have realized that courts establish legal rules and employ policy in doing so.[57] Even if the framers somehow held to the
naive understanding that courts do not establish legal rules and employ policy in doing so, that belief has not continued into our living
constitutional understanding. Considerations of structure, function,
and fairness do suggest that courts, unlike legislatures, may properly
employ only policies that have a requisite degree of social support
and meet certain other criteria, but they do not suggest that courts
should refrain from establishing legal rules or from employing policies in doing so.[58]

The argument from democracy in its elaborated form—that decisions concerning policies require comparisons of the nature and
intensity of different demands, which judges are not qualified to
make—has more force. In its full extension, however, this argument
mistakes the question whether policies may properly be formulated
by the courts with the question what criteria a policy must meet if
it is to be employed by the courts. The courts are not required to
formulate policy by comparing the nature and intensity of different

demands, but to determine what policies have a requisite degree of social support. It is true that judicial weighting—not of competing demands but of policies that reflect competing demands—may sometimes be required. For example, different policies, each with substantial support, may collide in a given case, or a policy may collide with a moral norm. But weighting may also be required where there is a collision between different moral norms, each with substantial social support. Furthermore, at least in regard to collisions between policies and moral norms, the court's judgment can often be guided. For example, Donald Regan has pointed out that "it is widely felt that avoiding harm is more important than promoting increases in welfare. In particular, it is widely felt that it is unfair to require a few individuals to suffer significant specialized harms in order to produce widespread benefits, even if the total benefit exceeds the total harm."[59] Accordingly, a preference for not suffering a particularized harm resulting from the violation of a moral norm should normally be accorded weight over a colliding preference for producing a generalized benefit through the effectuation of a policy.[60]

Of course, the former preference does not always trump the latter. A highly relevant policy might outweigh a weakly relevant moral norm. Furthermore, some policies are based on the concept that affording legal protection against certain individualized harms could lead to even more individualized harms. And it is often the case that the concept of individualized harm is not very salient in resolving a legal issue—for example, the issue whether an acceptance of an offer is effective on dispatch or on receipt. Ultimately, therefore, there will be some cases where the weighting of colliding policies and moral norms must lie within the court's judgment. There is no evidence, however, that courts are not competent to make this type of weighting. They do it daily, and have done it for several hundred years. The process of rendering judgment cannot be rendered judgment-free.[61]

Dworkin's argument from fairness, like the argument from democracy, is first stated in relatively simple form: "[I]f a judge makes new law and applies it retroactively in the case before him, then the losing party will be punished, not because he violated some duty he had, but rather a new duty created after the event."[62] It is then elaborated: If A does not have a right to recover against B, a court cannot justifiably impose liability against B simply on the ground that to do so would further the general collective welfare.[63]

These arguments are also misconceived. The employment of policies in common law reasoning is fair on both substantive and procedural grounds.

Substantively, a rule that reflects a policy that has the requisite social support is a rule that a substantial portion of the society will believe maximizes the general welfare. Every member of society has reason to want the society's legal rules to be conducive to that end and to expect others to act accordingly. It would be unfair for a member of the society to expect to benefit from such rules while avoiding their burden. A fair-minded member of society should therefore admit the relevance of policy in determining what constitutes proper behavior and what should be the content of legal rules established by the courts, including the rules that are applied to his case.[64]

The procedural argument, that policies should not be employed in adjudication because it is unfair to make new law and apply it retroactively,[65] also fails. I will show in Chapter 6 that almost any rule employed in a common law decision is new in the sense that the court must choose in every case whether to apply, extend, reformulate, or radically reconstruct relevant doctrinal propositions. As long as the courts follow a replicable process this feature of the common law is not unfair. Since every member of society has reason to know that the society's legal rules will reflect policies, and reason to know that a policy has the requisite social support, neither the policy nor judicial action reflecting the policy should normally involve unfair surprise.

Moreover, there is an anomaly in the procedural side of Dworkin's argument from fairness, which was latent in the rights thesis but has become explicit in his more recent work. Dworkin now argues that a judge should decide each case by determining what rules would satisfy some threshold test of fit with prior institutional decisions and then selecting, from among those, the rule he thinks best on the basis of his own moral and political convictions.[66] But it cannot be that the application of a policy with substantial social support would be objectionably retroactive while the application of the judge's personal convictions would not.[67]

To recapitulate, the employment of policies that have substantial social support in establishing common law rules is fair on both substantive and procedural grounds. Substantively, it is fair for a court to resolve a dispute by taking into account policies that characterize certain states of affairs as good or bad for the whole

community, when the parties themselves benefit from other court-
made rules that take policy into account, expect the law to reflect
such policies, and expect others to act accordingly. Procedurally, it
is fair for a court to take policies into account when there is an
established institutional principle that they should do so, the policies
have the requisite social support, and the process by which policies
are taken into account is replicable by the profession.

Experiential Propositions

Experiential propositions are propositions about the way the world
works. One major class of such propositions describes regular patterns of conduct followed in social subgroups. I shall refer to this
class of propositions as usages. Usages resemble legal doctrines and
moral norms, insofar as they are propositions concerning human
conduct. Unlike doctrines and norms, which tend to prescribe the
way people should act, usages in themselves only describe how
people do act. However, some usages take on a prescriptive aspect,
because they demonstrate how people think they should act, because the adoption of a usage often generates an expectation that
it will continue, and because of what has aptly been called the normative power of the actual.

Like other social propositions, usages figure in adjudication at
various levels. In some cases, an established legal rule specifically
provides for reference to usage. For example, under contract and
commercial law a relevant usage of a trade or community will be
legally implied in a contract unless negated, even though one of
the contracting parties is not aware of the usage.[68]

In other cases, the full meaning of a relatively general legal rule
can be developed only through the employment of usages. This is
often true, for example, in determining what constitutes negligence
in the conduct of an industry or a profession. The law normally does
not require that members of an industry or profession take every
possible precaution. Rather, the content of the negligence principle
is determined by striking a balance between the benefits of a precaution and its costs. The existence of a usage helps provide a base-
line rule of conduct in such a context, because it demonstrates that
those who bear the costs in the first instance have determined that
the costs are worth the benefit.[69] If most tugs have radar, it is reasonable to conclude that a tug-owner who doesn't install radar has
failed to use due care. If most physicians don't perform surgery un-

less they have undergone a surgery residence, it is fair to conclude that a general practitioner who performs surgery has failed to use due care. If most corporate directors study quarterly financial reports, it is fair to conclude that a director who doesn't has failed to use due care. Similarly, a corner of a trade or profession may be so arcane or technical that it is virtually impossible to say whether given conduct is negligent except by reference to usage—for example, what safety factor should be used in calculating the amount of wind a building should be able to withstand, or what kind of sutures should be used in various surgical procedures.

In still other cases, usages figure in the establishment of entirely new legal rules. Thus in the 1800s the California courts, in determining what constituted a valid mining claim, adopted miners' usages as rules of law.[70] Similarly, in determining when a whaler had a property right in a whale he had harpooned, the courts adopted whalers' usages as rules of law.[71]

Usages account for only a fraction of the experiential propositions that play a role in adjudication. For example, the laws of the physical and biological sciences are all experiential propositions—they all concern the way the world works—and so are descriptions of physical relations, such as the proposition that a railroad train, unlike a truck, cannot run to the door of a consignee.[72] For purposes of adjudication, undoubtedly the most important types of experiential propositions are propositions of psychology and sociology—more specifically, propositions that describe, predict, or explain individual and group response to incentives, deterrence, and institutional design, and individual and group capacity to process information. It is almost impossible to overstate the importance in adjudicative reasoning of these types of experiential propositions, whose major function is to mediate between policies (and to a lesser extent moral norms), on the one hand, and legal rules, on the other. Generally speaking, it is only through the mediation of experiential propositions that policies can be implemented, and the soundness of legal rules based on policies often rests as much on the validity of the propositions of psychology and sociology through which they are mediated as on the validity of the policies themselves.

This can be illustrated by the business-judgment rule and the rule against reviewing the adequacy of consideration. Under the business-judgment rule a corporate director is not liable for the loss resulting from a business judgment that was negligent, in the sense that it was a decision a reasonable person would not have made, if the judgment was made in good faith and on due inquiry and had a rational basis.[73] This rule rests in significant part on propositions of policy. One such policy is that it is undesirable to deter able persons from serving as directors.[74] That policy supports the business-judgment rule only if mediated by two psychological propositions. The first is that the imposition of ordinary negligence liability on directors would have a measurable deterrent effect on the willingness to serve on boards. This proposition seems relatively uncontroversial, but it is a matter of experience, not logic. (For example, the imposition of ordinary negligence liability on automobile drivers does not seem to have a measurable deterrent effect on the willingness to drive.) The second is that the imposition of ordinary negligence liability would have not only a measurable but a substantial deterrent effect, despite the financial and nonfinancial incentives for serving as a director and the corporation's ability to limit the deterrent effect of liability through the purchase of liability insurance. This is potentially a more controversial proposition, and only if this proposition is correct does the policy that able persons should not be deterred from serving as directors support the business-judgment rule.

A second policy on which the business-judgment rule is based is that directors should not be deterred from making risky decisions.[75] This policy supports the business-judgment rule only if mediated by the psychological proposition that reviewing directors' decisions under a regime of ordinary negligence would result in such deterrence.

Another basis for the business-judgment rule is an application of the administrability policy—that it is too difficult for a fact finder reliably to determine whether a business decision went bad because it was not a sensible risk or despite the fact that it was a sensible risk.[76] This policy supports the rule only through mediation of the psychological proposition that fact finders typically do not have the capacity to make this determination. That proposition may be correct, but it is not unchallengeable, and unless it is correct the policy would not support the rule.

A similar analysis is applicable to the rule that adequacy of consideration will not be reviewed, that is, the rule that bargains will be enforced according to their terms without inquiry into the fairness of the bargained exchange.[77] This rule also rests in part on policies. One of these policies is that there should be security in contracting, so that actors will not be unduly reluctant to enter into and plan on the basis of contracts.[78] This policy supports the rule only if mediated by the psychological proposition that actors would be unduly reluctant to enter into and plan on the basis of contracts if they believed the courts might later readjust the contracts' terms according to the fact finder's notion of fairness.

A second basis of the rule that adequacy of consideration will not be reviewed is an application of the administrability policy—that it is too difficult for a fact finder reliably to determine the fairness of a contractual exchange.[79] As in the case of the business-judgment rule, this policy supports the principle only through mediation of the proposition that fact finders typically do not have the capacity to make this determination.

Like propositions of morality and policy, experiential propositions that figure in adjudication should have a requisite degree of support. Unlike propositions of morality and policy, however, experiential propositions do not require support in the general community. Many or most experiential propositions concern either relatively technical issues with which the general community would rarely be familiar, or relatively specialized issues as to which some degree of expertness is required. Therefore, it can fairly be assumed that the community would normally prefer to confide decisions concerning the accuracy of such propositions to the judgment of the courts, subject to the check of discourse. Accordingly, such propositions should be supported by (or be propositions the court believes would be supported by) the weight of informed opinion—including informed opinion based on conclusions of the social sciences and the informed opinion of the courts themselves on matters in which they are expert, such as the capacity of fact finders.[80] The weight of informed opinion is a function of persuasiveness and authority, rather than the numbers of those lined up on each side. Ultimately the court itself must determine where the weight of persuasiveness and authority lies, although it should be cautious about establishing or changing legal rules on the basis of experiential propositions whose truth is hotly contested among experts.

Consider, by way of comparison with the position of the community toward the courts in this regard, the position of a person, O, who owns a number of enterprises, toward the managers of those enterprises. O subscribes to certain moral norms and policies relating to the conduct of business. For example, she holds as a moral norm that a business should be conducted well within the limits of the law, and she has a policy in favor of employee participation in decisionmaking. O wants her managers to follow the moral norms and policies to which she subscribes rather than those to which they subscribe. She believes, however, that her interests are best served by confiding to the judgment of each manager the determination of those experiential propositions necessary to the implementation of her moral norms and policies. For example, she believes that within the framework of her policy on employee participation each manager should decide what particular work rules the manager's enterprise will adopt, depending upon the manager's determination of such questions as the attitudes and motivations of the enterprise's workforce. O confides the determination of such questions to the judgment of her managers partly because she believes the questions are likely to involve technical issues with which she is not proficient, and partly because she believes that she will normally have less information on the relevant issues than any single manager, each of whom is specialized in just one enterprise.

The position of the community toward the courts, as respects experiential propositions, parallels the position of O toward her managers. The most efficacious implementation of the community's prevailing moral norms and policies through law is likely to be achieved by confiding to the courts' judgment the determination of the experiential propositions necessary to that implementation. Many experiential propositions are relatively technical, and most depend on specialized and changing information. A court, instructed by counsel, is more likely than the general community to have relevant and timely information at its disposal, and it is also likely to be more proficient on such questions as individual and group response to incentives, deterrence, and institutional design, and individual and group capacity to process information. Given the goal of implementing the community's prevailing moral norms and policies in common law adjudication, the community therefore should normally be deemed to have confided to the courts the determination of the experiential propositions necessary to mediate between those social standards and legal rules.

A court's judgment concerning the support for experiential propositions, like a court's judgment concerning the support for moral norms and policies, is subject to the check of discourse. A court that appears ready to rely on a mistaken experiential prop-

osition is likely to be corrected by counsel. If the court nevertheless reaches a decision based on such a proposition, its reasoning
and its decision are likely to be rejected in the larger arena following
the publication of its opinion, and the court is obliged to respond
accordingly.

Chapter 5

Standards for the Common Law

The key questions in common law reasoning concern the interplay of social and doctrinal propositions.

It is relatively easy to see why social propositions figure in common law reasoning. The common law is heavily concerned with the intertwined concepts of injuries and rights, and moral norms largely shape our perception of what constitutes an injury and a right. Judicial consideration of policies furthers the courts' function of enriching the supply of legal rules: if the courts are to establish legal rules to govern future social conduct, it is desirable for them to consider whether those rules will conduce to a good or a bad state of affairs. Experiential considerations are necessary to mediate between policies and moral norms on the one hand and legal rules on the other. Accordingly, few would object to the practice of basing common law rules on moral norms, policies, and experience.

I shall use the term *applicable social propositions* to mean those moral norms, policies, and experiential propositions that it is proper for a court to employ.[1] In some cases, at least, doctrinal propositions must lead to a rule and result that differ from the rule and result that would follow from applicable social propositions. Otherwise, there would appear to be little reason (except perhaps ease of administration) for considering doctrinal propositions at all. But if applicable moral norms, policies, and experience point, on balance, to rule A and result A', what justifies a court in ever establishing another rule or reaching another result? And what institutional principles govern the interplay between social and doctrinal propositions in the common law?

The resolution of these issues depends both on the foundational principles examined in Chapter 3 and on the standards that the common law should seek to satisfy. In this chapter I will examine those standards and develop two models of the common law in which they are reflected.

The Standards of Social Congruence and Systemic Consistency and the Model of Double Coherence

The first of these models is based principally on social propositions. I shall call it the model of double coherence. The term *coherence* has several senses, depending on the type of material to which it is applied. One sense of the term is the "integration of social and cultural elements based on a consistent pattern of values and a congruous set of ideological principles"[2]—or coherence as congruence. A second sense is a "systematic or methodical connectedness or interrelatedness [especially] when governed by logical principles"[3]—or coherence as consistency. The model of double coherence embodies two ideals, reflecting these two senses.

The first ideal is that the body of rules that make up the law should correspond to the body of legal rules that one would arrive at by giving appropriate weight to all applicable social propositions and making the best choices where such propositions collide. Attainment of this ideal helps assure that disputes will be resolved under, and law will be based upon, the society's prevailing standards; harmonizes legal outcomes with the reasonable expectations of private actors; and furthers the legitimacy of the law by demonstrating its substantive rationality. Call this the ideal of social congruence.

The second ideal is that all the rules that make up the body of the law should be consistent with one another. Attainment of this ideal promotes predictability and evenhandedness and furthers the legitimacy of the law by demonstrating its formal rationality. Call this the ideal of systemic consistency.

Social propositions play a central role in both ideals. It might appear that social propositions figure only in the ideal of social congruence. That is not so. Social propositions also normally determine whether the body of the law is systemically consistent. To illustrate, take the rule that bargains are enforceable. There are a number of exceptions to this rule. Generally speaking, the rule and its exceptions are consistent only if the exceptions reflect applicable social propositions. For example, one standard exception to the rule is that a bargain made by a minor is not enforceable against the minor. This exception is consistent with the rule because, and only because, applicable social propositions suggest that for purposes of contractual liability a distinction should be drawn between the consent of a minor and the consent of an adult. In contrast, suppose a court were to hold that a bargain made by a clergyman is not enforceable against the clergyman, even if the bargain is not religious in nature. This exception would undoubtedly be criticized as inconsistent with the rule. That criticism, however, would not be based on formal logic, but on the ground that applicable social propositions would not support a rule giving special status to clergymen for this purpose. It is easy to imagine social propositions that would support clergyman exceptions for other purposes or in another society or time. In the middle ages, for example, clergymen could be prosecuted for felony only in ecclesiastical courts, and therefore were not subject to capital punishment.[4] Even today, religious bargains made by clergymen might well be unenforceable. But applicable social propositions in contemporary society would not support a clergyman exception for secular bargains. That is the reason, and the only reason, why such an exception would be inconsistent with the bargain rule.[5]

(It is necessary here to draw a distinction between a strong and a weak meaning of systemic consistency. A legal rule is systemically consistent in a strong sense if it is consistent with other legal rules on the basis of applicable social propositions. Even if that condition is not satisfied, however, a legal rule may be said to be systemically consistent in a weak sense if it is supported by a general legal concept that is traditionally taken to justify differentiations that are not justified by applicable social propositions. A concept of this type normally takes the form of a deep doctrinal distinction. Examples include the distinctions traditionally drawn in our legal system between transactions in real and personal property, and between maritime and nonmaritime transactions. These distinctions may render different treatment of two socially comparable transactions consistent in a weak sense, because one transaction involves personal property and one involves real property, or because one involves transport by water and the other does not. The number of such distinctions is limited. Deep doctrinal distinctions that are not themselves supported by applicable social propositions usually originated in periods in which they were socially congruent. Distinctions that lose the support of applicable social propositions tend to dissolve over time, because they provide only an impoverished justification for different treatment of socially comparable transactions. For example, a well-known trend in modern law is the gradual dissolution of the deep doctrinal distinction between real estate contracts and other contracts.)

For reasons to be explored in the next section, a body of common law that satisfies the model of double coherence can be captured only in a mythical way. Imagine that a Federal Revolution has occurred, one of whose features is the abolition of state governments. The founding fathers of our reconstituted country wish to preserve the common law method in those subject-matter areas where it had previously prevailed, but do not wish to preserve the body of prerevolutionary common law. To achieve their objective, the founding fathers constitute a Master Court, and direct it to reconsider and redecide every prerevolutionary appellate case handed down in the previous thirty years and to issue all its decisions on a specified Decision Day. A corps of lawyers is appointed to argue each side of every case. The original parties to the redecided cases will be unaffected by the new decisions, but after Decision Day the rules established by the new decisions are to be treated as if they were received common law, and are then to be developed in traditional common law fashion. The Master Court is instructed that in arriving at its decisions it may not rely on prerevolutionary common law, except as a resource for suggesting possible rules, for indicating the implications of adopting one rule rather than another, and the like. A case decided under the prerevolutionary common law is to have no more and no less standing in the Master Court's deliberations than a case decided under Continental law, or, for that matter, than the views of a commentator.

The mythical body of the law as of Decision Day would reflect the model of double coherence. Presumably, in writing its opinions the Master Court would seek to construct a body of law that satisfied both the ideal of social congruence and the ideal of systemic consistency. The body of the law handed down on Decision Day would be socially congruent, in the sense that all applicable social propositions were given appropriate weight, and systemically consistent, in the sense that all the rules were consistent with one another.

Although the model of double coherence does not adequately capture our ongoing legal system, it is nevertheless reflected in two basic types of criticism of legal rules which together comprise a major portion of professional discourse. One type of criticism is aimed at showing that a legal rule is socially wanting, because it fails to give appropriate weight to applicable moral norms, policies, and experience. This type of criticism reflects the ideal of social congruence. The second type of criticism is aimed at showing that a legal rule is doctrinally wanting, because it is inconsistent with other legal rules. This type of criticism reflects the ideal of systemic consistency.

Because these two ideals provide the basis by which legal rules are evaluated, I shall hereafter refer to them as standards. Generally speaking, these standards apply in a continuous rather than a binary fashion—that is, the relevant question is usually not whether a given rule would be socially congruent and systemically consistent, but which of two competing rules would be more socially congruent and systemically consistent.

The Standard of Doctrinal Stability and the Real-World Model of the Common Law

The second model of the common law gives a major role to doctrinal as well as social propositions. This model reflects the fact that in the real world the courts must take into account not only social congruence and systemic consistency but also a third ideal, stability of doctrine over time.

The considerations underlying that ideal can most usefully be examined by considering the ideal's most significant expression, the institutional principle of stare decisis. Under that principle, as it is traditionally formulated, the "ratio decidendi" (ground of decision), "holding," or "rule" of a precedent is binding in subsequent cases, within broad limits, if the precedent satisfies certain formal conditions, such as having been rendered by a court at a designated level in the relevant jurisdiction.[6] This institutional principle is supported by a number of considerations.

Under the principles of support and replicability, the courts must establish and apply rules that are supported by the general standards of society or the special standards of the legal system, and must adopt a process of reasoning that is replicable by the profession. Reasoning from precedent satisfies both those principles.

Under the principle of objectivity, courts are obliged to reason from propositions that are universal, that is, propositions the courts are ready to apply not merely to the parties to the immediate dispute, but to all similarly situated disputants who may come before them in the future. Stare decisis gives effect to this concept too. Under stare decisis, a court is on notice that if it chooses to apply a given proposition to resolve a dispute between these litigants today, it may be obliged to apply the same proposition to all similarly situated disputants in the future. Thus stare decisis discourages a court from deciding cases on the basis of propositions it would be unwilling to apply to all similarly situated disputants.[7]

Another concept entailed by the principle of objectivity is even more salient in this area: the concept of evenhandedness, that like cases should be treated alike. The concept of universality instructs a court not to decide a case on the basis of a rule unless it is ready to apply the rule to all similarly situated disputants. The concept of evenhandedness instructs a court that all other things being equal, once the court has adopted a rule to decide a case it should indeed apply that rule to similarly situated disputants. (Evenhandedness is more complex than universality, however, partly because often all other things are not equal and partly because evenhandedness can be satisfied not only by the consistent disposition of like cases, but by the consistent application of the institutional principles that determine how cases should be decided. These two types of evenhandedness usually but do not always converge.)[8]

Stare decisis also serves as the foundation for the courts' function of enriching the supply of legal rules. A precedent is conceived of as law chiefly because it is binding under stare decisis. Thus stare decisis makes planning on the basis of law more reliable and private dispute-settlement on the basis of law easier. The most salient aspect of this role of stare decisis is the protection of justifiable reliance. Such reliance may be special or general.

By special reliance, I mean reliance by a litigant before the court who specifically planned his conduct on the basis of a legal rule. By general reliance, I mean reliance by members of a society, other than the litigants, who are likely to have planned their conduct on the basis of the system of legal rules. General reliance may take three different forms. First, although the litigant before the court has not planned his conduct on the basis of the rule in question, a significant number of other actors may be likely to have done so. Alternatively, a significant number of actors may be likely to have planned on the basis of other legal rules or institutional arrangements that reflect the rule in question. Finally, the court may be concerned that failure to follow the precedent that adopted the rule in question may be likely to make actors insecure about the reliability of other precedents.

The occurrence of either special or general reliance is not an argument for stare decisis, since in the absence of stare decisis reliance would not be justified. The *capacity* for reliance is an argument for stare decisis, however, because it is through stare decisis that the supply of legal rules becomes enriched. And once stare decisis is established, it is powerfully reinforced by the reliance it is partly intended to elicit.

A mirror image of the value of protecting justified reliance is the value of preventing unfair surprise to those who have justifiably relied upon legal rules.[9]

Not all legal reasoning that utilizes doctrinal sources is governed by the principle of stare decisis. Under stare decisis, a court is bound by its own precedents and those of higher courts in its own jurisdiction. However, courts also follow the practice of reasoning from other doctrinal sources, such as precedents decided by coordinate courts in their own jurisdictions, precedents from other jurisdictions, and secondary sources like commentaries. Courts follow this practice because the justifications of stare decisis also support the more expansive ideal that the courts should maintain the stability of doctrine over time. This ideal is reflected in a third basic type of legal criticism—criticism for failing to reason consistently over time. Because this ideal serves as a fundamental basis for professional criticism, I shall hereafter refer to it as a standard—the standard of doctrinal stability.

It can now be seen why the real-world model of the common law differs from the model of double coherence. In the real world a model of the common law must incorporate not only the standards of social congruence and systemic consistency, but also the standard of doctrinal stability. As a result, criticisms of a legal *rule* that are based on the model of double coherence may not be conclusive as to legal *reasoning* that applies the rule in a particular case. So, for example, we might criticize a legal rule on the ground that some alternative rule would be more congruent with applicable social propositions and more consistent with other legal rules, and yet conclude that under the standard of doctrinal stability a court reasoned properly in applying the rule.

Chapter 6

Modes of Legal Reasoning

The common law should seek to satisfy three standards: social congruence, systemic consistency, and doctrinal stability. Often, the three standards point in the same direction. The central problems of legal reasoning arise when they do not. These problems will be considered in this chapter and the next, which together will examine most of the basic modes of legal reasoning employed in the common law. I will show that the institutional principles that govern these modes rest on the foundational principles examined in Chapter 3, the interplay of applicable social and doctrinal propositions, and more specifically, the interplay of the three standards the common law should seek to satisfy.

Chapter 6 will explore reasoning from precedent, from principle, by analogy, from the professional literature, and from hypotheticals. Chapter 7 will explore overruling and other forms of overturning. Each of these modes has enough special characteristics to merit separate treatment, but it will be seen that although very different in form, they are often highly comparable in substance.

Reasoning from Precedent

Reasoning from precedent is perhaps the most characteristic mode of reasoning in the common law. In fact, commentators who speak of an "easy case" at common law usually have in mind a case that can be decided simply by the application of a rule established in a binding precedent, without the employment of social propositions (except insofar as the rule explicitly requires social propositions for its application). The principle of stare decisis, under which the rule of a precedent is binding if the precedent meets certain conditions, has already been examined in a preliminary way. In examining reasoning from precedent itself, two intertwined questions must be considered: (1) How does a court faced with a precedent determine what rule the precedent stands for? (2) What is meant by the concept, expressed in the principle of stare decisis, that the rule of a precedent is binding? For ease of exposition, I shall assume in the following discussion that the relevant rule is established in a single case and that this case meets the criteria of stare decisis and concerns a single issue. I shall call the court that decided this case the precedent court, and the court that is called on to consider the effect of this case the deciding court.

Establishing the Rule of a Precedent

As a practical matter, the force of the principle of stare decisis is inversely related to the extent of the deciding court's discretion to determine what rule a precedent stands for. This has led a number of commentators to formulate mechanical rules for making that determination, in an effort to suggest that the deciding court has no latitude in the matter. Even those who do not formulate mechanical rules often use a nomenclature that suggests the deciding court's latitude is extremely limited. For example, many commentators, and for that matter many courts, often speak of "interpreting" a precedent, as if all the deciding court does is to determine what the precedent court would have done if the later case had also been before it when it decided the precedent. This nomenclature is misleading. It is true that a deciding court will often take as given the rule expressly laid down by a precedent. It is also true that even when the deciding court reformulates the rule expressly laid down by a precedent, it may very well be doing what the precedent court would have done. As Joseph Raz has pointed out:

> [It is] tempting to say that the modified rule was really the rule the original court had in mind but which it failed to articulate clearly. Often enough this may indeed be the case. It may be that the [precedent] court . . . was influenced by [some feature that was present in the first case but not in the second] but somehow perhaps they took this feature too much for granted, they failed to specify its existence among the operative conditions of their *ratio*. . . . [C]ourts may be and often are a little careless in formulating rules.[1]

Nevertheless, it would be a strange kind of interpretation that allowed the interpreter to reformulate or radically reconstruct the text, and that is just the power of a deciding court in dealing with a precedent. Furthermore, the term *interpretation* misleadingly suggests that the intent of the precedent court governs. So, for example, Raz further states:

> A modified rule can usually be justified only by reasoning very similar to that justifying the original rule. . . . The *ratio* is binding in its basic rationale and as applying to its original context. Courts can, however, modify its application to different contexts so long as they preserve its fundamental rationale.[2]

In fact, however, the continued application of a rule adopted in a precedent may be rationalized on grounds very different from that employed in the precedent itself.[3] In actual practice, a determination of what rule a precedent stands for typically involves consideration not only of the intent of the precedent court, as revealed by its language taken in context, but also professional discourse concerning the precedent, changes in social propositions and in doctrine after the precedent was decided, and the judgment of the deciding court concerning what rule would be most socially congruent and systemically consistent. Accordingly, the role of the deciding court in determining what rule a precedent stands for is not so much to determine what the precedent was intended to stand for as to determine what it has or will come to stand for. To capture this process, I shall use the nomenclature *establishing the rule of a precedent*, which reflects the deciding court's decisive role far better than does the term *interpretation*.

Most theories of how the rule of a precedent is established by the deciding court tend to be variations on three basic approaches, which I shall call the minimalist, result-centered, and announcement approaches.

Under a *minimalist* approach, the rule of a precedent consists of that part of the rule announced by the precedent court's opinion that was necessary for the decision. The rule so established is characterized as the ratio decidendi or holding of the precedent, and is deemed binding. Anything else said in the opinion is characterized as dicta and is deemed not binding. Carried to its logical conclusion, such an approach cuts back the rule announced by the precedent court to a bare minimum.

Under a *result-centered* approach, the rule of a precedent consists of the proposition that on the facts of the precedent (or some of them) the result of the precedent should be reached. What is important under this approach is what the precedent court did, not what it said. It is often implicit in this approach that in the deciding court's view the precedent court's intuition was better than its rationalization.

On the surface, at least, minimalist and result-centered approaches both seem to be grounded in the by-product model of the courts' role in establishing legal rules, under which legal rules are generated only as a by-product of the dispute-settlement function. Perhaps because the courts often profess to follow this model, it is frequently taken as a rubric that the rule of a precedent is based less on what the precedent court said than on what it did. Minimalist and result-centered approaches fit neatly under this rubric. As full descriptions of judicial practice, however, both approaches come up short. Rules of law announced in precedents are only infrequently pruned back by a deciding court to the bare minimum necessary for the precedent court's decision. Even less frequently are they disregarded entirely in favor of a rule pieced together out of the facts of the precedent and its result. A major reason for this is that the rigorous use of either approach would render the law highly uncertain, because it is normally impossible to establish reliably a single rule of a precedent under these approaches. This is well illustrated by Julius Stone's critique[4] of the theory of Arthur Goodhart[5] that the rule of a precedent is the result reached on those facts of the precedent that the precedent court considered material. Goodhart attempted to develop mechanical rules to determine what facts the precedent court considered material, so that his theory would provide a mechanical test for establishing the rule of a case. Stone demonstrated that it was virtually impossible to apply Goodhart's theory, because every material fact in a case can be stated at different levels of generality, each level of generality will tend to yield a different rule, and no mechanical rules can be devised to determine the level of generality intended by the precedent court.

Stone used for his demonstration a famous British case, *Donoghue v. Stevenson.*[6] A friend of the plaintiff had purchased a bottle of ginger beer for her in a cafe. The bottle was opaque. After the plaintiff drank part of the ginger beer she discovered a decomposed snail in the bottle. She suffered shock and severe gastroenteritis, sued the manufacturer, and won. Before *Donoghue*, a manufacturer who negligently produced a defective product was ordinarily liable only to its immediate buyer. It is clear that *Donoghue* abandoned this rule, because it held the manufacturer liable although the plaintiff was not its immediate buyer. As Stone pointed out, however, under

Goodhart's theory it would be far from clear what rule the *Donoghue* court adopted, because the various material facts in the case could be characterized at vastly different levels of generality. For example, the vehicle of harm in *Donoghue* could be characterized as an opaque bottle of ginger beer, an opaque bottle of beverage, a bottle of beverage, a container of chattels for human consumption, a chattel, or a thing. The defendant could be characterized as a manufacturer of nationally distributed goods, a manufacturer, a person working on goods for profit, or a person working on goods. The injury could be characterized as a physical personal injury, a physical personal or emotional injury, or an injury. Under the Goodhart theory, therefore, *Donoghue* could stand for almost numberless rules constructed from permutations of the material facts at various levels of generality—for example, the rule that if a manufacturer of nationally distributed goods that are intended for human consumption produces the goods in a negligent manner, it is liable for resulting physical personal or emotional injury; or the rule that if a person working on goods for profit is negligent, he is liable for resulting physical personal injury if he packaged the goods in such a way that the defect was concealed.[7]

While Goodhart's theory is essentially a result-centered approach, it also has strong connections with the minimalist approach, and Stone's critique is applicable to the latter as well as the former. Thus suppose the court in *Donoghue* had stated the rule to be that if a manufacturer produces goods in a negligent manner it is liable for injury caused by defects in the goods. No element of this rule (except negligence) would have been strictly necessary for the decision, because every element could have been stated in a narrower way. For example, the court could have reached the same result by adopting the narrow rule that if a manufacturer produces food in a negligent manner, it is liable for a reasonably foreseeable physical injury produced by defects in the food, or the even narrower rule that if a manufacturer of nationally distributed food produces the food in a negligent manner and packages it so that reasonable inspection would not have revealed the defect, the manufacturer is liable for a reasonably foreseeable physical injury to a consumer or a person for whom the consumer purchased.

The third basic approach to establishing the rule of a precedent, which I shall call the *announcement* approach, avoids the force of

Stone's objections. Under this approach, the rule of a precedent consists of the rule it states, provided that rule is relevant to the issues raised by the dispute before the court.

In contrast to the minimalist and result-centered approaches, the announcement approach is implicitly grounded in the enrichment model of the courts' role in establishing legal rules. On the one hand, the announcement approach gives weight to the rules announced by the court just on the ground that they are announced, thereby recognizing that the enrichment of the supply of legal rules is a valued function in itself. On the other, the announcement approach insists on some relation between the rule and the dispute, thereby recognizing that the function of enriching the supply of legal rules, although valued in itself, is nevertheless connected in important ways to the function of dispute-resolution.

Partly in reflection of the descriptive power of the enrichment model, the descriptive power of the announcement approach is much greater than that of the minimalist and result-centered approaches. Few precedents would escape unscathed from a rigorous application of those approaches, but observation shows that courts usually reason from precedent by starting with the rule the precedent announced, rather than by pruning that rule back to its minimal contours or disregarding the rule entirely and instead constructing a rule out of the facts of the precedent and its result. The use of this approach is so common that it needs no extensive illustration. Pick up any reported case and examples will come readily to hand. (A particularly dramatic example is provided by cases involving the technique known as pure prospective overruling, in which a court overrules a line of prior cases but makes the new rule applicable only to transactions that arise after the new rule is announced.[8] Although the new rule is not applied to the parties before the court, and is therefore completely unnecessary to the decision of the case before the court, under the announcement approach it will be given the same regard by the profession as a rule that is crucial to a decision.)[9]

But despite its predominance the announcement approach does not describe all judicial practice. Many cases do deal with precedents in part by using moderate versions of the minimalist or result-centered approaches to reformulate the rule announced by the precedent court. More important, some cases, including a number of our most important cases, employ rigorous versions of these approaches to radically reconstruct the precedents and overturn the rule the precedents announce, while purporting to follow the precedents—a use of minimalist and result-oriented approaches that I shall refer to as *transformation*.

An example of the rigorous use of a minimalist approach to effect transformation is provided by the treatment of *Christensen v. Thornby*[10] in *Sherlock v. Stillwater Clinic.*[11] In *Christensen v. Thornby* Christensen alleged that his wife had experienced great difficulty with the birth of her first child and had been told that it would be dangerous to bear another. Thornby, a physician, advised Christensen that a vasectomy would protect his wife against conception and then performed that operation. Following the vasectomy, Thornby told Christensen that the operation had been successful and guaranteed sterility. Subsequently, Mrs. Christensen became pregnant and gave birth. Although his wife survived, Christensen experienced great anxiety and was subjected to considerable expense as a result of the pregnancy and birth. Christensen did not allege negligence, but brought suit based on the failure of the vasectomy to fulfill Thornby's representations. The trial court dismissed the complaint, and the Minnesota Supreme Court affirmed.

Much of the court's opinion was devoted to showing that a contract for a vasectomy did not violate public policy. The portion of the opinion that upheld the trial court's dismissal consisted of two paragraphs that made two separate points. The first point was that the complaint did not allege a wrong by Thornby. Although, said the court, Christensen insisted that his complaint was grounded on deceit, he had failed to allege that Thornby's representations were made with fraudulent intent:

> ... [The plaintiff] alleges that the operation he contracted for was performed. It is a matter of common knowledge that such an operation properly done in due course effects sterilization. ... Any competent physician or surgeon must necessarily have given plaintiff advice to that effect.[12]

The second point was that the birth of a healthy child to a healthy mother did not constitute an injury to Christensen:

> The purpose of the operation was to save the wife from the hazards to her life which were incident to childbirth. It was not the alleged purpose to save the expense incident to pregnancy and delivery. The wife has survived. Instead of losing his wife, the

plaintiff has been blessed with the fatherhood of another child. The expenses alleged are incident to the bearing of a child, and their avoidance is remote from the avowed purpose of the operation. As well might the plaintiff charge defendant with the cost of nurture and education of the child during its minority.[13]

A fair reading of the case suggests that the second point was relevant to the decision. It may have been necessary as well, since the result seems to rest as much on the conclusion that Christensen suffered no injury as on the conclusion that Thornby had committed no wrong. Indeed, the latter conclusion seems shaky. Although at the end of its opinion the court states that plaintiff insisted his complaint was grounded in deceit, earlier passages suggest that the action was for breach of contract.[14] Christensen's allegations seemed to raise legitimate issues whether Thornby had promised beforehand that the operation would be successful, whether he had guaranteed sterility thereafter, and whether the promise and guarantee were enforceable if made.

Sherlock v. Stillwater Clinic was a strikingly similar case that arose in Minnesota some forty years after *Christensen.* Following the birth of their seventh child, Mr. and Mrs. Sherlock consulted Dr. Stratte, a member of the Stillwater Clinic, and discussed with him the various medical alternatives available to ensure that their family would grow no larger. A decision was reached that Mr. Sherlock would undergo a vasectomy, and the operation was performed by Dr. Stratte in mid-December. The Sherlocks were advised that they should either refrain from sexual relations or take additional contraceptive measures until it was conclusively determined by postoperative testing that Mr. Sherlock's semen was free of sperm. On January 23, Mr. Sherlock brought a sample of his semen to the clinic for testing. Later that day, Dr. Stratte telephoned Sherlock and reported that the results of the test were "negative"—that is, his semen was free of sperm. Dr. Stratte's report was incorrect: the test had shown that Mr. Sherlock's semen did have some motile sperm. Relying on the erroneous belief that the vasectomy had been successful, the Sherlocks resumed normal sexual relations without contraceptives. Several months later, Mrs. Sherlock began to miss her menstrual periods. On August 5, Mr. Sherlock returned to the clinic for a second test, and this time he was correctly advised that the vasectomy had been ineffective. The following day, it was determined that Mrs. Sherlock was pregnant, and in due course she gave birth to a healthy baby.

Thereafter, the Sherlocks brought suit against Dr. Stratte and the clinic, claiming that the unplanned birth of their eighth child was a direct result of Dr. Stratte's negligent postoperative care. Damages were sought for Mrs. Sherlock's pain and suffering during pregnancy and delivery, the cost of supporting and educating the child until the age of majority, and Mr. Sherlock's temporary loss of his wife's consortium (that is, conjugal companionship). Employing a minimalist approach, the court set aside, as dicta, the conclusion in *Christensen* that the birth of a healthy child to a healthy mother did not constitute an injury—that "[a]s well might the plaintiff charge defendant with the cost of nurture and education of the child"—and held that the Sherlocks could recover the damages they sought. Indeed, using a scalpel finer than that of Dr. Stratte, the court radically reconstructed *Christensen* so that its rule *supported* the Sherlocks' complaint:

> Apart from the technical disposition made in [*Christensen*, the court in that case] expressly held that sterilizations were not contrary to public policy and that an action, if properly pleaded, could be maintained against a physician for the improper performance of such an operation.
>
> Viewed in its correct posture, the *Christensen* case stands solely for the proposition that a cause of action exists for an improperly performed sterilization.[15]

A leading example of the rigorous use of a result-centered approach to effect transformation is provided by Judge Cardozo's treatment in *MacPherson v. Buick Motor Co.*[16] of the New York precedents concerning manufacturers' negligence. *MacPherson* was decided in 1916. In America at that time, as in England before *Donoghue*, the general rule was that the negligent manufacturer of a defective product was ordinarily liable only to its immediate buyer. This rule was subject to an exception, however, where the product was of a type that was "inherently dangerous." *MacPherson* grew out of injuries suffered by the plaintiff as a result of the sudden collapse of a new Buick he had purchased. One of the car's wheels had been made of defective wood, and the car had collapsed because the spokes of the wheel had crumbled into fragments. The car had been manufactured by Buick Motor Company, which had sold it to a dealer, which had sold it to MacPherson. MacPherson sued Buick Motor. Buick Motor had not made the wheel, but instead had purchased it from another manufacturer. There was evidence, however, that reasonable inspection by Buick Motor could have discovered the defects. MacPherson won a jury verdict against Buick Motor, and Buick Motor appealed.

Cardozo began by reviewing the major New York cases concerning the liability of a negligent manufacturer to a person other than its immediate buyer, beginning with *Thomas v. Winchester*, decided in 1852.[17] In that case the defendant had negligently labeled a jar of belladonna, a poison, as dandelion, a medicine. The plaintiff bought the jar and was made seriously ill. The court held that a manufacturer can normally be sued in negligence only by its immediate buyer. "If A. build a wagon and sell it to B., who sells it to C., and C. hires it to D., who in consequence of the gross negligence of A., in building the wagon, is overturned and injured, D. cannot recover damages against A., the builder. A.'s obligation to build the wagon faithfully, arises solely out of his contract with B.; the public have nothing to do with it. Misfortune to third persons, not parties to the contract, would not be a natural and necessary consequence of the builder's negligence; and such negligence is not an act imminently dangerous to human life."[18] The court nevertheless imposed liability, on the ground that in the case before it the general rule was inapplicable because "The defendant's negligence put human life in imminent danger."[19]

Cardozo then turned to later New York cases. In *Loop v. Litchfield*,[20] decided in 1870, the defendant had negligently constructed the flywheel of a circular saw. After the saw had been leased out by the original buyer it flew apart and fatally injured the lessee. The plaintiffs alleged that the saw was, like the poison in *Thomas v. Winchester*, a dangerous instrument. The court rejected this argument and held that the manufacturer was not liable to the lessee.[21] In *Losee v. Clute*,[22] decided in 1873, the defendant had negligently constructed a steam boiler which exploded and injured property of the plaintiff, who was not the defendant's buyer. Again the court held the manufacturer not liable.

In contrast, in *Devlin v. Smith*,[23] decided in 1882, the defendant had negligently constructed painters' scaffolding which collapsed and caused the death of a worker. The court reiterated the general rule that "The liability of the builder or manufacturer for [defects caused by negligence] is, in general, only to the person with whom he contracted." It nevertheless held the defendant liable, on the ground that the defect rendered the scaffolding "imminently dangerous."[24] Similarly, in *Statler v. George A. Ray Manufacturing Co.*,[25] decided in 1909, the defendant had negligently constructed a restaurant-size coffee urn which exploded and severely scalded the plaintiff, who had purchased the urn from a jobber. The court held the defendant liable on the ground that the urn was "inherently dangerous" and the defendant's negligence made it "imminently dangerous."[26]

With this background, Cardozo in *MacPherson* affirmed the judgment for the plaintiff on the basis of the following rule:

> We hold, then, that the principle of *Thomas v. Winchester* is not limited to poisons, explosives, and things of like nature, to things which in their normal operation are implements of destruction. If the nature of a thing is such that it is reasonably certain to place life and limb in peril when negligently made, it is then a thing of danger. . . . If to the element of danger there is added knowledge that the thing will be used by persons other than the purchaser, and used without new tests, then, irrespective of contract, the manufacturer of this thing of danger is under a duty to make it carefully.[27]

This formulation adopted the cloak of the old rule, insofar as it made the manufacturer's liability turn on whether the product was "a thing of danger," but it completely changed the substance of the old rule. Under the formulation in *MacPherson*, the issue became not whether a product is of a type that is inherently dangerous to third parties regardless of negligence, but whether a product is dangerous to third parties if negligently made; and any product may be dangerous if negligently made. In effect, therefore, *MacPherson* adopted a straightforward negligence rule, under which the negligent manufacturer of a defective product is liable to any person who would foreseeably be injured as a result of the manufacturer's negligence, whether or not that person is the manufacturer's immediate buyer.

However, Cardozo did not formally overrule the old cases. Instead, he used a result-centered approach to transform the old rule by a radical reconstruction of precedent. *Thomas v. Winchester*, *Devlin v. Smith*, and *Statler v. Ray*, he concluded, supported the rule established in *MacPherson*, since all those cases had imposed liability on a negligent manufacturer—never mind that they did so on a different theory. *Loop v. Litchfield*, which had held in favor of the manufacturer of a defective circular saw, and *Losee v. Clute*, which had held in favor of the manufacturer of a defective steam boiler, were distinguished on the ground that the defendants in those cases were insulated by standard negligence defenses. Under all the circumstances of those cases, Cardozo implied, there might have been no lack of due care by the manufacturer, and even if there was, the manufacturer's immediate buyer had assumed or made himself responsible for the risk.[28]

Taken together with the great bulk of cases that use the announcement approach, cases like *Sherlock* and *MacPherson* show that the various approaches to establishing the rule of a precedent are not so much theories as techniques. The issue, which technique should be used by a deciding court in a given case, cannot be resolved by describing or enumerating the techniques, but must turn on independent institutional principles. The development of these principles must begin with the question: what is the meaning of the concept of "binding," as that concept is used in the principle of stare decisis?

The Meaning of Binding: *Formal Constraints*

Two relatively formal constraints imposed by the concept that a precedent is binding may be stated at the outset.[29] The first is that the rule established by the deciding court must be reconcilable with the result reached in the precedent. For example, the rule established in *Sherlock v. Stillwater,* that a parent could sue a negligent doctor for the expenses attendant upon a wrongful birth, was reconcilable with the result in *Christensen v. Thornby* because the plaintiff in *Christensen* had not alleged negligence. Similarly, the rule established in *MacPherson,* that a manufacturer is liable for negligence even to parties other than his immediate buyer, was reconcilable with the results in *Thomas v. Winchester, Devlin v. Smith,* and *Statler v. Ray* because all those cases imposed liability on the manufacturer, and was reconcilable with the results in *Loop v. Litchfield* and *Losee v. Clute* because, at least as Cardozo stated the facts of those cases, the manufacturers there were protected by standard negligence defenses. As *Christensen* and *MacPherson* illustrate, this first formal constraint is relatively weak, because a deciding court can usually massage the facts of relevant precedents in such a way as to reconcile their results with whatever rule the court proposes to adopt.

The second formal constraint is that the deciding court must either follow the precedent or distinguish it. This constraint is also weak, because the process of distinguishing precedent turns on establishing the rule of a precedent through precisely the same techniques as those employed in the process of following precedent.

Distinguishing tends to fall into two formats. One format involves establishing the rule of a precedent by the announcement technique and then showing that the announced rule is irrelevant to the case at hand. The second format involves taking an announced rule that appears to conflict with the deciding court's proposed decision and then using a minimalist or result-centered technique to reformulate or radically reconstruct the rule so that it will not conflict with that decision. The special feature of the process of distinguishing therefore lies not in the techniques that are used to establish the rule of a precedent, which are identical to the techniques that are used when the precedent is to be followed, but in the formal objective of the process. A deciding court may establish the rule of a precedent to achieve one of two formal objectives: to provide support for its decision, or to show that the rule of the precedent is not in conflict with its decision. We speak of a deciding court as following precedent when its objective in establishing the rule of a precedent is to show that the precedent supports its proposed decision. We speak of a deciding court as distinguishing precedent when its objective in establishing the rule of a precedent is to show that the precedent does not conflict with its proposed decision.

Since following and distinguishing precedent involve precisely the same techniques for establishing the rule of a precedent, and since two of those techniques allow the courts great latitude, the constraint that a deciding court must either follow a precedent or distinguish it imposes little if any limitation beyond the constraint that the rule established by the deciding court must be reconcilable with the result reached in the precedent.

The Meaning of Binding: Substantive Constraints

Considering how weak are the formal constraints imposed by the concept that a precedent is binding, if there were no substantive—no really meaningful—constraints on a deciding court, that concept would have only limited significance. Certainly, substantive constraints are not to be found in the menu of techniques from which a deciding court can select in establishing the rule of a precedent. Rather, the substantive constraints imposed by the concept that a precedent is binding—and, therefore, the full meaning of stare decisis—depend on further institutional principles of adjudication. In particular, those substantive constraints depend on the institutional principles that govern the interplay of applicable social and doctrinal propositions and, more specifically, the interplay of the standards of social congruence, systemic consistency, and doctrinal stability.

These further institutional principles must be considered in the practical contexts in which reasoning from precedent arises. To begin with, when a court reasons from a precedent, it normally begins with an announced rule that seems directly applicable to the case at hand. To put this differently, reasoning from precedent normally uses the announcement technique as a starting point. There are good reasons for this. As a symbolic matter, disregard of what precedent courts say, if widely engaged in, would imply less than full respect for courts by courts, an attitude hardly calculated to instill respect for courts by others. More important, as a practical matter the announcement technique tends to minimize judicial discretion and to maximize replicability. This may seem paradoxical, because the traditional view of stare decisis stresses that a precedent court's power to make law is reined in by the concept that what the court says is less important than what it does. Giving full effect to that view, however, would require a deciding court to use either a minimalist or a result-centered technique to establish the rule of a precedent. These techniques permit the construction of almost numberless rules from any single precedent. Therefore, if deciding courts were required or even encouraged to use these techniques as a matter of course, the law would be extremely uncertain. It is much easier for the profession to replicate a process of reasoning that normally starts with an announced rule than it would be to replicate a process that normally started with the application of minimalist or result-centered techniques.

Because the courts normally use announced rules as their starting points, as a practical matter the deciding court is likely to have a limited number of salient choices in dealing with a precedent. It can accept and apply the announced rule; it can determine that on close inspection the announced rule is not relevant; or it can use a minimalist or result-centered technique to reformulate or radically reconstruct the announced rule, and then apply or distinguish the rule it so establishes. Furthermore, because announced rules often seem desirable until a new issue arises (that is why they are announced), as a practical matter the problem of reasoning from precedent is often whether a rule that seemed desirable without regard to the issue raised by the new case still seems desirable when that issue is considered. Accordingly, the question for a deciding court usually is whether, in light of the new issue, the announced rule of a precedent should be (i) applied to a case that falls within the stated ambit of the rule, (ii) extended to a case that falls outside the rule's stated ambit, or (iii) reformulated or radically reconstructed so that the rule is not applied to a case that fell within its ambit as originally stated.

I shall now examine, within these practical contexts, some of the institutional principles that govern the interplay of the standards of social congruence, systemic consistency, and doctrinal stability and thereby figure in determining the substantive constraints imposed by the concept that a precedent is binding. At the same time I shall sketch out models of the development of common law rules reflecting these institutional principles.

(i) *An announced rule that fully satisfies the standards of social congruence and systemic consistency should be consistently applied and extended; the meaning of consistency; the linear model of development.* One such institutional principle is that if the rule announced in a precedent fully satisfies the standards of social congruence and systemic consistency, it should be consistently applied and extended. The reasons for this principle are self-evident: if an announced rule fully satisfies the standards of social congruence and systemic consistency, it should be consistently applied and extended even without regard to stare decisis. The application of this principle, however, raises two questions: how is it to be determined whether the announced rule of a precedent satisfies the standards of social congruence and systemic consistency, and what does consistent application and extension entail in this context?

The first question has already been addressed in Chapter 4. If necessary, the court can itself make the relevant judgment. In practice, however, much of the work will often have been done for the court before the case is decided, through discourse in the wider arena. If the announced rule lacks social congruence or systemic consistency, that is likely to have been brought out in treatises and law reviews, in cases in other jurisdictions, in statutes that modify the rule, and in other ways. Even if no such discourse has occurred in the wider arena, criticism or the lack of it in the narrower arena will help instruct the court. In the absence of significant criticism in these arenas it is normally a fair inference that the announced rule satisfies the standards of social congruence and systemic consistency, although of course that inference is not inescapable.

The second question is, what does consistent application and extension entail in this context? Obviously, it entails more than identical treatment of identical cases. Since no two cases are identical, if that is all a requirement of consistency entailed it would have no real bite. When we require consistency in everyday activities, we usually mean that any differences in the treatment of two cases must be justified by some relevant background propositions.[30] The same is true in common law reasoning, and here the relevant background propositions consist chiefly of applicable social propositions. Therefore, an institutional principle requiring a rule to be consistently applied and extended normally entails that the rule must be applied and extended to a new case if applicable social propositions do not justify different treatment of the two cases under the rule, given the social propositions that support the rule. (I refer here to the social propositions that support the rule now, not those that supported the rule in its origin.) So, for example, the rule that bargain promises are enforceable must be applied to secular bargains made by clergymen, because the rule fully satisfies the standards of social congruence and systemic consistency, and applicable social propositions do not justify treating the secular bargains of clergy differently from the bargains of others, given the social propositions that support the bargain rule.[31] Similarly, in early days, when the dominant carriers were ships and wagons, the rule was established that a person who held himself out as willing to carry the goods of any member of the public had the status of a common carrier and the obligations attached to that status.[32] After railroads were constructed the rule was applied to them as well,[33] because applicable social propositions did not justify different treatment, for this purpose, of ships and wagons on the one hand and railroads on the other.

In considering an institutional principle that governs common law reasoning, it can be useful to descriptively model the line of development generated when the principle is applicable. There is sometimes a tendency to describe the development of common law rules by the use of a single model. Typically, the model bears a strong resemblance to the classical model of Darwinian evolution: a rule develops by a series of incremental steps until so many small steps have been taken that a new rule can be said to have emerged.[34]

In reality, however, the development of common law rules proceeds along a number of different paths and can only be captured by a variety of models. The development of a legal rule under the principle considered in this section can be described by what might be called a linear model, that is, a model of consistent application and extension.

Examples of consistent application have already been considered. Here is an example of consistent extension: It is an established rule of contract law that if an employer wrongfully terminates an employment contract, the employee cannot recover his entire contract salary. Instead, he can only recover either (i) the difference between his salary under the contract and what he actually earned on a replacement job, together with amounts reasonably spent to search for the replacement job, or (ii) the difference between his salary under the contract and what he could have earned if he had used reasonable efforts to search out a comparable replacement job.[35] This rule reflects the general principle that the victim of a breach of contract is under a duty to use reasonable efforts to mitigate his losses. After the rule had been established it was held that an employee could recover amounts reasonably spent to search for a replacement job even if the search was unsuccessful.[36] This was a consistent extension of the rule. If the employee is under a duty to search for a new job for the purpose of mitigating the employer's damages, the employer should bear the expense of the search. Applicable social propositions would not justify different treatment of successful and unsuccessful searches for this purpose. (I will examine the extension of announced rules more fully later in this chapter, in the section "Reasoning by Analogy.")

(ii) *An announced rule that fully satisfies the standards of social congruence and systemic consistency should be reformulated when a case arises that falls within the stated ambit of the rule, but that requires different treatment given the social propositions that support the rule; the hiving model of development.* A second institutional principle that governs reasoning from precedent is that if the rule announced in a precedent fully satisfies the standards of social congruence and systemic consistency, and a case arises that falls within the stated ambit of the rule but that requires different treatment given the social propositions that support the rule, the announced rule should be reformulated accordingly. Here consistency requires not that the announced rule be applied or extended, but that an exception should be made. Exempting minors from the rule that bargain promises are enforceable provides an illustration. The rule that bargains are enforceable is supported partly by social propositions concerning the significance of consent, and applicable social propositions require a distinction to be drawn between the consent of a minor and the consent of an adult.

Here is another, more complex example: A standard way to conclude a contract is by offer and acceptance. Often the issue arises whether a response to an offer constitutes an acceptance or not. Suppose there is an announced rule that a response to an offer constitutes an acceptance if a reasonable person in the offeror's position would interpret the response as an acceptance, even if the offeree does not intend his response as an acceptance. Assume further that this rule is socially congruent and systemically consistent. It is congruent with moral norms because a person who intends something other than the reasonable meaning of his words has used language carelessly. It is congruent with policy because the security of transactions (and therefore the ability to plan reliably) would be undermined if a person could escape contractual liability by convincing a fact finder that he had subjectively attached some special, unreasonable meaning to his expressions. It is consistent with the body of the law because the law often measures conduct by a reasonable-person standard.

The following case now arises: A makes an offer to B, and B makes a response that he does not intend as an acceptance. A reasonable person with A's knowledge would interpret B's response as an acceptance. However, A does not so interpret it. B does not perform. A sues for breach of contract, falsely claiming that he interpreted B's response as an acceptance. The announced rule should be reformulated by making an exception for the new case, in which both parties share the same subjective understanding.[37] The announced rule is supported by moral norms concerning fault and by the policy favoring security of transactions. Moral norms concerning fault require an exception for the new case. B may have been at fault, but his fault caused no injury to A. Rather, it is A who is at fault for seeking to impose contractual liability on B even though A never believed that B intended to contract. An exception for the new case would not conflict with the security of transactions, because B can escape liability only by showing A's state of mind as well as his own. Application of the announced rule to the new case would also be inconsistent with the body of the law, because if applied to the new case the announced rule would impose liability in the absence of injury and with no justification in policy.

The line of development generated by the institutional principle considered in this section can be described by what might be called the hiving model. Under this model, development proceeds by hiving off certain types of activity from treatment under an established rule, in a manner that is consistent with the social propositions that support the rule. To illustrate, it is an established rule of corporation law that a holder of controlling stock may sell his stock at a premium over the market price, even though the premium is unavailable to noncontrolling shareholders.[38] This rule reflects the experiential proposition that controlling stock normally sells at a higher price than noncontrolling stock, and serves policy by facilitating the transfer of control from less efficient to more efficient hands. A number of exceptions have been hived off from this rule. For example, the seller must disgorge a premium that is paid because the buyer foreseeably plans to loot the corporation,[39] or a premium paid for the seller's agreement to transfer a corporate office.[40] These exceptions are consistent with the underlying rule. The premium in such cases reflects something other than the value of controlling stock, and requiring the seller to disgorge the premium in such cases will not inhibit the transfer of control to more efficient hands.

(iii) *An announced rule that substantially satisfies the standards of social congruence and systemic consistency should be consistently applied and extended.* If an announced rule substantially satisfies the standards of social congruence and systemic consistency, it should be consistently applied and extended even though some other rule would better satisfy those standards. Since small differences in social congruence and systemic consistency are likely to be highly debatable, difficult to perceive, or both, if the courts failed to apply and extend an announced rule consistently just because the rule was modestly less socially congruent and systemically consistent than a competing alternative, it would be very difficult to replicate the adjudicative process or to put much reliance on announced rules. Where the difference between the social congruence and systemic consistency of two competing rules is small, the values that underlie those standards are outweighed by the values that underlie the standard of doctrinal stability.

To illustrate, assume the following hypothetical, which bears at least a rough resemblance to the law:

In *Case A* the court announced the rule that an unrelied-upon donative promise is unenforceable. Call this the basic rule. Applicable social propositions provide strong support for this rule. The policy of social gravity is relevant, because the injury that results from the breach of an unrelied-upon donative promise is likely to be relatively slight and it is far from clear that such promises, taken as a class, implicate any important social interests. The policy of private autonomy is relevant, because donative promises might well be expected to fall within the realm of personal trust and confidence. The administrability policy is also relevant. If donative promises were enforceable it would often be hard to refute a false claim that such a promise had been made. Furthermore, the moral obligation created by a donative promise is normally excused by the promisee's ingratitude or the promisor's improvidence. What constitutes ingratitude and improvidence, however, is extremely difficult to determine. A rule that made donative promises enforceable, but subject to the defenses of ingratitude and improvidence, would create very difficult problems of administration. Finally, if a person is to come under a legal obligation simply by virtue of having exercised his will it might at least be required that his will has probably been exercised in a deliberative manner. However, because the actors involved in donative transactions are often emotionally involved, and a donative promisor tends to look mainly to the interests of the promisee, a donative promise is more likely to be uncalculated than deliberative.

After the basic rule was announced in *Case A*, the issue arose, in *Case B*, whether an exception should be made for an unrelied-upon donative promise that is in writing and states an explicit intent to be legally bound. A decision either way would have substantially satisfied the standards of social congruence and systemic consistency. If a promise is in writing the problem of dealing with false claims is not significant. If a promise includes an explicit statement that the promisor intends to be legally bound there is assurance both that the promisor acted deliberatively and that he did not want to leave enforcement of his promise to the realm of personal trust and confidence. Furthermore, once the concerns about false claims and deliberativeness are satisfied it may seem socially desirable to provide a facility by which an individual can make an enforceable donative commitment.[41] On the other hand, the difficulty of administering a regime in which improvidence and ingratitude constituted defenses would be substantial. The court in *Case B* therefore concluded that an exception to the basic rule should not be made for such a promise.

Another issue has now arisen in *Case C*. Should an exception be made to the basic rule if a written donative promise is deliberately (but falsely) cast in the form of a bargain? The deliberate false use of the bargain form serves the same function as a statement that the promisor intends to be legally bound. Therefore, applicable social propositions do not support a distinction, within the context of the basic rule, between a written donative promise that states an intent to be legally bound (*Case B*) and a written donative promise cast in the form of a bargain (*Case C*). In the view of the deciding court in *Case C*, the rule announced in *Case B*, that a written donative promise that states an intent to be legally bound is unenforceable, is less socially congruent than a rule that such a promise is enforceable. The deciding court would therefore have decided *Case B* the other way. Correspondingly, if the deciding court were writing on a clean slate, it would decide *Case C* by holding that a written donative promise cast in the form of a bargain is enforceable. Nevertheless, because the rule announced in *Case B* has substantial social congruence, and applicable social propositions would not support a distinction between *Case B* and *Case C* within the context of the rule, the deciding court should not distinguish *Case B* but should instead consistently extend the rule of *Case B* and hold that an un-relied-upon donative promise cast in the form of a written bargain is also unenforceable.

As a descriptive matter, the situation may be a bit different. If an announced rule does not fully satisfy the standards of social congruence and systemic consistency, it is predictable that courts will occasionally strain to get around the rule by placing a case into a category where it does not properly belong, but which leads to a more socially congruent outcome than the proper category. In *Case C*, for example, a court might strain to treat a promise that was a bargain only in form as if it were a real bargain and then enforce it on that ground.[42] Thus while a rule that substantially satisfies the standards of social congruence and systemic consistency should and generally will be developed in a linear manner, on a working level it is likely that some retrograde motion will occasionally occur.

(iv) *An announced rule that substantially fails to satisfy the standards of social congruence and systemic consistency should not be consistently applied and extended; the jagged model of development.* If an announced rule substantially fails to satisfy the standards of social congruence and systemic consistency it should not be consistently applied and extended. Major gains in social congruence and systemic consistency outweigh losses in the stability of doctrine over time. Nor is it material whether the rule was always socially incongruent and systemically inconsistent, or only later became so. Perhaps the rule substantially failed to satisfy the standards of social congruence and systemic consistency even when it was originally established. Perhaps the rule substantially satisfied those standards when it was originally established but no longer does so, because norms, policies, or experiential propositions have changed. Perhaps the actual effects of the rule undesirably differed from the effects that were reasonably expected when the rule was originally established. No matter. The point is not whether the rule was justified when it was adopted, but whether it is justified now.

An institutional principle that does not require the courts invariably to apply and extend doctrinal propositions in a consistent manner is consonant with the principles of support and replicability. Social congruence and systemic consistency both turn on objective support. Because such support is observable, the application of a principle that turns on substantial failure to satisfy those standards is replicable.

The courts use several different techniques to give effect to the institutional principle that an announced rule that substantially fails to satisfy the standards of social congruence and systemic consistency should not be consistently applied and extended.[43] Perhaps the most common of these techniques is to draw distinctions, in the form of exceptions, that seem plausible in form but are in substance either inconsistent with the announced rule, given the social propositions that support the rule, or impossible to administer in such a way that cases are treated in a consistent fashion. The courts will do this in an effort to save as much activity as possible from the announced rule's operation. Often too, the legislature will intervene in at least a partial way. The result is a model of development that can best be described as jagged, and a path of development characterized by disintegration and decay.

For example, under the legal-duty rule in contract law a bargain is unenforceable if one party's performance consists only of an act he had already contracted to perform.[44] As this area of law developed, however, the courts made a number of inconsistent exceptions to the rule. Under one exception, the rule is inapplicable if the duty under the prior contract is owed to a party other than the promisor.[45] Under another exception, the rule is inapplicable if the duty is to pay a debt whose total amount is disputed, even though the performance consists of paying the part that is admittedly due.[46] Some courts have held the rule inapplicable by concluding that in the cases before them the parties had "rescinded" their prior contract and then made a "new" one[47]—a conclusion that can be drawn, if a court so desires, in any case that falls within the rule. And under modern law the bargain is enforceable if it consists of a modification of the prior contract that is fair and equitable in view of circumstances not anticipated when the prior contract was made[48]—an exception that probably covers the great majority of the cases to which the legal-duty rule is purportedly applicable. The legislatures have also intervened. Many statutes provide that promises within the rule are enforceable if in writing,[49] and under the Uniform Commercial Code a promise modifying a contract for the sale of goods is binding despite the rule.[50]

The development of the legal-duty rule has followed a jagged path, characterized by disintegration and decay, because the rule substantially fails to satisfy the standards of social congruence and systemic consistency. The rule lacks congruence with moral norms because it condones promise-breaking. If A makes an uncoerced promise to B that because of rising prices he will increase the payment due B under a going contract, and then reneges, it is normally A who is perceived to have acted unfairly, not B. The same is true if A agrees to accept part payment in discharge of B's entire debt and, after having received the part payment, sues B for the balance. The rule lacks congruence with policy because the transactions rendered unenforceable by the rule normally have the social value attached to bargains or, at the least, the social value attached to promises that facilitate bargains. Because the rule is socially incongruent it is also inconsistent with other legal rules—specifically, the rule that bargains are enforceable according to their terms. (This is another example of how consistency with the body of law is normally dependent upon social congruence. If there were good social reasons to treat a bargained-for promise to perform a preexisting contractual duty differently from other bargained-for promises, the legal-duty and bargain rules would not be inconsistent.) Thus it is not surprising that the courts adopted inconsistent exceptions to the legal-duty rule and that the legislatures overturned the rule in many of its applications. Substantial social incongruence will lead the courts to adopt inconsistent exceptions, because the exceptions, at least, will be socially congruent. It will lead the legislature to intervene for the same reason.

Similarly, it was early established as a rule of corporation law that a director or officer could buy or sell stock without disclosing material inside information that he learned through his position.[51] As this area of law developed, however, the courts adopted an exception under which the rule did not apply if "special facts" were present.[52] Since there was no meaningful way to differentiate cases that involved "special facts" from those that did not, the exception either ate up the rule or made the rule impossible to administer in a consistent fashion. Eventually, the Securities and Exchange Commission adopted Rule 10b-5,[53] which was expansively interpreted by the federal courts to require directors and officers to make full disclosure in such cases. Development in this area followed a jagged path, characterized by disintegration and decay, because the announced rule substantially failed to satisfy the standards of social congruence and systemic consistency. The rule lacked congruence with moral norms, because it is unfair for an agent to exploit information he derives from his position for his own benefit and to the detriment of his ultimate principal. The rule lacked congruence with policy, because trading in inside information serves no useful social purpose and saps investor confidence in capital markets. Because the rule was socially incongruent, it was inconsistent with other legal rules concerning the fiduciary duties of directors and officers. Thus it is not surprising that the state courts adopted an exception that either ate up the rule or made it impossible to administer in a consistent fashion, that Rule 10b-5 was adopted, and that the federal courts interpreted Rule 10b-5 in a way that made the common law rule largely moot.

Still another illustration is provided by the pre-*MacPherson* rule that a negligent manufacturer of a defective product was ordinarily liable only to its immediate buyer. The exception made to this rule for "inherently dangerous" products was both inconsistent with the rule and impossible to administer in such a way that manufacturer's-liability cases were treated in a consistent fashion, as evidenced by the application of the exception to such products as painters' scaffolding and coffee urns. The rule developed in a jagged manner because it came to substantially lack social congruence and systemic consistency. The original justifications for the rule seem to have been a policy of protecting industry against extensive liability in its infant days, and a belief that in the absence of the rule the courts would be flooded with litigation. Perhaps too there was a belief that consumers, at least depended on the due care of those with whom they dea't, rather than the due care of some remote vendor. By the turn of the century, however, none of these policy and experiential propositions could have seemed valid. Industry had matured, and it is unlikely that there was substantial support for a policy that mature industry should have special protection against ordinary negligence liability. Flood-of-litigation arguments are always tenuous, and this one probably had little basis in reality from the very outset. And with the advent of nationwide distribution of brand-name merchandise, consumers had begun to rely more on manufacturers than on retailers. Because the rule came to be socially incongruent, it also came to lack consistency with the body of the law. When applicable social propositions seemed to provide good reasons for distinguishing the liability of manufacturers from the liability of others, special treatment for manufacturers was consistent with the negligence principle. When good social reasons for such a distinction could no longer be perceived, special treatment became inconsistent with the negligence principle. Thus it is not surprising that the courts adopted an exception that was inconsistent with the rule and impossible to administer in a consistent fashion.

A legal rule whose development follows a jagged path tends to be highly unstable. Such a rule will be unstable even before the jagged development begins, because it will substantially fail to satisfy the standards of social congruence and systemic consistency. As jagged development proceeds, the instability will markedly increase. First, the inconsistent exceptions will accentuate the failure to satisfy the standard of systemic consistency. Second, there will often be a failure to satisfy even the standard of doctrinal stability, because it will become difficult or impossible to determine whether a court will apply the rule, apply one of the inconsistent exceptions, or develop still another inconsistent exception. As a result of this marked instability, a jagged path of development normally terminates in legislative or administrative abrogation, as in the case of Rule 10b-5, or in full overturning, a process that will be considered in Chapter 7.

It can now be seen that the institutional principle that a precedent is binding has substantive meaning beyond the formal constraints that the rule established by the deciding court must be reconcilable with the result reached in the precedent, and that the deciding court must either follow the precedent or distinguish it. The substantive meaning is that if the rule announced in a precedent substantially satisfies the standards of social congruence and systemic consistency, it should be consistently applied and extended even though another rule would be marginally better. Since systemic consistency usually depends on social congruence, for most practical purposes this substantive meaning can be recast as follows: The announced rule of a precedent should be applied and extended to new cases if the rule substantially satisfies the standard of social congruence and a failure to apply or extend the rule to a new case would not be justified by applicable social propositions, given the social propositions that support the rule.

We can also now begin to see why social propositions are relevant in all common law cases, and why no case is easy in the sense that it can be decided solely on the basis of doctrinal propositions, without the employment of social propositions.

First, since no two cases are identical, every new case raises an issue whether the rule announced in a precedent can consistently be distinguished. Whether a precedent can consistently be distinguished turns chiefly on whether applicable social propositions justify different treatment of the two cases, given the social propositions that support the rule of the precedent.

Second, courts normally have considerable formal power to either apply, extend, distinguish (and thereby reformulate), radically reconstruct, or, for that matter, overrule any announced rule. Call a rule that substantially satisfies the standard of social congruence a socially congruent rule, and call a rule that substantially fails to satisfy that standard a socially incongruent rule. Whether a deciding court applies, extends, reformulates, radically reconstructs, or overrules an announced rule will always depend in part on whether the rule is socially congruent or incongruent. If an announced rule is socially congruent, the courts should and normally will apply and extend the rule consistently and adopt only those distinctions that are justified by applicable social propositions. If an announced rule is socially incongruent, the courts should and normally will follow some other course, such as drawing distinctions that are plausible in form but inconsistent in substance, radically reconstructing the rule through the use of minimalist or result-based techniques, or overruling.

Of course, many opinions do not refer to social propositions but simply apply the announced rule of a precedent. Typically this occurs because the announced rule is socially congruent. Applicable social propositions are taken into account in such cases, but they are taken into account tacitly rather than explicitly. Where a court applies an announced rule that is socially incongruent, it usually does so because the case to be decided cannot be even plausibly distinguished under the rule, and overruling is inappropriate. The latter judgment itself rests either explicitly or tacitly on social propositions concerning the relative weight to be accorded in the given case to the standards of social congruence and doctrinal stability, the extent to which the announced rule is socially incongruent, and the bearing of the moral and policy values that underlie stare decisis.[54] Thus the legal standing of every rule announced in a binding precedent depends not simply on the fact that it was announced, but on whether the rule is congruent with applicable social propositions, considered either explicitly or tacitly.

Reasoning from Principle

In the context of adjudicative reasoning, the term *principle* is sometimes used to mean a moral standard and sometimes used to mean a legal standard. Often it is unclear whether the term is being used in the first or the second sense.[55]

This lack of clarity might not be troublesome if the standards described by the two different senses of principle were coextensive, but that is not the case. Principles in the first sense—moral standards—figure in adjudicative reasoning but are not themselves law. Principles in the second sense—legal standards—are by hypothesis law. It is true that some standards are principles in both senses. An example is the standard that no person should unjustly enrich himself at another's expense. Many standards, however, are principles in only one of the two senses, because not all moral standards are adopted as law, and not all legal standards are grounded in morality. For example, that a promise should not be broken, and that one should rescue a person under hazard of death or injury if the rescue involves no risk, are standards of morality but not standards of the common law. Correspondingly, that an unrelied-upon donative promise is unenforceable, and that there is no liability for failure to rescue a stranger even though no risk is involved, are standards of the common law but not standards of morality.

Because many standards are principles in only one of the two relevant senses, it is critical, in analyzing adjudicative reasoning, to hold the two meanings in separation. To that end I reserve the term *moral norm* for moral standards and the term *principle* for legal standards.

Within the universe of legal standards there is no logical distinction between those that might be called principles and those that might be called rules.[56] For most purposes the term *legal rule* adequately describes all legal standards, and that is the terminology I have up to now employed. For some purposes, however, a useful working distinction can be drawn between principles and rules: principles are relatively general legal standards, and rules are relatively specific legal standards.[57] That distinction will be employed in this section.

When principles and rules are conceived in this way, principles may be seen as explanations for rules, in the sense that we commonly invoke more general propositions to explain those that are more specific. However, the force of principles is not merely explanatory. Principles, like rules, are binding legal standards, and often determine results without the mediation of rules. So, for example, simple accident cases are often resolved by application of the principle of negligence. It is true that a principle may not fully determine every case to which it is relevant. An actor who fails to use due care, as required by the principle of negligence, may nevertheless be free from liability under some special rule, such as the rule governing the liability of manufacturers prior to *MacPherson v. Buick Motor Co.* However, a principle can be binding even though it does not fully determine every case to which it is relevant. Rules, as normally stated, also do not fully determine every case to which they are relevant.[58] Thus a contract that fails to satisfy the rules of the Statute of Frauds, which make certain types of contracts unenforceable unless in writing and signed by the party to be charged, may nevertheless be enforceable under the principle of reliance.

It is possible to explain reasoning from principle on a narrow basis, as simply a special case of reasoning from precedent. For example, when a principle is first judicially established it is likely to be justified on the ground that it accounts for the results of the relevant precedents better than the reasons given in the precedents. This type of justification could be explained as a special case of the result-centered technique of establishing the rule of a precedent. Similarly, after a principle has once been judicially embraced, its subsequent employment could be explained as a special case of the announcement technique of establishing the rule of a precedent. These narrow explanations, however, would miss important characteristics of reasoning from principle. As a practical matter the judicial establishment of a principle seldom rests exclusively on the power of the principle to account for the results of the precedents. Similarly, the subsequent employment of a principle seldom rests on its having been announced in one or more precedents.

In considering the careers of principles, it is instructive to invoke the concept of a scientific paradigm developed by Thomas Kuhn in *The Structure of Scientific Revolutions*. Kuhn uses the term *paradigm* to mean a model, principle, or theory that explains most or all phenomena within its scope but that is sufficiently open-ended to leave room for the resolution of further problems and ambiguities. Characteristically, a paradigm is formulated by one or two theoreticians, partly as a way to explain phenomena that are anomalous under then-prevalent scientific principles. At the time of its formulation, a paradigm looks both backward and forward. Looking backward, the paradigm permits and indeed requires the reconstruction of prior explanations. Looking forward, the paradigm will be applied and extended, by further articulation and specification, to resolve additional problems and ambiguities and to uncover new or explain previously disregarded phenomena. As the paradigm is applied and extended in this manner, however, phenomena are uncovered that the paradigm cannot account for. At first, these phenomena are treated as anomalies, just because the paradigm does not explain them. If, however, anomalies persist and accumulate, eventually a new paradigm will be formulated to explain them.[59]

Similarly, new legal principles are often first explicitly formulated by one or two theoreticians, partly as a way to explain phenomena, in the form of precedents, that are anomalous under then-prevalent legal principles. For example, the reliance principle in contract law was first explicitly formulated in Section 90 of the *Restatement [First] of Contracts*,[60] authored principally by Samuel Williston, and in the landmark article "The Reliance Interest in Contract Law," authored principally by Lon Fuller.[61] A major justification of this principle was that it explained the results in cases that enforced certain nonbargain promises despite the prevalent theory that (with a few purely historical exceptions) only bargain promises were enforceable, and in cases that measured damages by the injured party's reliance (that is, by his output or forgone opportunities) despite the prevalent theory that damages for a breach of contract were to be measured by the injured party's expectation. The modern principle of unconscionability was first explicitly formulated in Article 2 of the Uniform Commercial Code, authored principally by Karl Llewellyn.[62] A major justification of this principle was that it explained the results in cases that policed bargains for fairness despite the prevalent theory that bargains were enforceable without regard to fairness. The principle of strict product liability was first explicitly formulated by Judge Roger Traynor in his concurring opinion in *Escola v. Coca Cola Bottling Co.*,[63] and in Section 401A of the *Restatement (Second) of Torts*,[64] authored principally by William Prosser. A major justification of this principle was that it explained the results in cases that imposed liability on the manufacturers of defective products despite the absence of either a warranty or an affirmative showing of negligence.

Since a newly formulated principle is often justified in large part on the ground that it explains cases that seem anomalous under then-prevailing principles, it is tempting to believe that the formulation and establishment of a principle results solely from the application to such cases of the result-centered technique of establishing the rule of a precedent. This temptation should be resisted. A newly formulated principle draws sustenance from anomalous precedents only if the precedents draw sustenance from applicable social propositions. Anomalous precedents tend to appear when prevalent principles lose their social congruence because of a change in applicable social propositions. The courts then begin to reach results based on current social propositions, but because those propositions are not yet reflected in the principles available to the courts as explanations, the law follows a jagged path of development. The consequence is the creation of an implicit body of law in which applicable social propositions find indirect expression. Eventually, this implicit body of law is metamorphosed into an explicit legal doctrine, in the form of a new principle, in which applicable social propositions find direct expression. So, for example, contract law implicitly protected reliance even before the principle of reliance was formulated, and implicitly refused to enforce unconscionable contracts even before the modern principle of unconscionability was formulated, while tort law implicitly imposed strict product liability even before the principle of strict product liability was formulated. Thus new principles are formulated and established not only because they explain anomalous precedents in a way that prior principles cannot, but also because they reflect applicable social propositions in a way that prior principles do not. In contrast, if precedents are anomalous simply because of judicial error, no principle will be formulated to explain them. Such precedents will not provide the basis of an implicit body of law, but instead will be cabined off from the body of the law and allowed to atrophy.

What is true of principles that are explicitly formulated by theoreticians is also true of principles that emerge gradually through incremental extension. All principles, however they emerge, draw vitality from applicable social propositions and will not long persist if they lose the support of such propositions.

The direct relationship between principles and applicable social propositions also helps to explain the roles played by principles after they are originally formulated and established. One such role is to serve as a basis for new legal rules. At one level, principles serve as the basis for new legal rules in the sense that relatively general standards serve as the basis for relatively specific standards. For example, the principle that on breach of a bargain contract the injured party is entitled to expectation damages has served as the basis for a variety of specific rules, such as the rule that if a buyer breaches a contract for services, the seller's damages are measured by the contract price minus the costs remaining to be incurred. At a deeper level, principles serve as a basis for new legal rules by mediating between legal rules and social propositions. Because principles rest in substantial part on applicable social propositions, they have the effect of internalizing those propositions in the law and making them into institutional values. Accordingly, when the courts draw on a principle as the basis of a new legal rule they draw directly on a doctrinal proposition (the principle) and indirectly on applicable social propositions (which generate the principle).

Another role played by principles after they are originally formulated and established is to serve as a basis for reexamining and refashioning previously established rules. In this role principles allow the courts to criticize, reexplain, and reformulate established rules in the light of institutionalized values. Because of the direct relationship between principles and applicable social propositions, by using new principles to reexamine established rules the courts can refashion relatively specific doctrinal propositions that fail to satisfy the standard of social congruence through an appeal to relatively general doctrinal propositions that do satisfy that standard. This use of new principles to critically reexamine and refashion established rules is reflected in the concept of the law working itself pure.

Because principles are used by the courts both to fashion new rules and to refashion old rules, the reach of a new principle, like that of a new paradigm, will typically be extended over time well beyond its original doctrinal justification. For example, in its origin the principle of reliance in contract law was doctrinally justified as an explanation of cases in which the courts had enforced nonbargain promises and awarded reliance damages. Later, however, the reach of the principle was extended to fashion new rules in such areas as offer and acceptance[65] and to refashion old rules in such areas as the Statute of Frauds.[66] Similarly, in its origin the modern principle of unconscionability was doctrinally justified as an explanation of cases involving the use of unfairly surprising terms, particularly in form contracts.[67] Later, however, the reach of the principle was extended to permit the courts to review bargains for other types of exploitation[68] and to refashion old rules in such areas as unilateral mistake.[69] Strict product liability was doctrinally justified in its origin as an explanation of cases involving consumers and users, but was later extended to bystanders.

The career of a principle typically involves limitation as well as expansion. Often, limitations arise from a collision between two principles that both have spheres of action in which they admittedly govern but that point in different directions in a sphere in which they overlap. In some such cases the courts extend the reach of the more important of the two principles and correspondingly limit the reach of the less important. For example, in the collision between the principle that donative promises are unenforceable and the principle that reasonable reliance should be protected, the rule emerged that relied-upon donative promises are enforceable to the extent of foreseeable reliance.[70] In other cases, as Raz has pointed out, the courts may weigh the extent to which the goal of each principle will be advanced by its application, or defeated by its rejection, and apply the less important principle, because to do so will "greatly advance the goal of [that] principle, while doing only little harm to the goal of the more important principle."[71] In still other cases, the courts fashion a rule that reflects both principles. For example, in the collision between the principle that the business of a corporation is to be managed by its directors and the principle that directors must deal fairly with their corporations, the rule emerged that if a transaction between a director and the corporation is approved by disinterested directors, the approval will affect the standard of fairness by which the transaction is judged but will not completely insulate the transaction from review for fairness.[72]

The result of collisions between principles is that classes of transactions are gradually hived off from a principle's full force through the formulation of special rules. Hiving off may also occur through the formulation of special rules that reflect the direct interplay between a principle and applicable social propositions. Special rules of this kind will be formulated when applicable social propositions give rise to the perception that a type of transaction that falls within the stated ambit of a principle is sufficiently special that it should be exempted from the principle's full force. For example, special rules have been formulated, on the basis of policy, to limit liability for negligence—that is, to limit the full force of the negligence principle—in cases involving the exercise of business judgment by directors or the exercise of the judicial function by a judge.[73] Similarly, special rules have been formulated, on the basis of policy and moral norms, to limit the full force of the principle of expectation damages in cases where an element of damage was not reasonably foreseeable at the time the contract was made, or the defendant failed to mitigate his damages.[74]

Principles serve a number of roles in adjudicative reasoning. They explain legal rules. They are themselves binding legal standards, and directly determine the results in some transactions. They mediate between applicable social propositions and legal rules.

Ultimately, the career of a principle rests on its congruence with applicable social propositions. If applicable social propositions change in such a way that a principle ceases to be socially congruent, newly decided cases will begin to diverge from the principle as the courts respond to the new social propositions. At first, the old principle is not abandoned and the new cases therefore seem anomalous. Eventually, however, a new principle is formulated that explains the anomalous cases and gives expression to the social propositions that generated them. The reach of the new principle is likely to be gradually extended. Until the principle has done all of its work, rules that were generated by the old principle may coexist with rules that are generated by the new. By the time the new principle has worked through the legal system pervasively, it may itself be in the process of displacement.

The development of principles involves not only extension but limitation. Limitation occurs as the courts formulate special rules whose effect is to hive off some transactions from the full force of a relevant principle. Such limitations may arise out of collisions between two principles, or as a result of the interplay between a principle and applicable social propositions. A major and ongoing task of legal reasoning is to determine what kinds of transactions are sufficiently special, under applicable social propositions, to justify their exemption from the full force of an otherwise relevant principle.

As a result of these various dynamics, over the course of time the reach of any given principle is likely to increase in some ways and decrease in others, as some transactions are covered by the principle's extension, others are hived off for special treatment by its limitation, and still others that were once hived off for special treatment are later reabsorbed. For example, within the last forty years the reach of the negligence principle has been greatly extended by the abolition of immunity rules that had insulated various actors against the full consequences of their fault. During the same period, however, the liability of manufacturers for defective products, which had once been hived off from the full force of the negligence principle under a special rule, and had then been reabsorbed under that principle through cases like *Donoghue* and *MacPherson*, was hived off once again for treatment under the principle of strict product liability. What was once seen as special under applicable social propositions, and therefore outside a principle, may later be seen as not special, and therefore within it. What was once seen as not special, and therefore within a principle, may later be seen as special, and therefore outside it.

Reasoning by Analogy

Reasoning by analogy in the common law is sometimes thought to consist simply of comparing similarities and differences between cases, or of reasoning "by example." If these conceptions were correct, reasoning by analogy would be qualitatively different from reasoning from precedent or principle, which both turn on reasoning from standards. These conceptions are, however, incorrect. Reasoning by analogy differs from reasoning from precedent and principle only in form.

The error of the first conception—that reasoning by analogy in the common law consists simply of comparing similarities and differences between cases—can easily be shown. Assume that (1) on January 1, 1987, (2) a manufacturer (3) of grouting machines (4) in Cleveland (5) sells a grouting machine (6) to a machine-shop operator (7) in Cleveland (8) who on March 1 (9) injures his hand while using the machine (10) as a result a defect in the machine. The court holds that the manufacturer is liable under the principle of strict product liability. Now a second case arises, which differs from the first only in that the injury does not result from a defect in the machine. Here there are nine similarities between the cases and only one difference, but obviously the difference is decisive, and it would be decisive if ninety more similarities were added. Cases are not determined in the common law simply by comparing similarities and differences.[75]

The second conception—that reasoning by analogy in the common law consists of reasoning by example—is at the core of Edward Levi's *An Introduction to Legal Reasoning*,[76] which characterizes not only reasoning by analogy but all of common law reasoning in this manner. Levi attempts to illustrate this conception by the line of cases concerning a manufacturer's liability for negligence that culminated in New York (and substantially, in America) in *MacPherson v. Buick Motor Co.*[77] and in England in *Donoghue v. Stevenson*.[78] In the early nineteenth century, the rule had emerged that the manufacturer of a defective product was liable for negligence only to his immediate buyer unless the product was of a type that was "inherently dangerous" even if carefully manufactured. Acting under this rule, English and New York courts had denied recovery against the negligent manufacturers of a defective horse-drawn carriage, a defective circular saw, a defective oil lamp, a defective boiler, and a defective soldering lamp, but had granted recovery against the negligent manufacturers of a purported medicine that was actually a poison, a defective coffee urn, a defective hair wash, a defective bottle of aerated soda, and defective scaffolding. In the early twentieth century, both American law, led by *MacPherson*, and English law, led by *Donoghue*, essentially dropped the special protection afforded to manufacturers and allowed suit for injuries resulting from negligently manufactured products without regard to whether the products were "inherently dangerous."

Using this vignette as a paradigm case, Levi argues that the common law develops through, and only through, "reasoning by example":

The steps are these: similarity is seen between cases; next the rule of law inherent in the first case is announced; then the rule of law is made applicable to the second case. This is a method of reasoning necessary for the law. . . .

What does the law forum require? It requires the presentation of competing examples. The forum protects the parties and the community by making sure that the competing analogies are before the court.[79]

Levi derides the idea that the law develops by reasoning from general propositions rather than by the comparison of examples:

It may be objected that this analysis of legal reasoning places too much emphasis on the comparison of cases and too little on the legal concepts which are created. . . .

The process . . . runs contrary to the pretense of the system. It seems inevitable, therefore, that . . . there will be the attempt to escape to some overall rule. . . . The rule will be useless. It will have to operate on a level where it has no meaning. . . . It is window dressing. Yet it can be very misleading. Particularly when a concept has broken down and reasoning by example is about to build another, textbook writers, well aware of the unreal aspect of old rules, will announce new ones, equally ambiguous and meaningless, forgetting that the legal process does not work with the rule but on a much lower level.[80]

Levi reserves special scorn for the concurring opinion of Brett, M.R., in *Heaven v. Pender*,[81] which formulated a general principle that foreshadowed *MacPherson* and *Donoghue:* whenever a supplier of goods should recognize that unless he used ordinary care and skill with regard to the goods' condition there would be danger of injury to the user, a duty arises to use ordinary care and skill. The statement of this principle, Levi says, constituted a "flight" by Brett "toward a rule above the legal categories which would classify the cases."[82] The flight was "concocted" by a judge so foolish as to think that " 'the logic of inductive reasoning requires that where two propositions lead to exactly similar premises there must be a more remote and larger premise which embraces both of the major propositions.' "[83]

A similar criticism is leveled against *MacPherson:*

[I]t would be a mistake to believe that the breakdown [of the inherently dangerous rule] makes possible a general rule, such as the rule of negligence. . . . A rule so stated would be equivalent to the flight of Brett. Negligence itself must be given meaning by the examples to be included under it. . . . The process of reasoning by example will decide.[84]

Levi's position is misconceived. It may be that example has a part to play in the intuitive leap of discovery. Courts, however, cannot leave matters at that. Courts must justify their results by objective reasons that meet certain criteria, and must reject intuitive conclusions that they cannot justify in this way. In a normative context, justificatory reasoning can proceed only from standards, and "reasoning by example," as such, is virtually impossible. Reason cannot be used to justify a normative conclusion on the basis of an example without first drawing a maxim or rule from the example (or, what is the same thing, without first concluding that the example "stands for" a maxim or rule).[85]

Indeed, in a normative context examples may not even lead to intuitive discovery. Imagine an enormous room in which are the following defective products, and nothing else: on the left-hand side, a horse-drawn carriage, a circular saw, an oil lamp, a boiler, and a soldering lamp; on the right-hand side, a coffee urn, a bottle of hair wash, a bottle of aerated soda, a purported bottle of medicine that is actually a poison, and some scaffolding. In the center of the room is a defective electric broiler. A judge is sent into the room and told that he cannot come out until he determines whether the broiler should be placed with the objects on the left or the right. The judge would probably go mad, and would surely starve, unless he mercifully ended his life by taking the poison. The same result would follow if the judge was told, about each of the objects, that the manufacturers who made those on the right were obliged to compensate injured persons but the manufacturers who made those on the left were not, and was asked to reason from these examples to a result concerning the liability of the manufacturer of the broiler.

Indeed, it is particularly ironic that Levi should have tried to illustrate his theory by the line of cases preceding *MacPherson*. Most of these cases did not even attempt to reason "by example." The court in *Losee v. Clute*[86] did not hold the negligent manufacturer of a defective steam boiler free from liability because a steam boiler resembles a circular saw. The court in *Statler v. George A. Ray Manufacturing Co.*[87] did not impose liability on the negligent manufacturer of a defective coffee urn because a coffee urn resembles scaffolding. Rather, these and most of the other pre-*MacPherson* cases tried to reason from a legal rule. Because that rule was both socially incongruent and made subject to an inconsistent and nearly incoherent exception, the pre-*MacPherson* cases provide not a paradigm of legal reasoning, but a paradigm of legal pathology that illustrates how trouble results whenever the courts try to reason from a socially incongruent and jagged rule.

If reasoning by analogy in the common law does not consist of either comparing the similarities and differences between cases or reasoning by example, of what does it consist? Essentially, reasoning by analogy in the common law is a special type of reasoning from standards, like reasoning from precedent and from principle. Like those processes, reasoning by analogy in the common law falls into several modes. At its core, reasoning by analogy is the mirror image of the process of distinguishing. In distinguishing, a court normally begins with a rule, announced in a prior case, that is in terms applicable to the case at hand, and then determines that there is good reason to treat the case at hand differently. The court therefore reformulates the announced rule (or, what is the same thing, formulates an exception) in a way that requires the two cases to be treated differently. In reasoning by analogy, a court normally begins with a rule, announced in a prior case, that is *not* in terms applicable to the case at hand, and then determines that there is no good reason to treat the case at hand differently. The court therefore reformulates the announced rule (or, what is the same thing, formulates a new rule) in a way that requires the two cases to be treated alike.

Consistent Extension

One mode of reasoning by analogy is as follows: A precedent court has announced rule r, which in terms covers matter X. The deciding court is now faced with a case that concerns matter Y. Matter Y does not fall within the stated ambit of rule r. Since matters X and Y are not identical, treating them differently might be consistent as a matter of formal logic. However, the deciding court determines that treating matters X and Y differently would be inconsistent as a matter of adjudicative reasoning, because neither applicable social propositions nor a deep doctrinal distinction justifies different treatment of the two cases. In effect, the deciding court determines that the statement of the announced rule in the relatively narrow form r, rather than in the relatively general form R, was or has become adventitious. Perhaps there never was any special reason for stating the rule in the narrower fashion. It may be, for example, that the facts involved in the precedent were narrow, and the precedent court stated a rule in a manner that addressed those facts without deliberately intending to limit the rule to those facts. Or perhaps there was a good reason to state the rule narrowly when it was announced, but applicable social propositions have changed, or a deep doctrinal distinction has dissolved, so that the narrow statement is no longer sensible. In either event, the deciding court concludes that the rule r, which covers only matter X, should now be deemed only a special case of the rule R, which covers both matters X and Y. It therefore reformulates the announced rule by generalizing it and decides the case at hand accordingly.

For example, prior to the end of the nineteenth century there was a rule that a husband could bring suit for the alienation (that is, estrangement) of his wife's affections by a third person. It was not entirely clear why the rule did not cover wives whose husbands' affections had been alienated. The narrow formulation might have had a substantive basis—the courts might have believed, based on then-applicable social propositions, that a wife did not suffer a legal injury when her husband's affections had been alienated. Alternatively, the narrow formulation might have been based on a procedural and a practical problem—a married woman could not then bring any type of suit in her own name, and a husband whose affections had been alienated would have no motive to bring suit against his paramour on his wife's behalf. After the law had been changed to allow married women to sue in their own name, the question had to be faced whether a wife suffered a legal injury if her husband's affections had been alienated. In *Bennett v. Bennett*[88] the New York court held that she did suffer such an injury, because applicable social propositions did not support treating a wife differently from a husband for this purpose:

> The actual injury to the wife from the loss of *consortium*, which is the basis of the action, is the same as the actual injury to the husband from that cause. His right to the conjugal society of his wife is no greater than her right to the conjugal society of her husband. Marriage gives to each the same rights in that regard. Each is entitled to the comfort, companionship and affection of the other. The rights of the one and the obligations of the other spring from the marriage contract, are mutual in character and attach to the husband as husband and to the wife as wife. . . . A remedy . . . has long existed for the redress of the wrongs of the husband. As the wrongs of the wife are the same in principle and are caused by

acts of the same nature as those of the husband, the remedy should be the same. What reason is there for any distinction? Is there not the same concurrence of loss and injury in the one case as in the other? Why should he have a right of action for the loss of her society unless she also has a right of action for the loss of his society? . . . Since her society has a value to him capable of admeasurement in damages, why is his society of no legal value to her? Does not she need the protection of the law in this respect at least as much as he does? Will the law give its aid to him and withhold it from her?[89]

In effect, the court concluded that the rule that a husband could bring an action for alienation of affections (rule r) should be deemed only a special case of the more general rule that a spouse could bring such an action (rule R). Perhaps the narrow formulation of the announced rule had been adventitious from the beginning, an artifact generated by the inability of a wife to sue in her own name. Perhaps—indeed, more likely—the narrow formulation was socially congruent at the outset but later became adventitious as social propositions changed. Under either explanation, the result is the same: the rule must be reformulated by generalizing from husbands to spouses, so that it covers both the precedents and the case at hand.

Oppenheim v. Kridel,[90] arising about thirty years after *Bennett v. Bennett*, shows even more clearly how reasoning by analogy takes hold because a narrow formulation that was once seen as justified is later seen as unjustified. The issue in *Oppenheim* was whether a wife could bring an action for criminal conversation. This was an action against a paramour based simply on adultery with the spouse; it did not require a showing that the spouse's affections had been alienated. Again, the traditional rule was that only a husband could bring such an action. In this case, however, it was clear that the reason for the narrow formulation of the rule was substantive. "The husband, so it was said, had a property in the body, and a right to the personal enjoyment of his wife, for the invasion of which right the law permitted him to sue as husband."[91] The wife, in the view that underlay the traditional rule, was deemed not to have a corresponding interest. The court in *Oppenheim* nevertheless reasoned by analogy to hold that a wife could bring an action for criminal conversation. If a husband could bring such an action so could a wife, because applicable social propositions did not justify treating husbands and wives differently for this purpose:

[W]hatever reasons there were for giving the husband at common law the right to maintain an action for adultery committed with his wife, exist to-day in behalf of the woman for a like illegal act committed with her husband. If he had feelings and honor which were hurt by such improper conduct, who will say to-day that she has not the same, perhaps even a keener sense, of the wrong done to her and to the home? If he considered it a defilement of the marriage-bed, why should not she view it in the same light? The statements that he had a property interest in her body and a right to the personal enjoyment of his wife are archaic unless used in a refined sense worthy of the times and which give to the wife the same interest in her husband. . . . The danger of doubt being thrown upon the legitimacy of the children, which seems to be the principal reason assigned in all the authorities for the protection of the husband and the maintenance of the action by him, may be offset by the interest which the wife has in the bodily and mental health of her children when they are legitimate. . . .

So far as I can see there is no sound and legitimate reason for denying a cause of action for criminal conversation to the wife while giving it to the husband. Surely she is as much interested as the husband in maintaining the home and wholesome, clean and affectionate relationships. Her feelings must be as sensitive as his toward the intruder, and it would be mere willful blindness on the part of the courts to ignore these facts. . . .[92]

It is often a difficult prudential question, in generalizing a previously announced rule, just how wide the generalization should be. In *Bennett v. Bennett* and *Oppenheim v. Kridel* the category of "spouse" presented a natural stopping point for generalization. Often, however, no natural stopping point is present. For example, in a much-commented-on English case, *D v. National Society for the Prevention of Cruelty to Children*,[93] the NSPCC was a voluntary body whose purposes included taking action to enforce laws for the protection of children. To that end, it was authorized by the Children and Young Persons Act to bring "care proceedings" in juvenile court. To assist in carrying out its purposes the NSPCC invited information from the public concerning children who might need protection from abuse. Its leaflets promised that such information would be kept confidential. The NSPCC's work was dependent on receiving information from members of the public concerning suspected child abuse, and without an effective promise of confidentiality neighbors and other informants would not provide such information. In December 1973, someone informed the NSPCC that D's daughter had been ill-treated, and the NSPCC sent an inspector to D's home. He found the child to be well cared for. D's health was affected by the false accusation against her. She sued the NSPCC for failure to exercise reasonable care in investigating the complaint before repeating it to her, and asked for an order requiring the NSPCC to disclose the informant's identity.

It was an established rule that the identity of police informants need not be disclosed in a civil action. The rationale was that if the identity of informants was liable to be disclosed in court, that source of information would dry up, and the police would be hindered in preventing and detecting crime. In an earlier case, the House of Lords had also established that the identity of informants to the Game Board was entitled to protection. On the basis of these two rules the NSPCC advanced a "broad submission" that wherever a party claims there is a public interest to be served by withholding information from disclosure the court must weigh that interest against the countervailing public interest in the administration of justice in the particular case, and refuse disclosure if the balance tilts that way. The House of Lords was unwilling to formulate so wide a rule. Reasoning by analogy, however, the House of Lords did extend the rule that protected persons who informed on suspected child abuse to the police, by reformulating in its place a more generalized rule that protected persons who informed on suspected child abuse to any agency, public or private, that was authorized to bring care proceedings:

> There are three categories of persons authorised to bring care proceedings in respect of neglected or ill-treated children: local authorities, constables and the NSPCC. The anonymity of those who tell the police of their suspicions of neglect or ill-treatment of a child would be preserved without any extention of the existing law. To draw a distinction in this respect between information given to the police and that passed on directly to a local authority or to the NSPCC would seem much too irrational a consequence to have been within the contemplation of Parliament when enacting the Children and Young Persons Act. . . .[94]

Although the House of Lord's preference here for generalizing at a relatively low level is not unusual, courts asked to reason by analogy often will formulate new rules at a relatively high level of generality. At its extreme, this technique is employed in cases that establish broad new principles by explaining—that is, rationalizing and extending—prior anomalous precedents. For example, estab-

lishment of the principle that reliance on a donative promise makes
the promise enforceable was based in part on a generalization from
cases holding that reliance on specific types of donative promises
(most prominently, promises to act as an agent, charitable subscriptions, promises in contemplation of marriage, bailment promises,
and promises to give land) made those types of promises enforceable.[95]

How should a court determine the appropriate level at which a
rule should be generalized? It is important to see that either too
high or too low a level may impose social costs. Let R_n stand for a
relatively narrow formulation of a rule, which would cover only a
limited number of instances, and let R_o stand for a relatively open
formulation of the rule, which would cover a large number of instances. Assume that R_n and R_o both permit certain conduct that
would otherwise seem to be prohibited; a court adopts the formulation R_n; over time the court expands the formulation, through
reasoning by analogy, to permit the specific activities $n + 1, n + 2$,
and $n + 3$, as new cases arise that the court believes cannot be consistently distinguished from R_n; and eventually the court shifts to
the formulation R_o. During the period before the adoption of R_o
some members of the profession may have erroneously advised their
clients that the specific activities $n + 4$ and $n + 5$, which are per-
missible under R_o, were prohibited. As a result, private actors may
have taken excessive precaution or refrained from activity they
would otherwise have engaged in. In that event, there could be a
cost in having adopted R_n rather than R_o at the outset.

On the other hand, assume that a court adopts at the outset the
formulation R_o and that over time the court restricts the rule by
establishing exceptions for activities $o - 1, o - 2$, and $o - 3$, as
cases arise that the court finds necessary to distinguish from R_o.
During the period between adoption of R_o and adoption of the exceptions, some members of the profession may have erroneously
advised their clients that activities $o - 1, o - 2$, and $o - 3$, which
would have been prohibited under R_n, were permitted. As a result,
private actors may have taken inadequate precaution or engaged in
activity they would otherwise have refrained from. In that event
there could be a cost in having adopted R_o rather than R_n at the
outset. (Of course, good lawyers may advise their clients correctly
under either R_n or R_o, but probably at least some members of the
profession will give different advice depending on the generality
with which a rule is formulated.)

Thus the optimal level of generality is likely to turn on the court's confidence that a relatively open formulation is sound and therefore unlikely to be subject to a number of exceptions. Obviously, the greater the number of specific rules that are accumulated before an open formulation is adopted, the more confident such an assessment may be. Even without the accumulation of a number of specific rules, however, a court may sometimes be confident that an open formulation is justified because that formulation is very strongly supported by applicable social propositions or by authoritative professional discourse such as a *Restatement*.[96]

Systemic Consistency

A second mode of reasoning by analogy in the common law, which is closely related to the first, proceeds by determining that one rule, rule A, should be adopted in preference to a competing rule, rule B, because neither applicable social propositions nor any deep doctrinal distinction would justify adopting rule B while adhering to some other previously announced rule. For example, in *Oppenheim v. Kridel* the court concluded that it would be inconsistent to retain the rule that a wife could not bring suit for criminal conversation while adhering to the rule, established in *Bennett v. Bennett*, that a wife could bring suit for alienation of affections:

> When we concede that a wife may maintain an action for alienating the affections of her husband, we virtually admit that she may also maintain an action for criminal conversation. While adultery is the sole basis of the latter, it is almost universally the chief element of evidence in the former.[97]

Similarly, in *Ploof v. Putnam*[98] Ploof alleged that he was sailing his sloop with his family when a violent tempest suddenly arose, which placed the sloop and the family in great danger. To avoid destruction or injury Ploof was compelled to moor the sloop to Putnam's dock. Putnam's agent unmoored it. Thereafter, the sloop was driven onto the shore by the tempest, its contents were destroyed, and Ploof and his family were injured. The court held that Ploof had stated a claim for relief. It reached this conclusion in large part by reasoning from cases holding that a person who was forced onto another's land by necessity was not a trespasser:

> A traveller on a highway, who finds it obstructed from a sudden and temporary cause, may pass upon the adjoining land without becoming a trespasser, because of the necessity. Henn's Case, W.

Jones, 296. . . . An entry upon land to save goods which are in danger of being lost or destroyed by water or fire is not a trespass. 21 Hen. VII, 27. . . . In Proctor v. Adams, 113 Mass. 376, 18 Am. Rep. 500, the defendant went upon the plaintiff's beach for the purpose of saving and restoring to the lawful owner a boat which had been driven ashore and was in danger of being carried off by the sea; and it was held no trespass. . . .[99]

The rule established in the cited cases might perhaps have been taken to directly determine the result in *Ploof*, on the theory that if a person is not a trespasser he has a right to be on the land. It would not have been inconsistent as a matter of formal logic, however, to hold that although a landowner cannot recover damages for unauthorized entry against an intruder who entered under necessity, he can use self-help to eject the intruder. Therefore, the question in *Ploof* was whether a rule that allowed a landowner to use self-help against an intruder who entered under necessity would be consistent as a matter of adjudicative reasoning with a rule that the intruder was not liable in damages for the unauthorized entry. The answer is no, because the two cases cannot be distinguished on the basis of applicable social propositions. The law denies a landowner damages for unauthorized entry against an intruder under necessity because the purpose of saving life or property is more important than the purpose of giving inviolate status to property, and it would be morally improper for the landowner to deny entry. Those reasons apply equally well when the issue is whether the landowner can use self-help to eject the intruder. Accordingly, damages and self-help cannot be distinguished for this purpose. It would therefore be inconsistent to adopt a rule that the landowner can use self-help while adhering to the rule that he cannot recover damages.[100]

It should now be clear that reasoning by analogy and reasoning from precedent are substantively equivalent. Whether a court reasons by analogy or from precedent depends largely on the generality with which the rule announced in the precedent was stated.

For example, suppose that at a given time there was an established rule that the revocation of an offer was effective on receipt, but there was as yet no rule on whether an acceptance was effective on receipt or on dispatch. A court was then confronted with *Case* A, which involved the following sequence of events: The course of post is two days. On Monday, Vary mailed an offer to Steadfast.

Steadfast received the offer on Wednesday morning. On Wednesday afternoon, Steadfast mailed an acceptance. On Thursday morning, Vary revoked his offer by telegram. Steadfast received the telegraphic revocation Thursday afternoon, and Vary received the mailed acceptance on Friday. Steadfast claims that a contract was formed; Vary says it was not. Under the established rule, the telegraphic revocation was effective on Thursday, when it was received. Accordingly, if the acceptance was effective on dispatch (Wednesday), a contract was formed, but if it was effective on receipt (Friday), no contract was formed. The court held that a contract was formed.

Case B then arises. Here an offer was mailed by East in one state and received by West in another. West promptly mailed an acceptance. The acceptance reached East on time, and there was no revocation, so that a contract was definitely formed, but a dispute has arisen concerning the scope of East's obligation under the contract. There is a difference between the law of the states in which East and West live. If the law of East's state governs, East wins. If the law of West's state governs, West wins. Under established rules, a contract is governed by the law of the state in which it is formed, and a contract is formed when an offer has been accepted. Which state's law governs therefore depends on whether West's acceptance was effective on dispatch, in West's state, or on receipt, in East's.

Assume that the rule announced in *Case A* was the broad rule that "an acceptance is effective on dispatch." The deciding court will then reason from precedent. Its reasoning will take the form of applying the broad rule announced in *Case A* unless applicable social propositions require that a distinction be drawn between (i) cases that raise the issue, if an acceptance crosses with a revocation, when is the acceptance effective, and (ii) cases that raise the issue, if an acceptance is mailed in one state and received in another, which state's law governs.

Suppose now that the rule announced in *Case A* was the narrow rule that "if an acceptance crosses with a revocation, the acceptance is effective on dispatch." The deciding court will then reason by analogy. Its reasoning will take the form of extending the rule announced in *Case A* to *Case B* if applicable social propositions would not justify a distinction between the two cases. The *form* of the court's reasoning in *Case B*, therefore, will differ according to the level of generality at which the announced rule in *Case A* was formulated. Substantively, however, the court's reasoning in *Case B* should be identical whether the rule announced in *Case A* was formulated at a high level of generality, so that the *Case B* court is required to reason from precedent, or at a low level of generality, so that the *Case B* court is required to reason by analogy. The substantive issue in either case is whether *Case A* and *Case B* are distinguishable under applicable social propositions.

It should also now be clear that the institutional principles that govern reasoning from precedent also govern reasoning from analogy. All the reasons that underlie the doctrine of stare decisis, in particular, and the standard of doctrinal stability, in general, apply as fully to reasoning by analogy as they do to reasoning from precedent. Like reasoning from precedent, reasoning by analogy advances the values reflected in the principles of replicability and support. Like reasoning from precedent, reasoning by analogy helps assure that like cases are treated alike. Like reasoning from precedent, reasoning by analogy is replicable by the profession, so that the courts' use of that process enriches the supply of legal rules and thereby makes planning on the basis of law more reliable and dispute-settlement on the basis of law easier.

Most important, because reasoning by analogy differs from reasoning from precedent only in form and not in substance, the integrity of the institutional principles that govern the latter practice could not sensibly be preserved unless those principles governed the former practice as well. Accordingly, if the announced rule of a precedent substantially satisfies the standards of social congruence and systemic consistency, and should therefore be applied to cases that fall within the stated ambit of the rule and cannot be consistently distinguished, so too should the rule be extended to cases that do not fall within the stated ambit of the rule but cannot be consistently distinguished. Precedents that meet the requirements of stare decisis are as binding by analogy as they are in direct application.[101]

Reasoning from Doctrines Established in the Professional Literature

Reasoning from precedent normally begins with precedents that were handed down in the deciding court's jurisdiction and are binding on the deciding court. Call these local precedents. Reasoning by analogy also normally begins with local precedents, and so in most cases does reasoning from principle. Often, however, the courts reason from doctrines found in texts that are not formally binding on the deciding court but are nevertheless generally recognized by the profession as authoritative legal sources. These texts include official sources, such as cases decided by courts outside the jurisdiction or by lower or parallel courts, and secondary sources authored by members or students of the profession, such as *Restatements*, treatises, and law review articles. I shall refer to these texts individually as professional sources and collectively as the professional literature. This literature makes up a substantial portion of the professional discourse in the wider arena. Its significance is suggested by a study of opinions in sixteen state supreme courts during 1940–1970, which found that citations to out-of-state cases accounted for about one-fourth of all citations to state cases and that secondary sources were cited in almost half the opinions.[102]

In many cases the professional literature is cited by the courts chiefly because of its bearing on local precedents—because, for example, the literature criticizes rules announced in those precedents or is relevant to determining what rule those precedents establish. Often, however, the professional literature not only criticizes or interprets local precedents, but embraces certain doctrines as law, and the courts correspondingly draw on that literature not simply as a source of criticism and understanding, but as a source of doctrine. This is most obviously true where the literature consists of cases decided by nonlocal courts, but it is also true of secondary sources, like *Restatements* and treatises.

In considering the employment, in common law reasoning, of doctrines drawn from the professional literature, it is necessary to distinguish between doctrines that are supported in the literature and doctrines that are established in the literature. Whether a doctrine is established or merely supported in the professional literature depends on the number and character of the sources that embrace the doctrine, the weight the profession attaches to each source, and whether the sources are mutually reenforcing.

A doctrine may be said to be *supported*, rather than established, in the professional literature if it is embraced as law by only a few professional sources, although not contradicted by others, or the sources in which the doctrine is embraced are not accorded great weight by the profession, or the doctrine is embraced as law by a number of sources but rejected by others. If a doctrine is supported in the professional literature, under the principle of responsiveness a court should take the doctrine seriously, at least in the absence of a contrary local precedent. At a minimum, the court should explain why it rejects the doctrine, if it does.

A doctrine may be said to be *established* in the professional literature if it is embraced as law by a number of nonlocal cases and weighty secondary sources (like the relevant *Restatement* and the leading treatises), and the sources are not in material conflict. In the absence of a contradictory local precedent, doctrines that are established in the professional discourse are treated as law in virtually the same way as local precedents. Cases that embrace such doctrines will be included in the national casebooks used at almost every law school. Law students will be taught that these doctrines are law—not just the law of the states where they are established in local precedents, but law generally. When these students become practicing lawyers and judges, they will carry with them both the specific doctrines they have learned as law and the institutional principle that doctrines established in the professional literature are to be treated as law in virtually the same way as local precedents. For example, if there is no local precedent governing the issue whether an acceptance that crosses a revocation is effective on dispatch or on receipt, and the dispatch rule is established in the professional literature, a court will employ that rule in virtually the same way as if the rule had been established in a local precedent.

Indeed, doctrines established in the professional literature will characteristically be treated as law even if they lead to a result different from that suggested by local precedent, as long as local precedent is not flatly contradictory. If local precedent establishes the rule that a donative promise is unenforceable, courts will nevertheless characteristically employ the rule, established in the professional literature, that a donative promise is enforceable if relied upon. If local precedent establishes the rule that a firm offer is revocable, courts will nevertheless characteristically employ the rule, established in the professional literature, that a firm offer is enforceable if relied upon. If local precedent establishes the legal-duty rule, courts faced with a case that falls within an inconsistent exception established in the professional literature will characteristically apply the exception rather than the rule.

The practice of treating doctrines established in the professional literature in virtually the same way as local precedents reflects the broad standard of doctrinal stability and the elements that underlie that standard. For one thing, the practice enormously enriches the supply of legal rules in any single jurisdiction and thereby facilitates planning and dispute-settlement on the basis of law. For another, the practice promotes a special aspect of the ideal of consistency—consistency on a national level. The result of the practice has been aptly summarized by Martin Shapiro, looking at tort law from the perspective of a political scientist. "[W]hat makes tort so interesting for the study of organizational policy-making . . . is that there are not fifty-two bodies of tort policy but in a very real sense a single body of . . . tort law that runs throughout . . . the United States, with local variations to be sure, but with a remarkably uniform core."[103] This is as it should be. We are, after all, one country. The concept that otherwise equivalent transactions can properly be given different treatment simply because they occur on either side of a state boundary is in a sense simply one more deep doctrinal distinction, unsupported in the present day by the standard of social congruence except where applicable social propositions themselves differ from state to state.

Reasoning from Hypotheticals

Reasoning from hypotheticals is a common method of adjudicative reasoning, and a central method of teaching law and legal reasoning to law students. As in the modes of reasoning considered earlier in this chapter, applicable social propositions play a central role in reasoning from hypotheticals.

One common form of reasoning from hypotheticals proceeds in the following manner: A court is faced with a case that presents admitted difficulty in choosing between competing rules. The court then states a hypothetical that has, at least in the court's view, three critical characteristics. First, the hypothetical differs from the case. Second, the hypothetical seems easier to decide than the case—in the hypothetical, one of the competing rules seems clearly preferable. Third, although the hypothetical differs from the case, the case cannot be distinguished from the hypothetical under applicable social propositions. Accordingly, if one of the competing rules should govern the hypothetical, it should govern the case as well.

For example, in *Vincent v. Lake Erie Transportation Co.*[104] Lake Erie Transportation had tied its vessel to Vincent's dock for the purpose of discharging the vessel's cargo. During the unloading, a violent storm arose. To avoid damage, Lake Erie retied the vessel to the dock with stronger lines and kept the vessel tied even after unloading had been completed. However, the waves caused by the storm struck the vessel with such force that it was constantly thrown against the dock, resulting in damage to the dock of five hundred dollars. The court tacitly concluded that Lake Erie had a right to keep its vessel tied to the dock under the doctrine of necessity. It nevertheless held that Lake Erie was liable for the damage. The court arrived at this result largely by reasoning from hypotheticals:

> Theologians hold that a starving man may, without moral guilt, take what is necessary to sustain life; but it could hardly be said that the obligation would not be upon such person to pay the value of the property so taken when he became able to do so. . . .
> Let us imagine in this case that for the better mooring of the vessel those in charge of her had appropriated a valuable cable lying upon the dock. No matter how justifiable such appropriation might have been, it would not be claimed that, because of the overwhelming necessity of the situation, the owner of the cable could not recover its value.[105]

Often, as in *Vincent* itself, a court leaves implicit both why a hypothetical is easier than the actual case, and why the differences between the hypothetical and the case do not justify distinguishing the two. Usually, however, the court's implicit reasoning can be explicated with a fair degree of confidence. In *Vincent* that explication seems to be as follows.

First, the hypotheticals differ from the case. In the case: (i) defendant's wealth was maintained but not augmented, (ii) defendant did not take possession of plaintiff's goods, and (iii) there was no intent by the defendant to appropriate part of the plaintiff's wealth. In contrast, in the hypotheticals there was: (i) an augmentation of the defendant's wealth at the plaintiff's expense, (ii) through taking possession of the plaintiff's goods, (iii) by the defendant's intentional act of appropriation.

Second, the hypotheticals seem easier to decide than the case. Surely one who appropriates another's goods, even for the best of reasons, should make compensation.

Third, the case cannot be distinguished from the hypotheticals under applicable social propositions. Applicable social propositions do not support distinctions: (i) between a diminution of A's wealth that results in an increase of B's, and a diminution of A's wealth to prevent a diminution of B's, (ii) between taking possession of another's goods, and using another's goods in a manner that foreseeably results in a diminution of their value, or (iii) between a diminution in A's wealth that results from B's intentional appropriation and a diminution in A's wealth that results from an action by B that was likely (although not intended) to cause the diminution that in fact occurred.

Accordingly, since liability should follow in the hypotheticals, it should follow in the case.

A second common form of reasoning from hypotheticals is to show that a proposed rule should be rejected because it would be un-suitable when extended to like hypothetical cases. In the first form, the object is to show that a rule should be adopted because the case cannot be distinguished from hypotheticals in which the rule seems clearly proper. In the second form, the object is to show that a rule should be rejected because the case cannot be distinguished from hypotheticals in which the rule seems clearly improper. Reasoning in the second form proceeds in the following manner: First, the hypothetical differs from the case. Second, the hypothetical seems easier to decide than the case. Third, the hypothetical cannot be distinguished from the case under applicable social propositions. Therefore, if the court decides the case in a certain way it would have to decide the hypothetical the same way if the hypothetical became a real case in the future. Since the hypothetical future case should not be decided that way, neither should the real present case.

For example, in *Roberson v. Rochester Folding Box Co.*[106] the plaintiff alleged that the defendant, which was engaged in the man-ufacture and sale of flour, had used the plaintiff's picture for ad-vertising purposes without her consent. As a result, the plaintiff was greatly humiliated, made sick, and suffered a severe nervous shock. Plaintiff sued on the theory that defendant had invaded her right of privacy. The court denied relief, partly on the basis of hy-potheticals:

> If such a principle be incorporated into the body of the law through the instrumentality of a court of equity, the attempts to logically apply the principle will necessarily result . . . in litigation bordering upon the absurd, for the right of privacy, once established as a legal doctrine, cannot be confined to the restraint of the pub-lication of a likeness but must necessarily embrace as well the publication of a word-picture, a comment upon one's looks, conduct,

domestic relations or habits. And were the right of privacy once legally asserted it would necessarily be held to include the same things if spoken instead of printed, for one, as well as the other, invades the right to be absolutely let alone. . . .

[A] distinction between public and private characters cannot possibly be drawn. On what principle does an author or artist forfeit his right of privacy and a great orator, a great preacher, or a great advocate retain his? Who can draw a line of demarcation between public characters and private characters, let that line be as wavering and irregular as you please? . . . Or is the right of privacy the possession of mediocrity alone, which a person forfeits by giving rein to his ability, spurs to his industry or grandeur to his character? A lady may pass her life in domestic privacy when, by some act of heroism or self-sacrifice, her name and fame fill the public ear. Is she to forfeit by her good deed the right of privacy she previously possessed? These considerations . . . serve to make more clear . . . the absolute impossibility of dealing with this subject save by legislative enactment, by which may be drawn arbitrary distinctions which no court should promulgate as a part of general jurisprudence.[107]

A problem that can easily arise in reasoning from hypotheticals is that the hypotheticals may in fact be distinguishable from the case. For example, the hypotheticals in *Roberson*, which involved the communication of true information, were distinguishable from the case, which involved making the plaintiff into an involuntary and unpaid model for the defendant's goods. Particularly in the second form, the technique of reasoning from hypotheticals must be used with caution.

Reasoning from hypotheticals is comparable in form to reasoning by analogy, since it turns on the question whether two cases can be distinguished, but it differs in substance from both reasoning by analogy and the other modes of reasoning previously considered in this chapter. While those modes depend on an interplay between applicable social propositions and actual doctrinal propositions and cases, reasoning by hypothetical depends on an interplay between applicable social propositions and conceivable doctrinal propositions and cases. Thus reasoning from hypotheticals is not directly supported by either the specific principle of stare decisis or the general standard of doctrinal stability. It might therefore seem that such reasoning is a rhetorical rather than a decisionmaking device. So it may be, in some cases. However, the central role played by such reasoning in teaching law, where the object is normally not to persuade but to instruct, suggests that reasoning from hypotheticals can legitimately serve to advance a court's decisionmaking process. Reasoning from hypotheticals may, for example, enable a judge to move from a social proposition with which he is naturally empathetic, because it involves everyday experience, to a social proposition that is initially more remote from his experience, but to which his awakened empathy can then be transferred. Alternatively, reasoning from hypotheticals may serve as a sort of standard of doctrinal stability run in reverse from the future to the present. By means of such reasoning the court can spin out the alternative legal regimes that would follow, under the standard of doctrinal stability, from the adoption of competing legal rules, and then choose the rule that promises to produce the best of these regimes.

Chapter 7

Overruling and Other Modes of Overturning

This chapter concerns *overturning*, by which I mean modes of reasoning that lead to the partial or complete abolition of a previously established doctrine. The most dramatic type of overturning is overruling. Overruling occurs when a court fully overturns an established doctrine and announces that it has done so. I will begin by examining conventional overruling and then turn to prospective overruling, transformation, overriding, and the drawing of inconsistent distinctions.

Overruling

On its face, overruling appears to be radically discontinuous with other modes of legal reasoning, both as a process and as an event in the history of a doctrine. This appearance, however, is deceiving. As a process, overruling is comparable to other modes of legal reasoning. As an event in the history of a doctrine, overruling often involves no sharp change of course.

Like other modes of legal reasoning, overruling is governed by institutional principles. In this section I will first develop two principles that state conditions under which overruling should occur. I will then turn to the technique of signaling that overruling is likely to occur, and the effect on overruling of deep doctrinal distinctions.

The Basic Overruling Principle

The first principle that governs overruling is as follows: A doctrine should be overruled if (i) it substantially fails to satisfy the standards

of social congruence and systemic consistency, and (ii) the values
that underlie the standard of doctrinal stability and the principle of
stare decisis—the values of evenhandedness, protecting justified
reliance, preventing unfair surprise, replicability, and support—
would be no better served by the preservation of a doctrine than
by its overruling. Call this the basic overruling principle.

Jagged doctrines. I will begin by examining the application of the
basic overruling principle to doctrines that have been made subject
to inconsistent exceptions. Call these jagged doctrines. (Recall that
whether a rule and its exceptions are consistent depends largely on
whether applicable social propositions justify treating cases falling
under the exceptions differently from cases falling within the rule,
given the social propositions that support the rule.) Jagged doctrines
meet the first condition of the basic overruling principle. They are
socially incongruent; that is why they have become subject to inconsistent exceptions. They are systemically inconsistent, partly
because of the inconsistency between the doctrine and the exceptions and partly because, by reason of their social incongruence,
they are inconsistent with other doctrines. I will show that jagged
doctrines also normally meet the second condition, because the values of evenhandedness, the protection of justified reliance, the prevention of unfair surprise, support, and replicability are normally
no better served by preserving a jagged doctrine than by overruling it.

I observed in Chapter 5 that the ideal of evenhandedness can be
satisfied by the consistent disposition of like cases—consistent outcomes—or by the consistent application of the institutional principles that determine how cases should be decided. I shall focus
here on the former sense of evenhandedness. When a doctrine has
become jagged, evenhandedness in this sense will be no better
served by preservation than by overruling. The preservation of a
jagged doctrine may lead to consistency of outcomes between present and past cases, insofar as persons to whom the doctrine is now
applied may be treated like persons to whom the doctrine has been
applied in the past. (This may not always be so: different outcomes
at different times can be consistent, if they result from a change in
applicable social propositions.) However, the preservation of a jag-

ged doctrine will lead to inconsistency of outcomes among present cases. Because a jagged doctrine is subject to inconsistent exceptions, its preservation will result in a lack of consistency between the treatment of those persons to whom the doctrine is applied and the treatment of those persons to whom the exceptions are applied. Because a jagged doctrine substantially fails to satisfy the standard of systemic consistency, its preservation will result in a lack of consistency between the treatment of persons to whom the doctrine is applied and the treatment of persons to whom other, inconsistent doctrines are applied.

The history of the charitable-immunity doctrine, which culminated in widespread overruling beginning around the 1940s, provides a useful example of the way in which the value of evenhandedness would be no better served by preservation of a jagged doctrine than by its overruling.[1] Under the general rules of tort and agency law, a principal is liable for its own wrongs and vicariously liable for wrongful acts by persons in its employ committed within the scope of their employment. Prior to the 1940s, it was a well-established exception to this rule that a charitable institution was immune from liability in tort. A variety of explicit reasons were advanced to support the charitable-immunity doctrine, the most significant of which were as follows: (i) An award of tort damages out of a charitable fund would violate the trust purpose (this was often referred to as the trust-fund theory). (ii) The principle of vicarious liability is applicable only to profit-making institutions. (iii) The beneficiaries of charity waive or assume the risk of a tort. (iv) Imposing tort liability on a charity would dissipate the charitable fund, deprive the favored class and the public of the charity's benefit, and discourage contributions to charity.

These explicit reasons reflected a series of implicit experiential, moral, and policy propositions that seemed to prevail at the time the charitable-immunity doctrine originated. The implicit experiential propositions were that most charities were relatively small nonbureaucratic institutions that would not remain economically viable if they had to absorb liability claims, and that in an era when governmental welfare programs were relatively sparse, the maintenance of a given charity was often essential to community welfare. The paradigm was the lone hospital in a small community, and indeed hospitals were involved in a very large proportion of the cases in which the doctrine was developed and applied. The implicit moral and policy propositions, which built on the experiential propositions, were that it was better that a few persons should suffer their losses than that a community should be deprived of essential services; that "accidents happen"; and that a charitable beneficiary who proposed to take an action that threatened to force the charity to close down was guilty of ingratitude.

By the middle of this century, both the explicit and the implicit reasons had lost most or all of their force and the doctrine had come to be widely criticized in the professional literature. (i) The trust-fund theory, that an award of tort damages out of a charitable fund would violate the trust purpose, largely assumed its own conclusion. In all likelihood, charitable donors have no intention to exempt charitable institutions from the normal operation of law or to provide that donated funds cannot be used to compensate for injuries caused by the institution's tortious acts. (ii) The argument that the principle of vicarious liability is applicable only to profit-making institutions assumed too narrow a justification for the principle. Although vicarious liability may rest in part on the fact that a principal stands to profit from the activity of persons within his employ, it also rests on such other elements as the principal's right to control those persons' conduct, the desirability of internalizing the costs generated by the tortious activities of an enterprise, the difficulty of proving lack of care in selecting and overseeing employees, and the fact that a corporate organization can normally act only through others. (iii) The argument that charitable beneficiaries waive or assume the risk of tortious activity simply had no support in fact, insofar as it was based on a premise of consent. (iv) Finally, the concerns that liability would dissipate the charitable fund, deprive the favored class and the public of the charity's benefit, and discourage contributions to charity were allayed by the development and eventual widespread availability of liability insurance. These concerns had also been vitiated by other kinds of experience. Profit-making counterparts of charitable institutions, such as proprietary hospitals, seemed to prosper even though they had no immunity. Charities in states that did not confer the immunity seemed no worse off than charities in states that did.[2]

Perhaps more fundamentally, there had been a change in the implicit experiential, moral, and policy propositions underlying the charitable-immunity doctrine. The availability of liability insurance made tort liability seem to be just one more ordinary cost of charitable activity, much like salaries and supplies. Many charities had become large, bureaucratic, well-funded organizations, often administered by full-time executives, engaged in the same type of careful planning as profit-making institutions, and unlikely to be felled by tort liability. The paradigm was now the urban medical complex that had a budget in the tens or hundreds of millions of dollars, was run by professional administrators, and was difficult to distinguish in organizational terms from a business enterprise. At the same time, massive governmental welfare programs and the development of private health insurance had made the survival of any given charity less essential.[3]

Moral and policy outlooks had also changed. In comparing injuries to the few with the needs of the many, increased weight was given to the former. The view had become prevalent that every enterprise, private or public, ordinarily should bear the costs of injuries caused through the fault of its employees, particularly where the enterprise was in a position to spread the risk of such injuries and the individual was not. And asking to be compensated for an injury caused by the tort of a charitable institution seemed not ungrateful but quintessentially reasonable.[4]

By the 1940s, therefore, applicable social propositions no longer seemed to support the charitable-immunity doctrine, and as a result the doctrine was widely criticized in the professional literature and had become subject to a number of inconsistent exceptions. In many jurisdictions the doctrine was made inapplicable to claims against the charity by its employees or by persons who were neither charitable beneficiaries nor employees, and to claims based on "administrative" or "managerial" negligence. In some jurisdictions the doctrine was made inapplicable to "noncharitable" revenue-raising activities carried on by a charity, to claims by paying beneficiaries (such as paying patients in a charitable hospital), and to claims that could be enforced against "nontrust" property. Some of these exceptions were inconsistent with virtually every ground on which the doctrine was justified, and all were inconsistent with one or more of those grounds. Some or all were also difficult if not impossible to administer in a coherent fashion. For example, the New York courts had held that placing an improperly capped hot-water bottle on a patient was "administrative," so that the immunity was inapplicable, but keeping a hot-water bottle on a patient too long was "medical," so that the immunity barred suit. Giving blood to the wrong patient was administrative, but giving the wrong blood to the right patient was medical. Using an improperly sterilized needle for an injection was administrative, but giving an injection improperly was medical. Failing to place sideboards on a bed after having decided they should be used was administrative, but failing to decide that sideboards should be used was medical.[5] The New Jersey courts had held that a mother who fell while visiting her child in a hospital was a charitable beneficiary,[6] but a fireman who brought a patient into a hospital and fell while getting a stretcher was not,[7] and that a Girl Scout who was injured on the stairs of a church where her troop met in rooms for which it had made a "donation" was a charitable beneficiary,[8] but a woman who fell on the stairs of a church while attending a social event for which she paid a fee was not.[9] The Ohio courts had held that a member of a church who fell after a service while on her way to the basement, where the church sold religious articles, was a beneficiary, so that the immunity barred her suit,[10] but that it was a jury question whether the immunity applied to a suit by a church member who ate a paid dinner while attending a church fund-raising bazaar.[11] The Missouri courts had held that the immunity barred suit for injuries in a building that a charity owned and maintained, part of which the charity occupied but half of which it rented out,[12] but that the immunity did not apply to a building a charity owned and maintained but did not occupy, although the building's revenues were spent solely on the charity's home for the aged.[13]

Because the charitable-immunity doctrine substantially failed to satisfy the standard of social congruence, it had become not only internally but externally inconsistent—that is, the doctrine was inconsistent not only with its exceptions but also with other doctrines. When applicable social propositions supported the proposition that the tortious activity of charitable institutions was different, for liability purposes, from the tortious activity of profit-making institutions, it was consistent to hold that profit-making institutions were liable in tort but that charitable institutions were not. When applicable social propositions failed to support the proposition that the tortious activities of the two types of institutions were different for liability purposes, it became inconsistent to hold one type of institution liable in tort but not the other. So, for example, by the 1940s it had become inconsistent to impose liability on a private hospital for injury to a patient resulting from the negligence of a surgeon but to refuse to impose liability on a nonprofit hospital for injury to a patient resulting from the negligence of a surgeon.[14]

In short, by the 1940s charitable immunity had become a jagged doctrine lacking both internal and external consistency, and consistency of outcomes was no more likely to be achieved by preserving the doctrine than by overruling it. True, preservation would have promoted consistency of outcomes insofar as present cases in which the immunity defense was successfully raised would be treated like past cases in which it was successfully raised, but preservation would have frustrated consistency of outcomes in two other, more important ways. First, there would be a lack of consistency among cases involving charitable institutions, because the exceptions were inconsistent with the doctrine and often difficult if not impossible to administer in a coherent fashion. Second, there would be a lack of consistency between cases that involved charitable institutions and cases that did not.

The coupled values of protecting justified reliance and preventing unfair surprise are also normally no better served by preserving a jagged doctrine than by overruling it.

It will be recalled that for purposes of the principle of doctrinal stability, reliance may be either special or general. Special reliance occurs when a litigant before the court has specifically planned his conduct on the basis of a legal rule. General reliance consists of reliance by members of the society, other than the litigants, who are likely to have planned their conduct on the basis of the system of legal rules. For reasons to be made clear, only general reliance need be considered by the courts.

One type of general reliance consists of the likelihood that a significant number of actors who are not before the court will have planned their conduct on the basis of a legal doctrine. In determining whether to preserve a legal rule, reliance of this type is important only if it is justified, relatively confident, and legally well-founded. Reliance that is unjustified, shaky, or legally unfounded does not provide a weighty reason for preserving an incongruent and inconsistent rule. In the case of a jagged doctrine, the requisite kind of reliance is very unlikely.

Assume a class of persons who might conceivably have relied on a jagged doctrine. Suppose first that some members of the class did not consult a lawyer before engaging in the relevant transaction. Certainly, persons cannot claim to have relied on a socially incongruent doctrine if they had no idea there was such a doctrine. The case will often be not much stronger as to persons who had an idea there was such a doctrine but formed that idea without consulting a lawyer. In most areas the common law is too complex to be reliably determined by laymen, and there's not much reason to protect a lucky guess.

Suppose next that some members of the class consulted lawyers but got wrong advice on the state of the law. Here again, reliance should not be a concern. It cannot be allowed to matter, in establishing the law, that some persons have relied on bad advice. In determining whether reliance on a doctrine argues against overruling, the issue cannot be what advice some persons happened to receive (which is in any event indeterminate), but what a well-informed lawyer would have determined the law to be.

Suppose finally that some members of the class consulted well-informed lawyers, that well-informed lawyers should have rendered one of the following two opinions, and that the lawyers did render one of these opinions: (1) There is a doctrine on the books that is applicable on its face to the transaction in which you propose to engage. However, the conditions for overruling are satisfied in the case of this doctrine, and in my opinion it is no longer the law. (2) There is a doctrine on the books that is applicable on its face to the transaction in which you propose to engage. However, the doctrine is subject to inconsistent exceptions, and although in my opinion the doctrine is still law and governs the transaction in which you propose to engage, I hold that opinion with a relatively low degree of certainty.

Persons whose lawyers rendered the first opinion cannot claim to have relied on the doctrine. Persons whose lawyers rendered the second opinion might have relied, but their reliance is unlikely to be confident, legally well-founded, and justified. Confident and legally well-founded reliance cannot be placed on a doctrine if it is subject to inconsistent exceptions (particularly exceptions that cannot be coherently administered) and its continued vitality is open to substantial doubt. Even if the reliance could somehow be thought of as confident and legally well-founded, it would typically not be justified. A doctrine becomes jagged because it lacks substantial congruence with applicable social propositions. Conduct that an actor has reason to know is inconsistent with norms and policies that have substantial social support will not often be morally justified.

Furthermore, in some cases the doctrine at issue does not lay down a rule of primary conduct, but relates only to such elements as remedies or standing to sue. If a doctrine is of that nature, so that overruling would not change an established rule of primary conduct,

a claim of justified reliance may be especially thin. As Justice Harlan
stated in *Moragne v. States Marine Lines, Inc.*:

> The confidence of people in their ability to predict the legal con-
> sequences of their actions is . . . threatened least by the announce-
> ment of a new remedial rule to effectuate well-established primary
> rules of behavior. . . . "If the new remedial doctrine serves simply
> to reenforce and make more effectual well-understood primary ob-
> ligations, the net result of innovation may be to strengthen rather
> than to disturb the general sense of security."[15]

Consider also, in this connection, the perspective of an actor who
does not know the law. Actors who do not know the law are likely
to act on the belief that the law normally requires compensation for
an injury that society treats as socially wrongful and does not impose
liability for conduct that society treats as socially rightful. Action
on the basis of such a belief is itself a type of reliance. This type
of reliance is frustrated by preserving a doctrine that is socially incongruent, and is protected by overruling such a doctrine.

The analysis of the first type of general reliance has an important
bearing on the issue of special reliance. It shows that the presence
or absence of special reliance should normally be irrelevant in determining whether a doctrine should be preserved or overruled. A
decision whether to preserve or overrule a legal doctrine will affect
the whole society. Whether well-advised persons would have been
likely to justifiably rely on a doctrine is relevant in making that
decision. What a particular person thought the law to be is not. In
the balance of this chapter, therefore, special reliance will not be
taken separately into account.

A second type of general reliance consists of the likelihood that
a significant number of actors who did not actually plan their conduct
on the basis of a doctrine nevertheless planned on the basis of other
legal rules or institutional arrangements that reflect the doctrine.
In the case of a jagged doctrine, this is also unlikely. A doctrine
that substantially fails to satisfy the standards of social congruence
and systemic consistency, and that is externally and internally inconsistent, is unlikely to serve as a reliable foundation for other
legal rules or institutional arrangements.

Finally, a court may be concerned that failure to follow the precedent that adopted the doctrine in question may be likely to make
actors insecure about the reliability of other precedents. But that
concern should be satisfied if overruling is governed by institutional
principles that can be applied in a replicable fashion. The basic

overruling principle can be so applied. Jagged doctrines will almost invariably have been widely criticized in the professional discourse, and the drawing of inconsistent distinctions is itself both a type of professional criticism and a marker for locating doctrines that should be overruled. Accordingly, the overruling of jagged doctrines should not make other legal doctrines significantly less reliable.

What has been said of reliance is also generally applicable to the mirror-image value of preventing unfair surprise. The overruling of a jagged doctrine is unlikely to be surprising at all, because it will characteristically have been foreshadowed by the inconsistent exceptions, by criticism of the doctrine in the professional literature, and by the institutional principles that govern overruling. Even if some actors were to be surprised by the overruling, it is unlikely the surprise would be unfair, because characteristically the actors will have acted in a manner that they knew or should have known did not conform to moral norms and policies with substantial social support. And the preservation of a socially incongruent doctrine will itself lead to unfair surprise, insofar as the application of such a doctrine defeats the reasonable expectations of actors who don't know the law.

The charitable-immunity doctrine provides a useful example of the way in which the values of protecting justified reliance and preventing unfair surprise would be no better served by preservation than by overruling in the case of jagged doctrines. First, the likelihood of confident and legally well-founded reliance on the doctrine was low. In most jurisdictions a well-informed lawyer would have advised that the exceptions made the doctrine highly unreliable. As stated in one of the leading cases that refused to follow the doctrine:

> [T]he "rule" has not held in the tests of time and decision. Judged by results, it has been devoured in "exceptions." Debate has gone on constantly, not so much as to whether, but concerning how far it should be "modified," with ever widening modification.
>
> . . . If we look at results . . . rather than words or forms of statement in opinions, for the test of what is "the law" or "the prevailing rule," immunity is not "the rule" and liability "the exception." The rule has become merely a relict in the multitude of departures.[16]

And, of course, once overruling began in some jurisdictions, the doctrine became increasingly unreliable in others.

Furthermore, even if a well-informed lawyer would have advised that the charitable-immunity doctrine was reliable, the likelihood of actual and justified reliance would have been low. Since liability was vicarious, presumably the only way in which a charitable institution could have changed its primary conduct in reliance on the doctrine was by decreasing the amount of care it took in selecting and supervising subordinates. In jurisdictions that had adopted the managerial or administrative exception, such a course of conduct would not have been protected by the immunity in any event. In jurisdictions that had not adopted that exception, such a course of conduct would have been morally unjustified. On the other side of the equation, the doctrine itself defeated the interests of those who transacted with charitable institutions and, not knowing of the doctrine, expected that the law would effectively require compensation for injuries caused by the wrongful acts of the agents through whom the institution acted.

A somewhat more substantial question would be raised by the possibility that in reliance on the doctrine a significant proportion of charitable institutions had chosen not to obtain liability insurance. That, however, was very unlikely. Most charities obtained liability insurance, either because they remained exposed to liability under the exceptions to the doctrine or because they believed it was morally proper to provide compensation for the victims of their employees' torts.[17] Indeed, many charities obtained liability policies in which the insurer specifically agreed not to avail itself of the immunity defense except with the charity's consent.[18]

A related question would be raised by the possibility that liability insurers relied on the charitable-immunity doctrine in setting their rates. Here too, however, justified reliance would have been unlikely. Liability insurers know that all common law doctrines are subject to being overturned. A rational liability insurer therefore will not determine its premiums on the assumption that all immunities are written in stone, but according to the probability that a relevant immunity will be preserved or overturned in whole or in part. Indeed, a person who procures liability insurance normally wants coverage not only against obvious legal risks but against risks due to changes in the law. Therefore, far from relying on the immutability of doctrine, a rational liability insurer will charge a premium that is based in part on the risk of a change in doctrine. If a liability insurer does not want to insure against liability resulting from a change in doctrine, it is free to avoid doing so by appropriate and conspicuous provisions in the policy. Few informed buyers would purchase such insurance, but that only shows that a change in doctrine is one of the events against which insureds want protection. Thus overruling of the charitable-immunity doctrine would not have defeated the justified reliance of liability insurers, because these insurers undoubtedly knew that the doctrine was subject to overturning, set their rates accordingly, and were paid for assuming that very risk.[19]

What has been said about justified reliance also applies to unfair surprise. On the one hand, the charitable-immunity doctrine itself was unfairly surprising to those who transacted with charitable institutions in the belief that the law would effectively require compensation for injuries caused by the wrongful acts of the agents through whom the institution acted. On the other, charitable institutions should not have been unfairly surprised by overruling. The doctrine's operation was unpredictable. The immunity substantially lacked congruence with applicable social norms and policies. Overruling the immunity did not change a socially accepted rule of primary conduct. Finally, overruling had been foreshadowed by a course of inconsistent distinctions, by explicit criticism of doctrine in the professional literature, and, once the process had begun, by decisions in other states. Insurers would not have been unfairly surprised for the same reasons, and also because if they were rational they had taken the risk of overruling into account in setting their premiums.

If a doctrine is jagged, the principles of replicability and support are also no better served by preserving the doctrine than by overruling it. Replicability is no better served by preservation than by overruling, because when a doctrine is subject to inconsistent exceptions it becomes difficult or even impossible to determine when a case falls within the doctrine and when it falls within an exception. Furthermore, the principle that jagged doctrines should normally be overruled can itself be applied in a replicable fashion. And while preservation of a jagged doctrine has the support of those cases that adopted and applied the doctrine, overruling will have the support of applicable social propositions, of those legal rules with which the doctrine is inconsistent, and of the inconsistent exceptions to the doctrine.

The charitable-immunity doctrine is again illustrative. Overruling was supported by applicable social propositions, by the principle of vicarious liability (since applicable social propositions did not support the charitable exception to that principle), and by the inconsistent exceptions to the doctrine. The profession as well as the courts could determine that the conditions for overruling had been satisfied.

The story of the charitable-immunity doctrine—which through overruling has become at best only a minority rule[20]—could be told of other jagged doctrines, including those that were fully overturned through a technique other than overruling. Take, for example, the doctrine, overturned in *MacPherson*, that a manufacturer was not liable to persons other than his immediate buyer for injuries caused as the foreseeable result of his negligence, unless the goods were inherently dangerous.[21] To begin with, consistency of outcomes was no more likely to be achieved by preservation of the doctrine than by its overturning. Because applicable social propositions did not support a distinction for this purpose between manufacturers and nonmanufacturers, there was a lack of consistency between the treatment of persons injured by the negligence of a manufacturer and the treatment of persons injured by the negligence of a nonmanufacturer. Because applicable social propositions did not support a distinction for this purpose between immediate buyers and ultimate buyers, there was a lack of consistency between the treatment of immediate buyers injured by a manufacturer's negligence and the treatment of ultimate buyers injured by a manufacturer's negligence. Because the "inherently dangerous" distinction was both inconsistent with the underlying doctrine and incapable of coherent application, there was a lack of consistency in the treatment of different ultimate buyers.

The protection of justified reliance and the prevention of unfair surprise were also no better served by preservation than by full overturning. Confident and legally well-founded reliance was unlikely. The doctrine was unreliable because of the incoherence of the exception and the doubt the exception cast on the doctrine's validity, and full overturning of the doctrine had been foreshadowed by the development of the exception and its application to products like coffee urns and painters' scaffolding. Even if reliance could somehow be seen as confident and legally well-founded, a manufacturer would not have been morally justified in deliberately failing to use due care. Indeed, due care was the legal rule of primary conduct even for manufacturers; the doctrine merely limited the classes of persons who could bring suit for failure to use due care.[22]

The principles of support and replicability were also no better served by preservation than by full overturning. Full overturning was supported by applicable social propositions, by the negligence principle (since applicable social propositions did not support excepting manufacturers from that principle), by the "inherently dangerous" exception to the manufacturer's liability doctrine, and by cases, like *Devlin*[23] and *Statler*,[24] which had negated the doctrine under the guise of applying the exception. The profession as well as the courts could determine that the conditions for full overturning had been satisfied.

The institutional principles of adjudication considered up to now have been both normative and descriptive. The principle that jagged doctrines should be overruled may seem to be an exception, because it is easy to find jagged doctrines that still prevail. Of course, at any moment in time some doctrines will have only recently become jagged. Those doctrines do not present a problem, because the principle that a jagged doctrine should be overruled assumes that the inconsistent or incoherent exceptions have become relatively well established. However, some doctrines, such as the legal-duty rule,[25] have remained in a jagged state for a long period of time. This may suggest that the principle that jagged doctrines should be overruled is not descriptive of judicial practice.

There are, however, other possible explanations. For one thing, a principle that describes social phenomena, unlike a scientific law, is not necessarily invalidated by a few outlying cases. An institutional principle of adjudication may be treated as descriptively accurate if it explains most judicial practice even though it does not explain every instance.

Moreover, a doctrine may seem to be jagged only because its exceptions reflect a principle that has not yet been stated at the appropriate level of generality. For example, at one time the doctrine that donative promises were unenforceable was subject to exceptions for certain types of relied-upon promises—most prominently, promises to act as an agent, charitable subscriptions, bailments, and promises to give land.[26] The exceptions appeared to be inconsistent with the doctrine, because applicable social propositions did not justify treating these particular types of promises differently from donative promises generally. Eventually, however, the exceptions were subsumed under a general principle (foreseeable reliance makes a donative promise enforceable) that was consistent with the underlying doctrine.

Furthermore, on close analysis at least some jagged doctrines that appear to have survived for a long time may have been so eroded by their exceptions that for most practical purposes their survival is nominal rather than real. For example, prior to the 1960s the survival of the legal-duty rule in contract law probably owed much to the fact that contract law had not developed a full-fledged doctrine of unconscionability. In the absence of such a doctrine, the courts normally lacked explicit power to review a bargain for fairness. In the absence of such a power, the next-best solution was to smuggle in fairness tests through other doctrines. The legal-duty rule was one such doctrine. It served as a crude surrogate for an explicit fairness review, because bargains in which one party's performance consists of an act he had already contracted to perform often involve unfairness. Under modern contract law, the fairness underpinning of the legal-duty rule has explicitly surfaced in the form of an exception: the rule is inapplicable to a contract modification that is fair and equitable in view of unanticipated circumstances. For most purposes this exception transforms the rule from a crude surrogate for fairness into an explicit fairness doctrine. Explicit overruling would still be preferable, both because of the clarity that would result and because the fairness exception, as conventionally stated, is not applicable to every case to which the rule applies. Nevertheless, the adoption of the fairness exception, together with numerous other exceptions and statutory modifications, have so eroded the rule that it has been overturned for most purposes, and the need for explicit overruling is correspondingly less insistent.

Nonjagged doctrines; criticism in the professional literature. Not all doctrines that substantially fail to satisfy the standards of social congruence and systemic consistency are jagged, partly because not all doctrines are easily made subject to inconsistent exceptions. Jaggedness is only an administrative aid, not a condition, to applying the basic overruling principle. An alternative aid is significant criticism of a doctrine in the professional literature, including judicial opinions other than local precedents. If a doctrine substantially lacks social congruence and systemic consistency, and that has been brought out in the professional literature, the values that underlie the standard of doctrinal stability and the principle of stare decisis will normally be no better served by preservation than by overruling, even if the doctrine is not jagged. Consistency of outcomes is unlikely to be better achieved by preservation than by overruling, because by hypothesis the doctrine is inconsistent with other doctrines. The principle of support is unlikely to be better served by preservation than by overruling, because overruling will have the support of applicable social propositions, those parts of the law with which the doctrine is inconsistent, and the professional literature. Justified reliance and unfair surprise are also unlikely. Confident and legally well-founded reliance is unlikely, because significant criticism in the professional literature will bring the legal reliability of a doctrine into serious question and foreshadow its eventual demise. If reliance does occur, it is unlikely to be morally justified, because by hypothesis the doctrine is socially incongruent. Finally, in many areas with which the law is concerned, planning on the basis of legal advice is rare and overruling would not change a socially accepted rule of primary conduct.[27] Therefore, the basic overruling principle is also applicable to doctrines whose failure to satisfy the standards of social congruence and systemic consistency has been brought out by significant judicial and scholarly criticism.

An example is provided by the widespread overruling, after the mid-1940s, of the prenatal-injury doctrine. Under this doctrine suit could not be brought on behalf of a child who had been born deformed or injured as a result of damage inflicted by negligence during the fetal state. Two reasons were usually given in support of the doctrine: a duty of care could not be owed to a person who was not in existence; and allowing suit would invite fraudulent claims because of the difficulty of proving a causal connection between the negligence and the deformation or injury. By the mid-1940s, it had become apparent that these reasons, and the doctrine they supported, substantially failed to satisfy the standard of social congruence. The danger of fraudulent claims did not seem much greater than in many other negligence cases, particularly in light of advances in medical knowledge. The argument that a duty of care could not be owed to a person who was not in existence largely assumed its own conclusion, because the issue was whether a fetus *is* in existence for this purpose or, even if it is not, whether a duty can be owed to a fetus. Furthermore, the premise of the argument seemed wrong. The general social view is that a fetus is a being in existence, and this view is particularly strong where the fetus has become viable (that is, capable of living apart from its mother), a condition normally achieved well before birth.

The prenatal-injury doctrine also substantially failed to satisfy the standard of systemic consistency. Because the doctrine was socially incongruent, it was inconsistent with general principles of negligence. It was also inconsistent with the legal status accorded to a fetus in property law, criminal law, procedural law, and equity:

> [I]n contemplation of the common law, life begins when the child is able to stir in the mother's womb. It can have a legacy, can own an estate, and a guardian can be assigned to it. . . . to make available processes of the law for the protection and preservation of the properties belonging to the child. . . . It would . . . be an unwarranted reflection upon the common law itself to attribute to it a greater concern for the protection of property than for the protection of the person. . . . If the killing of the unborn child is regarded by the law as being sufficient injury to society to justify taking the life of the perpetrator of the crime, then, to be logical . . . the law must allow [the injured child] to employ legal process and recover damages for the injury inflicted upon it. . . .[28]

> Let us see, what this non-entity can do. . . . He may be an executor. He may take under the Statute of Distributions. . . . He may take by devise. He may be entitled under a charge for raising portions. He may have an injunction; and he may have a guardian.[29]

Accordingly, by the mid-1940s the doctrine had been widely criticized in the professional literature, and jurisdictions that had not already adopted the doctrine generally refused to do so when the opportunity arose.

Under these conditions, the values underlying the standard of doctrinal stability and the principle of stare decisis were no better served by preservation of the prenatal-injury doctrine than by overruling. Because the doctrine substantially failed to satisfy the standard of social congruence, its application resulted in a lack of consistency between the treatment of those who were deformed or injured as a result of a negligent prenatal injury and the treatment of those who were deformed or injured as a result of a negligent postnatal injury. There was also a lack of consistency between the treatment of fetuses under the law of tort, on the one hand, and under the law of property, crimes, procedure, and equity, on the other. Overruling had the support of applicable social propositions, of the negligence principle, and of the professional literature, and the profession as well as the courts could determine that the conditions for overruling had been satisfied. Justified reliance and unfair surprise were very unlikely. Overruling had been foreshadowed by the criticism in the professional literature, including decisions in jurisdictions that had not previously adopted the doctrine, and (as the process of overruling began) by overruling in other states. Even if reliance on the doctrine could somehow be seen as confident and legally well-founded, an actor would not have been morally justified in deliberately failing to use due care. Indeed, such conduct normally would not have been legally authorized. The doctrine did not excuse a failure to use due care, but provided only that such a failure would not render a defendant liable to the child. In many prenatal-injury cases the defendant had clearly violated his legal duty to the mother, and the only issue was the extent of his liability.

By the mid-1940s, therefore, the prenatal-injury doctrine fell within the basic overruling principle. As a result, the doctrine was overruled in most jurisdictions that considered the issue, at least where viable and surviving fetuses were involved, and today is at best a minority rule in such cases.[30]

A Second Overruling Principle and the Technique of Signaling

Most cases in which a doctrine substantially lacks social congruence and systemic consistency will fall within the basic overruling principle. Some, however, will not. For example, overruling will often be inappropriate if a doctrine is neither jagged nor the subject of significant criticism in the professional literature. The lack of an objective marker makes it more difficult for the profession to determine that the conditions for overruling have been satisfied, and makes justified reliance more likely. The absence of such a marker may also suggest that the doctrine might not in fact substantially lack social congruence and systemic consistency.[31] Usually, the prudent course under such circumstances is to employ a technique of partial overturning, such as drawing an inconsistent distinction.[32] A decision that employs such a technique provides other courts with support for full overturning, while allowing the deciding court to draw back later if its view commands no following.

Even if a doctrine that substantially lacks social congruence and systemic consistency has been criticized in the professional literature, overruling may be inappropriate if the doctrine concerns an area in which planning on the basis of law is common, certainty is particularly important, and justified reliance is very likely. This may be true, for example, of rules of property law governing the legal effect of dispositions of real estate, or other questions of title. Here lawyers are commonly consulted before action is taken by third parties who acquire rights after the original disposition, security of title and use is a paramount value, and reliance by third parties may be legally well-founded and morally justified.[33]

To put the problem in more general terms, there may be some cases in which a doctrine substantially fails to satisfy the standards of social congruence and systemic consistency, and yet the basic overruling principle is not satisfied because the values underlying the standard of doctrinal stability and the principle of stare decisis would not be as well served by overruling as by preservation. In these cases a second overruling principle comes into play: Such a doctrine should be overruled if, but only if, the advantages of making the legal rule socially congruent and systemically consistent outweigh the costs of not serving the values that underlie doctrinal stability and stare decisis.

The application of this principle will tend to perpetuate social incongruence and systemic inconsistency in areas in which planning on the basis of law is common and certainty is particularly important. However, signaling can be employed to facilitate overruling even in those areas.

Signaling is a technique by which a court follows a precedent but puts the profession on notice that the precedent is no longer reliable. By the use of this technique, a court paves the way for overruling a doctrine it believes would otherwise have to be preserved because of justified reliance. A good example is provided by a series of Massachusetts cases concerning a corner of property law. Real estate deeds often contain covenants restricting the uses to which land can be put. If certain conditions are satisfied, a restrictive covenant is said to run with the land, which means that it is enforceable by the holder of the dominant parcel (the land that is benefited by the covenant) against the holder of the subordinate parcel (the land that is burdened by the covenant) even if the two holders have no direct contractual relationship. One condition is that the benefit of the covenant must "touch and concern" the dominant parcel.

A common type of restrictive covenant prohibits any use of a sub-

ordinate parcel that would compete with a use of the dominant parcel. Outside Massachusetts, this type of covenant was deemed to
touch and concern the dominant parcel. In Massachusetts, however,
a contrary rule had been established in *Norcross v. James*,[34] decided
in 1885 by Justice Holmes. *Norcross* held that such a covenant does
not touch and concern the dominant parcel and therefore does not
run with the land and cannot be enforced by a transferee.

The *Norcross* doctrine was criticized by the commentators and
conflicted with decisions in other states. Even in Massachusetts the
doctrine was not applied to covenants in leases, although a distinction between leases and deeds for this purpose could not be
justified under applicable social propositions. Nevertheless, in 1927
the Massachusetts Supreme Court followed the doctrine in *Shade
v. M. O'Keefe, Inc.*[35] The issue arose again in the 1960s, in *Shell
Oil Co. v. Henry Ouellette & Sons Co.*[36] Ouellette owned one
hundred acres of land. It conveyed twenty acres to certain trustees
in 1962, and promised on behalf of itself and its successors that the
remaining eighty acres would not be used in a way that competed
with a contemporaneous use made of the twenty acres it conveyed.
In 1963, the trustees sold part of the twenty acres to Shell, which
constructed a service station on the land. In 1965, Ouellette granted
an option to Mobil to buy part of Ouellette's remaining eighty acres
for the construction of a service station that would compete with
Shell's. Shell then brought suit against Ouellette and Mobil to enforce the restrictive covenant. The court indicated that it agreed
with the criticisms of the *Norcross* doctrine:

> If we were without precedent, we might (in 1967 conditions) reach
> a conclusion different from that of our predecessors. . . . We rec-
> ognize that there may be substantial reasons for permitting those,
> having privity of estate with a covenantee of a reasonable covenant
> restricting competition, to enforce such a covenant in equity against
> a person having (a) actual or constructive notice of the covenant,
> and (b) privity of estate with the covenantor.[37]

The court nevertheless refused to overrule *Norcross*, on the ground
that the "fact of bar reliance in the past . . . must be given weight
where a rule affecting real estate is involved," and that "in this
case, as in probably numerous other past transactions, there may
reasonably have been reliance" on *Norcross* and *Shade*.[38]

Seven years later, the issue arose once again in *Gulf Oil Corp.
v. Fall River Housing Authority*.[39] This time the Massachusetts court
avoided the force of the *Norcross* doctrine by drawing an incon-

sistent distinction. The owners of the dominant and the subordinate parcels both traced their titles back to the Fall River Housing Authority. The court distinguished *Norcross, Shade,* and *Ouellette* and enforced a noncompetition covenant, on the ground that the reason for the covenant in *Gulf Oil* was to assure the orderly and mutually beneficial development of the entire area, and that a covenant restricting competition for that reason did touch and concern the land.

Five years later, the issue arose once more in *Whitinsville Plaza, Inc. v. Kotseas.*[40] This time, the Massachusetts court overruled the *Norcross* doctrine. The court reviewed the history of the doctrine, dwelt on the scholarly criticism and the rejection of the doctrine in most other states, pointed out the inconsistency in applying the doctrine to deeds but not to leases, and confessed that the distinction it had drawn in *Gulf Oil* was untenable. It concluded that overruling had been adequately signaled by *Ouellette* and *Gulf Oil*, and made the new rule retroactive to the date on which it was foreshadowed in *Ouellette:*

> We believe that parties who, after the date of the *Ouellette* decision, executed restrictive covenants of the kind involved in this case could reasonably have relied on the expectation that on the next appropriate occasion thereafter this court would overrule the *Shade* and *Norcross* decisions, as we have done by our present decision. We believe further that parties who executed such covenants after *Ouellette* could not reasonably expect that the covenants would continue to be unenforceable under the rule of the *Shade* and *Norcross* decisions. We therefore hold that our overruling of the rule of the *Shade* and *Norcross* decisions shall apply to all such covenants executed after the *Ouellette* decision.[41]

The Effect of Deep Doctrinal Distinctions

In some cases a doctrine substantially lacks social congruence but is systemically consistent in at least a weak sense, because it is justified by a deep doctrinal distinction that is traditionally taken to justify otherwise unsupported differentiations. Examples of such distinctions include those between real and personal property and between maritime and nonmaritime transactions. These distinctions can render different treatment of two socially comparable transactions consistent in a weak sense simply because one transaction involves personal property and one involves real property, or because one involves transport by water and the other does not.

Call a group of rules that turns on a deep doctrinal distinction, like real estate or admiralty law, a legal subsystem; a given rule within the subsystem R_1; and the counterpart rule of general law R. That R_1 differs from R does not mean that R_1 is socially incongruent. Perhaps R_1 is justified by the social difference reflected in the deep doctrinal distinction, although other special rules of the subsystem are not. Perhaps R_1 is socially congruent when taken in conjunction with some other rule of the subsystem. Perhaps it is R that is socially incongruent. Perhaps R is preferable to R_1, but R_1 is nevertheless substantially congruent. For example, there is a duty to rescue under admiralty law, but not under general law. It may be that the admiralty rule is justified by special considerations applicable to ships at sea, or that the admiralty rule is preferable to the general rule, or that the general rule is preferable but the admiralty rule is substantially congruent.

Suppose, however, that R_1 substantially lacks social congruence. In such cases it might be thought that overruling will not lead to consistency of outcomes, because bringing R_1 into compliance with R will make R_1 inconsistent with the balance of the subsystem. That is not the case. A deep doctrinal distinction does not require the rules of the subsystem to differ from those of general law, but merely provides a weak justification for such differences. Still, the case for overruling a socially incongruent doctrine that is justified by a deep doctrinal distinction will not be quite as compelling as it would be in the absence of such a distinction. Because the doctrine will not completely lack systemic consistency, there may not be a visible marker to the profession that the conditions for overruling have been satisfied, or a marker may exist but be disregarded out of deep-seated professional respect for the deep distinction. Legally well-founded reliance may therefore be more likely, and the courts may be less ready to find that the conditions for overruling have been satisfied.

Nevertheless, rules that are socially incongruent and that would be systemically inconsistent except for a deep doctrinal distinction tend to erode over time, because such a distinction provides only an impoverished justification for the different treatment of socially comparable transactions. It is therefore to be expected that while change may come at a slower pace where socially incongruent doctrines are supported by deep doctrinal distinctions, overruling will eventually occur. For example, among the rules of general contract law are that a merchant impliedly warrants that his goods are fit for the ordinary purposes for which such goods are used, and that a person injured by a breach of contract is under a duty to mitigate his damages. Until recently, however, there were special rules of real property law on both issues. Under one rule, a landlord did not impliedly warrant the habitability of an apartment. Under the other, if a residential tenant broke a lease the landlord was under no duty to mitigate his damages, so that he was not obliged to try to relet the apartment or even to take an offer from a substitute tenant, and could instead let the apartment stand idle and sue for the entire rent. Both special rules were socially incongruent and were justified only by a deep doctrinal distinction between leases and other contracts. Within recent years, the limits of the courts' patience with this distinction became exhausted, and cases holding that a residential landlord does not warrant the habitability of an apartment and is under no duty to mitigate his damages have been widely overruled.[42]

Conclusion

As a process, overruling is comparable in important respects to other basic modes of legal reasoning, which, like overruling, involve an interplay between the standards of social congruence, systemic consistency, and doctrinal stability. Indeed, overruling may serve the values that underlie the standard of doctrinal stability and the principle of stare decisis as well as or better than preservation. The principles of overruling and stare decisis are not inherently opposed.

As an event in the history of a doctrinal proposition, overruling may or may not represent a sharp change in course. Under the traditional model of the history of doctrine, which bears a strong resemblance to the classical model of Darwinian evolution, a doctrinal proposition develops by a gradual series of incremental steps until so many small steps have been taken that a new doctrine can be said to have emerged. Certainly this model describes many instances of overruling, particularly those in which overruling is preceded by a course of inconsistent distinctions. In other cases, however, overruling results in a sharp discontinuity in the history of a doctrine, at least if that history is written separately for each state. One day, there is a doctrine in state A that suit cannot be brought on behalf of a child born deformed or injured as a result of negligence while the child was a fetus. The next day, there is a doctrine in state A that such a suit can be brought. In cases like these, the model of the history of doctrine is that of punctuated rather than gradual evolution, at least on the local level.

Even in these cases, however, there is often an important sort of continuity, if history is written on a national basis and account is taken of the professional discourse. Typically, even when overruling is not preceded by a course of inconsistent distinctions it is preceded by a course of criticism in the professional literature. Furthermore, once overruling of a doctrine begins, it often diffuses rapidly through the states. This is not surprising. Under the practice of reasoning from the professional literature, the status of a doctrine in one state becomes very unstable once it has been overruled in others. Because of its foreshadowing effect, overruling in other states diminishes the likelihood of confident and legally well-founded reliance on the local doctrine, and provides a final signal to the local profession, if such a signal were still necessary, that the time for reaping is at hand. Therefore, even when overruling seems discontinuous if we read history microscopically by looking only at the precedents of the local jurisdiction, continuity will probably be found if we read history through a lens that takes in professional criticism and national law.[43]

Prospective Overruling

Common law decisions are normally retroactive, in the sense that the rule established by a case is applied to a transaction that occurred before the case was decided, and is applicable to all comparable transactions that occurred before the decision but are still open to legal challenge. This retroactivity is both justified and made tolerable by the principle of support, under which newly announced rules are rooted in accessible doctrinal and social sources, and the principle of replicability, under which the process by which the court establishes a rule can be replicated by the profession even before the rule is announced.[44] Retroactivity also serves to ensure that the rule a court announces is sufficiently well considered that the court is willing to apply the rule to individuals who stand before it.

Increasingly in recent years, however, the courts have adopted a technique, known as prospective overruling, in which overruling is made less than fully retroactive. In the simplest case the new rule is made applicable to the immediate transaction (that is, the transaction in the case to be decided), but not to any other transaction that occurred before the date of the decision.[45] There are a number of variations. In some cases, the new rule is not made applicable even to the immediate transaction.[46] This variant is sometimes called pure prospective overruling. In some cases, the new rule is made applicable only to transactions that occur after a designated future date. This variant is sometimes called prospective prospective overruling. So in *Spanel v. Mounds View School District No. 621*[47] the Minnesota court overruled the municipal-immunity doctrine, which provided an immunity for municipal units (cities, school districts, and the like) very similar to that provided for charities under the charitable-immunity doctrine. However, the court not only refused to apply the new liability rule to the immediate transaction, but delayed the new rule's effective date to the end of the next session of the Minnesota legislature.

Other, intermediate variations are sometimes adopted. For example, in *Molitor v. Kaneland Community Unit District No. 302*[48] the Illinois court overruled the municipal-immunity doctrine in a case involving a suit on behalf of a child, Thomas Molitor, who was injured in a school-bus accident. The original opinion held that the new rule would not apply in any case, except Thomas's, based on transactions prior to December 16, 1959, the date of the decision. Subsequently, however, the court extended the application of the new rule to seven other children who were passengers in Thomas's school bus—three of whom were his siblings—on the theory that the parties had envisaged that the decision concerning Thomas would determine the rights of the other children, although there had been no formal agreement to that effect.[49] In *Li v. Yellow Cab Co.*[50] the California Supreme Court overruled the doctrine of contributory negligence and substituted the rule of comparative negligence in its place. The new rule was made applicable to all cases in which a trial had not begun before the date of the decision, but not to cases in which trial had begun, unless the case was reversed on appeal for other reasons. The technique used in *Whitinsville Plaza*, in which overruling was made retroactive only to the date on which a signal was given, might also be viewed as a special case of prospective overruling. Indeed, signaling itself can be viewed as a special case of prospective overruling, at least where the signal is unambiguous. So, for example, in *Tucker v. Budoian*,[51] which involved the liability of a landowner for damage caused by diverting water onto the land of others, the Massachusetts court applied the prior Massachusetts doctrine to the immediate transaction (partly because neither party had argued for overruling), but stated its intention to apply a new rule in future cases.

It was shown in Chapter 2 that the social functions of courts include not only dispute-settlement but enrichment of the supply of legal rules. No judicial technique brings out the latter function as sharply as does prospective overruling, particularly when the new rule is not made applicable to the immediate transaction. Similarly, no judicial technique brings out the announcement technique of interpreting precedent as sharply as does prospective overruling. At least in cases where the new rule is not made applicable to the immediate transaction, the rule announced by the court is absolutely unnecessary to the decision, but it will be given the same regard by the profession as a rule that is crucial to a decision.

Prospective overruling has obvious benefits. Assume a case in which a doctrine substantially fails to satisfy the standards of social congruence and systemic consistency, but justified reliance on the doctrine seems very likely and the value of protecting that reliance outweighs the value of making the legal rule socially congruent and systemically consistent. Ordinary overruling would then be inappropriate. If, however, prospective overruling can be properly employed, the court can overcome the reliance barrier and thereby make the law more socially congruent and systemically consistent than it would otherwise be.

The costs of prospective overruling, while not as obvious as the benefits, may nevertheless be substantial. Ordinary overruling typically increases the consistency of outcomes, by eliminating inconsistencies associated with the overruled doctrine. Prospective overruling, in contrast, often involves severe inconsistency of outcomes. Take, for example, *Molitor v. Kaneland*, the school-bus case. Under the court's decision, the outcomes for persons injured through municipal negligence before December 16, 1959, other than the children in Thomas's bus, would be different from the outcomes for the children in Thomas's bus, although the accident involving that bus occurred almost two years before December 16, 1959. Even the other children in Thomas's bus—even Thomas's siblings—would have had outcomes different from Thomas's, if the court had not been able to discover an agreement that all the children in that bus would be treated the same way. Similarly, where the new rule is made applicable only as of some future designated date, cases involving persons who engaged in transactions just before the designated date will have outcomes different from those of cases involving persons who engaged in comparable transactions just after that date, although the court already will have announced that the treatment to be accorded the former cases is a bad treatment.

In one important type of case, however, prospective overruling may increase consistency of outcomes. Assume a court has reason to believe that its overruling will itself be legislatively overturned. (This was often the prospect, for example, in municipal-immunity overrulings. The best rule might have been one that was suitable for legislative but not judicial adoption, such as a rule that made municipal units liable, but only up to a certain limit or only under certain conditions.) Assume further that if the legislature does overturn the overruling, the new legislative rule will govern only transactions that occurred after the rule was adopted. Under these circumstances, ordinary overruling would have the following consequences: transactions that were litigated to conclusion before the overruling will have been disposed of under the overruled doctrine, X; transactions that occurred before adoption of the new legislative rule and are still open to litigation will be disposed of under the overruling doctrine, Y; and transactions that occur after adoption of the legislative rule will be disposed of under either rule X or a third rule, Z.

Some cases have used prospective overruling to avoid precisely such a result. A leading example is still another Massachusetts decision, *Whitney v. City of Worcester*, in which the court used signaling as a functional substitute for prospective overruling, and stated its "intention to abrogate the doctrine of municipal immunity in the first appropriate case decided by this court after the conclusion of the next . . . session of the Legislature, provided that the Legislature at that time has not itself acted definitively as to the doctrine."[52] The court explained:

> [L]egislative action on the subject of sovereign immunity is almost sure to follow any action on our part. . . .
>
> In virtually every jurisdiction in which the doctrine of sovereign immunity has been judicially abrogated, judicial action has been followed by legislative action which modified, and in some cases completely nullified, the action of the judiciary. . . . [W]e think it unfair to create in this area expectations which the Legislature may nullify. Nor do we have any wish to promote unnecessary possibilities of unequal treatment among litigants, as caused by the chance of dates of injuries or lawsuits, as related to the sequence of judicial and legislative actions.[53]

Other costs of prospective overruling are institutional in nature. Take the question whether the newly announced rule in a prospective-overruling case should be made applicable to the immediate transaction. If the court applies the new rule to that transaction, as in *Molitor*, it not only raises difficult issues of consistency but undermines its own reasoning in using prospective rather than retroactive overruling. The major justification for prospective overruling is the protection of justifiable reliance. If the reliance on the old rule is so worthy of protection that a retroactive application of the newly announced rule would be unjust, it seems equally unjust to apply that rule to the immediate transaction. On the other hand, if the court adopts the technique of pure prospective overruling and refuses to apply the new rule even to the immediate transaction, it breaks the intimate tie between the dispute-settlement and rule-enrichment functions. Pure prospectivity also removes the assurances that follow from the willingness of a court not only to announce a rule but to apply the rule to individuals who stand before it. Furthermore, a regular use of pure prospective overruling would diminish the incentive to argue for overruling in future cases, because the litigating party would bear the cost of the litigation but would not benefit from its result. Thus a universe in which pure prospective overruling was widely employed would tend to diminish the role of a crucial mechanism for growth in the law.

An even more pervasive institutional cost concerns the impact of prospective overruling on the role of the bar in determining the law. In a universe in which overruling is normally retroactive, the bar must view the common law as a developing enterprise. In contrast, in a universe in which all overruling was fully prospective, the incentive to view the common law as a developing enterprise would be reduced. Rather than keeping apprised of case-law trends and professional discourse, lawyers in such a universe might well advise their clients to rely on old local precedents, no matter how eroded and criticized, on the premise that when a precedent is officially overruled the overruling will not affect past transactions. The effects of such a practice on social conduct would be highly undesirable. As Louis Kaplow has pointed out:

> Although behavior prior to [a] rule change cannot be altered after the fact, transition policy can nonetheless influence such behavior ex ante. [For] example, firms making initial . . . product design decisions will have made earnings projections that took into account expected liabilities. If it was known that tort liability would ensue when a product or production process caused substantial harm, decisions might have been substantially different than if it was likely that the firm would be immune. . . . Thus, when the risk of . . . liability depends in important ways on the evolution of tort law . . . the expectation that future evolution in the law will be made

applicable to harms arising . . . prior to the announcement of new rules will have a desirable effect on behavior. . . .

. . . To the extent that a given transition policy mitigates the impact of future reforms on preexisting investment, those currently making investment decisions will not have the proper incentive to take into account the prospects of future reform. . . . [I]t is desirable for investors to be influenced by the prospects of future government action, however uncertain, in making current decisions.[54]

In practice, the present institutional costs of prospective overruling seem marginal, partly because the technique is used in only a very small fraction of overturnings. Prospective overruling in the common law is normally appropriate, if at all, only if justifiable reliance is unusually likely notwithstanding that the rule is socially incongruent and systemically inconsistent, or there is a substantial likelihood that a judicial overruling will itself be legislatively overturned. These requirements are seldom met. Accordingly, common law overruling is still normally made fully retroactive. Furthermore, overruling is only a special case of overturning, and other types of overturning are rarely if ever made less than fully retroactive. However, the institutional costs of prospective overruling would be increased if the courts failed to use the technique with great discrimination. The courts should not assume the existence of justified reliance without a meticulous consideration of whether the area in question is one in which actors commonly plan on the basis of law, whether overruling had been foreshadowed, and whether reliance was morally justified.[55] The courts should also be careful to consider not only the advantages of prospective overruling in a particular case, but also the costs that would be entailed if the technique was used in a number of cases.

Transformation

Transformation occurs when a court fully overturns an established doctrine but does not announce that it has done so. In *MacPherson v. Buick Motor Co.*,[56] for example, Cardozo substituted a new rule, that the principle of negligence was fully applicable to manufacturers, for the old rule, announced in a number of precedents, that it was not. Rather than overruling, however, Cardozo radically reconstructed the precedents through a result-based technique and then purported to follow them. Similarly, in *Sherlock v. Stillwater*

Clinic[57] the Minnesota court substituted a new rule, that a negligent physician was liable for wrongful birth, for the old rule, announced in *Christensen v. Thornby*, that he was not. Rather than overruling, however, the court radically reconstructed *Christensen* through a minimalist technique and then purported to follow it.

Since both transformation and overruling involve the full overturning of an established doctrine, the distinction between the two modes is often formal rather than substantive. In overruling, the court explicitly announces that a doctrine is being abolished; in transformation, it does not. In some cases the two modes can be distinguished substantively, on the ground that in transformation the newly announced rule is consistent with the results reached in the precedents, while in overruling it is not. Often, however, this difference is largely the result of stage management, because the apparent consistency, in transformation, between the newly announced rule and the results reached in the precedents is achieved only by singling out features of the precedents that the precedent courts did not themselves consider material. In *MacPherson*, for example, Cardozo achieved apparent consistency between his newly announced rule and precedents that had refused to hold manufacturers liable, by suggesting that when the facts in those precedents were properly considered, the manufacturers were either not negligent or could have established a standard negligence defense. That may or may not have been true, but it was not how the precedent courts conceived the cases before them.[58]

Assuming that a court can choose between transformation and overruling, how should that decision be made?

Overruling and transformation might be said to reflect two different realities of full overturning. Overruling reflects the reality that a newly announced doctrine is being substituted for an old one. Transformation reflects the reality that by the time a doctrine is fully overturned, often it will already have been overturned in substantial part. (Thus prior to *MacPherson* the New York cases had whittled away most of the doctrine limiting a manufacturer's liability for negligence by holding that even goods like coffee urns and scaffolding fell within the "inherently dangerous" exception to that doctrine.) In theory, therefore, the choice between transformation and overruling might depend on which reality is stronger in a given case. As a practical matter, however, the choice usually seems to depend on the importance a court places on two matters of appearance.

One matter of appearance is brought out in a comment on this section by Peter Westen:

> ... [T]ransformation involves one *volteface* by courts, while overruling involves two. Transformation and overruling both involve implicit confessions of error by a court that it made mistakes in its earlier formulations of doctrine: they both involve a court's repudiation of its earlier reasoned explanations of the judgments it was entering. But overruling involves an additional confession of error that transformation does not—a confession by a court that it erred not only in its earlier *explanations* of the judgments it was entering, but also in the *judgments themselves*. Overruling is a confession by a court that it erred not only in its reasoning, but also in its judgment—a confession that it formerly ruled in favor of a party who really should have lost, and against a party who really should have won.
>
> Thus, the difference between *MacPherson v. Buick Motor Co.* and *Whitinsville* is that while both courts confessed to have changed their minds about doctrine, they had radically different views about the justice of their prior judgments: Cardozo explicitly asserted the New York Court of Appeals had ruled for all the right parties over the years, while the Massachusetts Supreme Judicial Court had to confess that it had ruled against many covenantees over the years who should in justice have won. . . . [59]

The second matter of appearance that may cause a court to choose transformation rather than overruling is a desire to maintain the impression that the standard of doctrinal stability is an extremely powerful constraint on judicial decisionmaking. From this perspective, the advantage of transformation is that it appears to be different from what it is. *MacPherson* is a masterly example. The overturning in that case was accomplished with such subtlety that law students, on reading the opinion for the first time, seldom realize what Cardozo really did.

The disadvantages of transformation are the obverse side of its advantages. In some cases, even lower-court judges may not realize that the doctrine has been abolished. This is exactly what happened after *MacPherson*. For a time, some New York trial-court judges failed to understand what Cardozo had really done, and went on blithely applying the special manufacturer's liability rule that *MacPherson* had overturned.[60] Furthermore, what strikes a court as a prudent concern for appearances may strike others as simply disingenuous. Perhaps most important, the clarity of overruling is more likely to lead to coherent development of the new rule than is the deliberately opaque nature of transformation.

On balance, there are few cases in which transformation is preferable to overruling. It is widely perceived that the pace of overruling has dramatically increased in the last forty years. Undoubtedly one reason for this phenomenon is a shift in the institutional principles of adjudication, but it is also likely that doctrines that once would have been transformed are now being overruled.

Overriding

Overriding occurs when a court narrows the ambit of an established doctrine in favor of a rule that has arisen after the earlier doctrine was established. Prior to the 1930s, for example, there was an established doctrine that donative promises were unenforceable.[61] In 1932 the *Restatement [First] of Contracts* adopted, in its famous Section 90, the principle that donative promises were enforceable if relied upon. Thereafter, the courts overrode the earlier doctrine by applying the new principle and limiting the ambit of the old doctrine to unrelied-upon donative promises.[62] Up through the 1940s there was an established doctrine that an offer that was accompanied by a promise to hold the offer open for a fixed period of time—a "firm offer"—was revocable despite the promise, unless the promise was separately paid for.[63] Beginning in the 1950s the courts overrode that doctrine by applying the reliance principle to firm offers and limiting the ambit of the old doctrine to offers that were not relied upon.[64] Up through the 1950s there was an established doctrine that bargains were not reviewable for fairness, but beginning in the 1960s the courts overrode that doctrine by applying the unconscionability principle to review bargains for certain types of unfairness.

In theory, overriding can be merely a special case of hiving off through consistent distinctions,[65] in which the court deals with a type of transaction that was not involved in the precedents that established the earlier doctrine and concludes that, given the social propositions that support the earlier doctrine, the transaction in question should be hived off for treatment under the later. In practice, however, when a court overrides an established doctrine it often deals with exactly the types of transactions that were involved in the precedents. Before Section 90 was adopted, for example, the doctrine that a donative promise was unenforceable had been applied to cases in which the promisee had clearly relied on the promise.[66] Before the reliance exception to the firm-offer doctrine became established, some courts explicitly held that reliance did not make a firm offer irrevocable.[67] Before the unconscionability principle became established, some courts enforced bargains that would now fall under that principle.[68] In such cases overriding is a form of overturning.

Overriding as a form of overturning resembles transformation in that the court characteristically does not announce that any overturning has occurred. It resembles overruling in that the new rule cannot be reconciled with the old results. It differs from both overruling and transformation in that the overturning is frequently only partial. In some cases, however, the ambit of the overriding principle may so swamp the overridden doctrine that the latter is effectively displaced. This extreme version of overriding is sometimes referred to as implied overruling. With its connections to hiving off at one end, and overruling and transformation at the other, overriding can be viewed as a bridge between the modes of legal reasoning described in the last chapter and those described in this one.

The Drawing of Inconsistent Distinctions

Another process by which the courts overturn established doctrines is the drawing of inconsistent distinctions—that is, distinctions that are inconsistent with the underlying rule, given the social propositions that support the rule. This process resembles overruling and transformation in that it involves overturning an established doctrine that substantially fails to satisfy the standards of social congruence and systemic consistency. It differs from those processes in that the overturning is only partial. Typically, even after an inconsistent distinction is established there will remain at least some cases in which the courts apply the underlying rule, either because the distinction is not all-encompassing or because it cannot be administered in a coherent fashion.

Since inconsistency does not seem to be a desirable attribute of legal rules, it might be thought that the drawing of inconsistent distinctions is improper and that the courts should either consistently apply, extend, and distinguish a rule or fully overturn it. In his book *Law's Empire*, Ronald Dworkin makes an argument that could be interpreted to lead to this conclusion. A central thesis of *Law's Empire* is that the law should have "integrity"—a term Dworkin defines in a special sense and calls an interpretive concept:

According to law as integrity, propositions of law are true if they figure in or follow from the principles of justice, fairness, and procedural due process that provide the best constructive interpretation of the community's legal practice. . . .

. . . The program [that law as integrity] holds out to judges deciding hard cases is essentially . . . interpretative. . . .

. . . [A judge faced with a new case] must find, if he can, some coherent theory about legal rights . . . such that a single political official with that theory could have reached most of the results the precedents report.[69]

Dworkin sharply distinguishes between the role of the integrity principle in the legislature and in the courts. Although the legislature should be guided by the integrity principle, "it does not follow that the legislature must never, in any circumstances, make law more inconsistent in principle than it already is."[70] Rather, the legislature, unlike a court, can also take into account considerations of policy and justice (by which Dworkin means, in this context, the ideal distribution of resources and opportunities), without regard to whether those considerations provide the best constructive interpretation of the community's past legal practice.[71] For the courts, in contrast, the integrity principle is "decisive."[72]

The drawing of inconsistent distinctions might be deemed improper under the integrity principle, because when an inconsistent distinction is drawn, no substantive rule will justify both the results reached by application of the underlying rule and the results reached by application of the inconsistent distinction. Part of the program of *Law's Empire* is to argue that jurisprudence should explain the legal practices of a society in their best light. Since the practice of inconsistent distinguishing is well established, something would be amiss, under that program, with a conclusion that a court cannot properly draw such distinctions. That conclusion, however, would follow only from a conception of integrity that is restricted to results or outcomes, and is therefore narrower than the ordinary meaning of the term. Integrity in its ordinary meaning can, like evenhandedness, be satisfied not only by consistency of results or outcomes, but by the consistent employment of the institutional principles that generate outcomes. Usually, the consistent employment of institutional principles will generate consistent outcomes. Certain institutional principles, however, may generate outcomes that are inconsistent in the sense that under these principles, cases that cannot be distinguished on the basis of applicable social propositions are nevertheless treated differently. The institutional principles of overruling, for example, may generate present outcomes that are inconsistent with past outcomes. As this example shows, the consistent employment of institutional principles does not lack integrity and evenhandedness simply because it generates inconsistent outcomes.

It might be argued that from the perspective of integrity drawing inconsistent distinctions differs in kind from overruling: The institutional principles of overruling justify the establishment of inconsistent legal standards at different times. In contrast, when a court draws an inconsistent distinction there are two inconsistent legal standards on the books at the same time—the underlying rule and the inconsistent exception.

If this argument was based on a concern with outcomes, it would have only limited force. If, for example, a court is deciding *Case B*, which seems to be controlled by an earlier precedent *Case A*, the outcome in *Case B* is the same whether the court overrules *Case A* or inconsistently distinguishes it. But, the argument might continue, overruling *Case A* would change the outcome in some later case that falls within the *Case A* rule but not the *Case B* exception. That argument would be mistaken: the later court could overrule *Case A* even if the *Case B* court did not. In short, once it is agreed that *Case B* can, with integrity and evenhandedness, be decided inconsistently with *Case A* through overruling, a prohibition on drawing inconsistent distinctions would not in itself change any outcomes. Such a prohibition would not compel a different outcome in *Case A* (which has already been concluded), *Case B* (which could still be decided inconsistently with *Case A* by overruling), or any later case (which could overrule *Case A* even if *Case B* did not).

It nevertheless remains true that as a result of inconsistent distinguishing, a rule and an inconsistent exception are simultaneously law. What justifies courts in following this messy practice, rather than attaining a clean picture through overruling?

Undoubtedly, one reason for the practice is a desire to preserve the impression of doctrinal stability: although overruling in fact accords with the standard of doctrinal stability, it has the appearance of discord. This desire to maintain appearances is not necessarily manipulative. Judges themselves believe strongly in the value of doctrinal stability and undoubtedly have a sincere preference for solutions that appear to accord with that value, all other things being equal.

There are other and stronger reasons that justify the practice of inconsistent distinguishing. To begin with, a court may properly decide that if it is uncertain about how given conduct should be treated it may give effect to its uncertainty by carving out only a portion of the conduct, on a provisional basis, provided the line it carves is rationally related to the purpose. Call this the institutional principle of provisionality. For example, a court may believe that a doctrine substantially lacks social congruence and systemic consistency and yet may not be confident that its belief is correct. The court may then properly draw an inconsistent distinction as a provisional step toward full overturning. Alternatively, a court may properly formulate an exception at a level of generality below that necessary for the exception to be fully principled, as a provisional step toward full generality. For example, a court faced with a relied-upon bailment promise in the early twentieth century might have made an exception to the rule that donative promises were enforceable, but limited the exception to bailment promises, because it was not yet sufficiently confident to formulate a broad reliance principle.

A court that applies the institutional principle of provisionality acts with integrity and evenhandedness although the rule it adopts is inconsistent with the body of present law. Overruling is final, and, if the court is wrong in its view of a doctrine, would be a serious mistake. Establishing an exception at too high a level of generality may also have substantial costs.[73] Over time, the professional discourse should make clear whether the court's provisional view of a doctrine is correct and whether the court has articulated an exception at the best level of generality. Over time, a court can adjust its provisional position by fully overruling a doctrine, pulling back from an exception, or generalizing it further. Meanwhile, the provisional quality of the court's action will have allowed the issues to percolate, and the discourse to continue, in a way that overruling or a broad formulation of an exception would not.

Inconsistent distinguishing may also be used as a technique for dealing with the problem of justified reliance. Inconsistent distinguishing allows the courts to protect at least those who relied on the core of a doctrine, that is, that part of a doctrine that cannot be even plausibly distinguished. This may be particularly important where the doctrine has not yet been made subject to inconsistent distinctions or to significant criticism in the professional literature. At the same time, a case that employs the technique of inconsistent distinguishing itself becomes part of the professional literature and puts the profession on notice that the underlying doctrine has been advanced to candidacy for overruling. It may sometimes be best to move to the best rule in steps, even at the price of inconsistency during the transition. By using the technique of inconsistent distinguishing, a court may simultaneously move the law toward social congruence, protect past justified reliance on the core of a doctrine, diminish the likelihood of future justified reliance, and prepare the way for an overruling that might not have otherwise been proper.

Integrity, in the ordinary sense of that term, is therefore not compromised by the practice of inconsistent distinguishing. However, integrity does have a special role to play in this practice. Its role is not to prohibit the practice, but to shape it by urging candor. If the court draws an inconsistent distinction because it is tentative about the social congruence of the underlying doctrine, it is well to say so. If the court draws a distinction at a very low level of generality because it is unsure about the appropriate level of generality, it is well to say so. If the court is concerned about justified reliance, it is well to say that too. Those messages are normally implied in any event, but if the provisionality that justifies inconsistency is to be fully vindicated, the message is better made explicit.

Noninterpretive Elements of the Common Law

The concept of law as integrity, in the special meaning Dworkin gives that term, finds expression in two claims about the nature of law and adjudication that extend well beyond the issue of inconsistent distinguishing. It is useful to examine these claims at this point, as a bridge to Chapter 8.

The first claim is that courts determine cases on the basis of legal rights and duties, rather than making law in a legislative capacity. This claim is correct. A court does not say, "We establish this legal duty for the first time today, and we impose liability on you for not performing the duty yesterday." Rather, a court says, "You were under a legal duty to do this, and we impose liability on you because you didn't."[74]

The second claim, which I will call the convictions thesis, has a general and a special part. The general part is that adjudication is essentially an interpretive enterprise and that the task of the judge is to give the best possible interpretation of prior institutional decisions. The special part is that a judge properly decides common law cases by first determining what rules would satisfy a threshold degree of fit with prior institutional decisions and then selecting, from among those rules, the one he thinks best on the basis of his own convictions of political morality, excluding his convictions on policy.[75] This second claim is incorrect in both its general and special parts.

To begin with, the criteria the convictions thesis lays down, in its special part, for the employment of social propositions are completely inverted: In establishing common law rules, courts should and do employ policies, and should not and do not employ their personal convictions. I have shown why both these points are so in Chapter 4, and I shall return to the latter point in Chapter 8. Therefore, I will focus here on some deeper problems with the convictions thesis.

There is a theory of law and adjudication that a court decides a "hard case" by constructing the legal rule that will best fit prior institutional decisions, without regard to social propositions.[76] Call this the pure-fit theory. Dworkin has explicitly disavowed this theory,[77] and rightly so. The theory is not only wrong in both descriptive and normative terms, but is essentially incoherent. In any given case any number of rules can be constructed on the basis of fit. What fit is the best fit must depend on what criteria the fit should satisfy and on how to select among competing rules when no single rule best satisfies all the relevant criteria. Therefore, any theory that employs fit to determine law must answer such questions as whether the fit should be based on past outcomes or on the rules by which the outcomes were arrived at, how far back in time and over how many fields of law the fit should extend, which kinds of facts and statements in prior decisions may be properly emphasized and which submerged, how many decisions may be left unaccounted for and on what basis, and how different criteria of fit should be ranked when they are in conflict. These questions cannot be answered by the pure-fit theory.

Dworkin's convictions thesis attempts to avoid this pitfall partly by employing a test of threshold or sufficient fit, rather than best fit, and partly by supplementing the concept of fit with answers to some of the criteria questions. Under his thesis, fit may be based on either rules or outcomes, although where the two diverge a fit based on outcomes seems preferable; the judge must take into account whether the decisions that support one rule seem more important, fundamental, or wide-ranging than the decisions that support others; and a rule cannot be said to fit unless it states a principle of justice (by which Dworkin means, in this context, that the rule must be connected to some more general moral or political considerations) and does not rest solely on considerations of policy.[78] The assumption is that this supplemented-fit test, unlike a pure-fit test, imposes meaningful constraints on judicial decision, so that the judge's personal convictions will not be alone decisive. Indeed, it is largely through this assumption that Dworkin maintains the argument that law is an interpretive enterprise, because if the judge's personal convictions were alone decisive, interpretation would have nothing at all to do with judicial decisions.

In fact, however, even the supplemented-fit test doesn't impose much of a constraint in common law cases. The common law presents a judge with a huge mass of data. The leeway for fit based on outcomes is particularly great, as illustrated by *MacPherson* and *Sherlock*, both of which managed to turn prior rules on their head while purporting to follow precedent.[79] It's true that in any given case, some conceivable rules would not satisfy Dworkin's supplemented-fit test, and the judge might therefore not be free to select the rule he thinks is the best of all conceivable rules. In most cases, however, a number of competing rules would pass the supplemented-fit test, and in many cases at least two of those rules would produce diametrically opposed outcomes. For example, in the case Dworkin uses as a paradigm of common law reasoning, *McLoughlin v. O'Brian*,[80] he concludes that at least two competing rules would satisfy the supplemented-fit test, only one of which would be likely to render the defendant liable.[81] Since under the convictions thesis the judge is free to select between competing rules on the basis of his personal convictions, provided the threshold test is met, and since a number of competing rules would normally meet that test, the judge's personal convictions would normally determine the contours of the rule he establishes and would frequently determine the outcome as well.[82] Indeed, under the convictions thesis the judge's personal convictions enter even the determination of fit, because whether a rule reflects a principle of justice, as required by the supplemented-fit test, itself turns on the judge's personal convictions. There is undoubtedly something compelling about a vision of an individual who acts on his personal convictions, but a judge who established legal rules and determined outcomes according to his personal convictions would be untrue to his office. The convictions thesis describes neither what judges claim to do, what they actually do, nor what they should do.

Another deep problem with the convictions thesis stems from its general part, that adjudication is essentially an interpretive enterprise and that the task of the judge is to give the best possible interpretation of prior institutional decisions. That may be true of those areas of adjudication that involve canonical texts, but it is not true of all adjudication, because it is not true of the common law. Certain modes of common law reasoning do heavily involve the consistent application and extension of rules announced in prior institutional decisions. Other modes, however, do not. For example, although the formulation of a new general principle often rests in part on previously anomalous precedents that the principle is able to explain, the basic support for a new principle lies not in such precedents but in applicable social propositions.[83] Similarly, both new rules and consistent distinctions from established rules are often formulated on the basis of applicable social propositions, with few or no roots in prior institutional decisions. All the modes of overturning fundamentally rest on a determination that a rule is socially incongruent. Even the employment of those modes of common law reasoning that do heavily involve the consistent application and extension of announced rules normally depends on a prior determination, explicit or tacit, that the announced rule is substantially congruent with applicable social propositions.

Dworkin defends the theory that the task of the judge is to give the best possible interpretation of prior institutional decisions partly by constructing and then criticizing a model of adjudication that he calls legal pragmatism. Under this model, a court concerns itself only with the function of establishing legal rules, disregards the function of settling disputes, takes policy into account, and places no value on consistency as such.

> [According to legal pragmatism,] judges do and should make whatever decisions seem to them best for the community's future, not counting any form of consistency with the past as valuable for its own sake. . . .
>
> [The pragmatist] finds the necessary justification for coercion in the justice or efficiency or some other contemporary virtue of the . . . decision itself, as and when it is made by judges. . . .
>
> . . . [P]ragmatism . . . finds [the best interpretation of judicial practice in the] story of judges as independent architects of the

best future, free from the inhibiting demand that they must act consistently in principle with one another.[84]

That no judge or commentator subscribes to the model of pragmatism is perhaps not important, if the model serves to bring out ideas about the law. One way the model serves that purpose is by bringing out Dworkin's own ideas. Although a judge who followed the model of pragmatism would be subject to a number of legitimate criticisms, Dworkin's criticisms are off point. One of those criticisms is that a pragmatist judge would not treat consistency with the past as valuable "for its own sake." But consistency with past institutional decisions has only limited value for its own sake; it has substantial value only if it serves some fairness or policy goal. We may sometimes accept, but we never treasure, consistency with bad past decisions. Consistency with past institutional decisions does serve the fairness goal of arriving at like outcomes in like cases over time, but it can frustrate the fairness goal of arriving at like outcomes in like cases across the law, and the even more important fairness goal of arriving at the outcomes that would be generated by the best possible legal rules. If the law is sometimes willing to frustrate the latter kinds of fairness goals in the interest of doctrinal stability, it is partly to serve the fairness goal of arriving at like outcomes over time, but more fundamentally to serve the policy goal of making the law reliable to facilitate planning and dispute-settlement.

Dworkin's criticisms of the model of pragmatism rest on the premise that courts that don't take into account past institutional decisions can't act consistently in principle. That premise is false. It would be wrong for courts to follow the model of pragmatism— wrong, for example, to have no concern with the dispute-settlement function or with the moral and policy values that underlie the standard of doctrinal stability—but it would not be unprincipled to do so. Each rule a pragmatist court adopted would be based on a just rule that was consistent with all other just rules that should be adopted at the moment of decision. Both the enterprise of determining rules on that basis and the individual rules themselves would be no less principled than an enterprise and individual rules based on threshold fit and the judge's personal convictions. Whether a theory of law and adjudication is principled does not depend on whether it produces rules and outcomes consistent with past rules and outcomes, desirable as that may be all other things being equal. Rather, it depends on whether rules and outcomes are generated by the consistent application of appropriate institutional principles of adjudication. Continuity with the past can be assured by methods other than consistency with prior rules and outcomes. Overruling, inconsistent distinguishing, and other forms of overturning do not necessarily involve discontinuity, even though they yield rules and outcomes that are inconsistent with the past, because the present is tied to the past through continuity in the institutional principles that generate those rules and outcomes.

Chapter 8

The Theory of the
Common Law

A theory of the common law is implicit in the theory of adjudication developed in Chapters 1–7. Essentially, this theory is that the common law consists of the rules that are generated at the present moment by application of the institutional principles of adjudication. I shall call this theory the generative conception of the common law. In this chapter I will develop that conception and contrast it with conceptions I call text-based theories. I will also develop two fundamental properties of the common law that are closely associated with the generative conception: that common law rules are not absolutely certain, and that there is a legal answer to every question that takes the form "What is the law concerning this matter?"

Text-based Theories of Law

I shall begin by considering some aspects of the theories of law and adjudication of two leading modern positivists, H. L. A. Hart and Joseph Raz. Hart's theory of law begins with the thesis that law consists of "a union of primary and secondary rules." Primary rules are rules of obligation—rules that state how people are obligated to behave.[1] Secondary rules are rules about establishing, changing, and applying primary rules; they "specify the ways in which the primary rules may be conclusively ascertained, introduced, eliminated, varied, and the fact of their violation conclusively determined."[2] The most fundamental type of secondary rule is a rule of recognition. A rule of recognition is a rule that tells how to recognize that some other rule is a legal rule. It specifies "some feature or features possession of which by a suggested rule is taken as a conclusive affirmative indication that it is" a legal rule.[3] It is a rule "for conclusive identification of the primary rules of obligation."[4] To say that a given rule is valid "is to recognize it as passing all the tests provided by the rule of recognition."[5] Thus a given rule is a valid legal rule if but only if its pedigree can ultimately be traced under a rule of recognition. In contrast, a given rule is a rule of recognition if but only if it is accepted by the society, and perhaps more particularly by its officials.

Compared to his theory of law, Hart's theory of adjudication is fairly rudimentary. Central to that theory is a binary conception in which adjudication is viewed as consisting of two almost wholly different processes. Under this conception, cases are either "clear" or "indeterminate."[6] In clear cases, the courts decide simply by applying rules that were adopted in past precedents or canonical texts to transactions that fall within the "core meaning" of the rules. Social propositions will be irrelevant to determining the law in these cases.[7] However, rules adopted in past precedents or canonical texts "will, at some point where their application is in question, prove indeterminate; they will have what has been termed an *open texture*."[8] This gives rise to a second class of cases, in which a large field is left open "for the exercise of discretion by courts . . . in rendering initially vague standards determinate . . . or in developing and qualifying rules only broadly communicated by authoritative precedents."[9] In deciding these cases, a court may determine what rule best fits existing doctrinal materials, but it may also act like a legislature and with a legislature's discretion, "striking a balance, in the light of circumstances, between competing interests."[10]

Raz's theories of law and adjudication stem from but refine and extend those of Hart. An important element of Raz's theories is that law is an institutionalized normative system,[11] and for Raz the institution most central to the existence of law is the court.[12] Thus Raz's theory of law gives primacy to the theory of adjudication, and his theory of adjudication is much more elaborate than Hart's. In the balance of this chapter I shall therefore focus on Raz's theory of adjudication, but most or all of what is said about that theory, and its relation to Raz's theory of law, applies to Hart's theories of law and adjudication as well.

Like Hart, Raz adopts a binary conception in which adjudication is viewed as consisting of two almost wholly different processes, one in which the court applies law, and one in which the court makes law through the exercise of a legislative discretion. Raz expresses this binary conception by drawing a central distinction between "regulated" and "unregulated" disputes.

A dispute is "regulated," for Raz, if the law is clear and cannot be changed by the court.[13] In regulated disputes, one particular solution is "required by law."[14] In such cases there is no gap in the law. The court decides the case by applying preexisting and legally binding rules which it is under a duty to apply.[15] To decide such cases, the court uses purely "legal skills."[16] The judge "can be seen here in his classical image: he identifies the law, determines the facts, and applies the law to the facts."[17]

A dispute is "unregulated," for Raz, if the law does not provide a clear answer or the law can be changed by the court.[18] All unregulated disputes are due to intended or unintended indeterminacy of language and intention.[19] In regulated disputes, one solution is required by law. In unregulated disputes, there is a "gap" in the law.[20] The court decides the case by using moral skills to fill the gap and make new law.[21] In making new law, the court has full (or in some cases guided) discretion to decide the case according to its own perception of what is right.[22] The relevant image here is that of the legislator. "[W]ithin the admitted boundaries of their law-making powers courts act and should act just as legislators do, namely, they should adopt those rules which they judge best. . . . [E]ssentially it is true that in the exercise of their law-making power the courts should . . . act as one expects Parliament to act."[23] The only difference between court and legislature, as regards unregulated disputes, stems from the fact that judicial lawmaking is usually piecemeal. A court may and sometimes should decline to reform the law simply because piecemeal reform would make the law discordant. In contrast, a legislature can avoid choosing between piecemeal reform and discordance because it can instead go down the path of thoroughgoing reform.[24]

At the core of Hart's and Raz's theories of law and adjudication is a conception of law as the body of doctrinal propositions that have been promulgated in past texts by officials of the relevant jurisdiction (together, perhaps, with doctrines that can be developed from such propositions by internal operations, like logical deduction).[25] So, for example, Raz states, "Laws are laws because they were enacted by legal institutions. . . . Even legal custom is not law until it is recognized and declared to be law by the courts. . . . [R]ecognition by law-applying organs [is] a necessary condition of the existence of laws. . . . [A] law is part of the system only if it is

recognized by legal institutions."[26] I shall refer to doctrinal propositions promulgated in past texts by officials of the relevant jurisdiction as doctrinal propositions adopted in past texts, and I shall
refer to theories of law and adjudication based on the concept that
law consists of such doctrinal propositions as text-based theories.
A central tenet of such theories is that a rule has force, and a court
is under a duty to apply a rule to a case that lies within its ambit,
just because the rule was officially adopted, without regard to the
rule's justification. Again, Raz:

> [M]arking a rule as legally binding is marking it as an authoritative
> ruling. This marking-off of authoritative rulings indicates the ex-
> istence in [the] society of an institution or organization . . . holding
> [members of the society] bound to conform to certain standards
> just because [the standards] were singled out by that purported
> authority regardless of whether or not they are justifiable standards
> on other grounds. Since it is of the very essence of the alleged
> authority that it issues rulings which are binding regardless of any
> other justification, it follows that it must be possible to identify
> those rulings without engaging in a justificatory argument, i.e., as
> issuing from certain activities and interpreted in the light of pub-
> licly ascertainable standards not involving moral argument.[27]

The adoption of a text-based theory of law helps to explain why
Raz conceives of the law as "gappy"—doctrinal propositions adopted
in past texts don't cover all questions. It also helps to explain the
conception of adjudication as a binary process, in which either (i)
cases fall under doctrinal propositions adopted in past texts (the
law), and the courts are under a duty to apply those rules regardless
of their justification ("clear" or "regulated" cases), or (ii) cases do
not fall under doctrinal propositions adopted in past texts, and courts
have a legislative discretion to establish the legal rules they think
best on the basis of the moral norms and policies they think best
("indeterminate" or "unregulated" cases).

I will consider the first part of this conception in the next section.
The second part—that courts have a legislative discretion in establishing common law rules when cases do not fall under doctrinal
propositions adopted in past texts—is a generalized counterpart of
the more specific theory, analyzed in Chapter 4, that in establishing
common law rules courts may employ the moral norms they think
best. The grounds for rejecting the more specific theory also apply
to the generalized counterpart—for reasons of social function,
structure, fairness, and replicability, a legislator may properly establish those legal rules he thinks best on the basis of those moral

norms and policies he thinks best, but a judge may not. To recapitulate the analysis in Chapter 4:

In terms of social function, the courts are the institution to which
a member of society is entitled to go to resolve a dispute growing
out of a past transaction and deriving from a claim of right based
on the society's existing standards. Therefore, it is those standards
from which the courts should reason when they resolve disputes.
If the courts resolved disputes by reasoning from those moral norms
and policies they think best, there would be no institution to which
a member of the society could go to vindicate a claim of right based
on existing standards.

In terms of structure, the combination of a representative conception, highly diverse training and experience, and responsiveness
and accountability to the citizenry on an ongoing basis provides
legitimacy to legislative rules that are adopted because the legislature thinks them best on the basis of the moral norms and policies
it thinks best. In contrast, courts are not conceived as representative,
are made up of a handful of members with relatively homogenous
training and experience, and are deliberately structured to limit their
accountability and responsiveness to the citizenry. The legitimacy
of the judicial establishment of legal rules therefore depends in large
part on the employment of a process of reasoning that begins with
existing legal and social standards rather than with those standards
the court thinks best.

In terms of fairness, requiring courts to employ moral n⬚ ⬚ ns and
policies with the requisite social support, rather than the standards
they think best, alleviates (although it does not eliminate) the retroactivity dilemma by ensuring that decisions are rooted in standards that the disputants either knew or had reason to know at the
time of their transaction, albeit standards that had perhaps not been
officially recognized as legal rules.

In terms of replicability, since moral norms and policies are relevant to the decision of all common law cases, if courts were free
to employ whatever norms and policies they think best, the profession would be unable to replicate the adjudicative process and could
not reliably determine the law for purposes of either planning or
dispute-settlement. The employment of a replicable process of reasoning employing existing standards also further alleviates the retroactivity dilemma, by enabling the profession to determine that
a proposition will be recognized by the courts as a legal rule even

though it has not yet received such recognition at the time of the transaction.

In short, courts do not have a legislative discretion to establish the rules they think best on the basis of the moral norms and policies they think best. Rather, they can properly establish legal rules only by employing doctrinal and social propositions that have the requisite degree of support, in the manner required by the institutional principles of adjudication.

Justification and the Content of the Law

Of more interest for present purposes is the concept that there is a large class of cases—"clear" or "regulated" cases—in which one particular solution is required under doctrinal propositions adopted in past texts, and justification and social propositions are irrelevant in determining the law. This concept misconceives common law adjudication by failing to accord to justification a role in determining the law, by failing to appreciate the extent to which social propositions figure in determining the law, and by failing to distinguish between the body of doctrinal propositions adopted in past texts and the content of law.

It is a central tenet of text-based theories that the content and force of legal rules can be determined without regard to the rules' justification.[28] In evaluating this tenet, as applied to the common law, it is necessary to distinguish between two types of judicial ruling and two types of justification. The term *ruling* may refer either to a court's final judgment (that is, a court's decision on which party prevails and what remedy will be granted) or to the rule the court establishes to support its final judgment. The term *justification* may refer either to critical morality and right policy, on the one hand, or to social congruence and systemic consistency, on the other.

Neither type of justification normally figures in determining the content and force of a final judgment. The content of a final judgment normally depends simply on its text, and its force depends neither on whether it is justified by critical morality and right policy or on whether it is socially congruent and systemically consistent. The issue is different, however, as regards a common law rule announced in support of a final judgment. The content and force of such a rule does depend on whether the rule is socially congruent and systemically consistent.

It is true that an announced common law rule may be deemed "valid" or "binding" even though it is socially incongruent and systemically inconsistent. The concept of validity, however, is of only very limited value in considering legal rules. On a linguistic level, that concept normally adds nothing to the term *legal*. How, after all, could a rule be a legal rule and not be a valid rule? Generally speaking, in describing legal rules the term *valid* is useful only as a rhetorical alternative to the term *legal*. For example, it may be rhetorically useful to employ the terms *valid* and *invalid* when inquiring whether a rule that has the surface indicia of a legal rule was duly adopted by a duly constituted body acting within the limits of its authority. Analytically, however, the issue in such an inquiry is not whether the rule is a valid rule but whether it is a legal rule.

On a deeper level, the concept of validity often captures only a weak and relatively formal dimension of legal rules. Whether a rule that has the surface indicia of a legal rule is valid (whether, that is, the rule is a legal rule) depends on such issues as whether it was duly adopted by a duly constituted body acting within the limits of its authority. That issue is seldom salient in determining the common law. The working issue for a deciding court considering a common law issue is almost never whether a rule announced in a precedent is "valid"; the working issue is the force of the rule. A rule announced in a precedent may be valid, in a weak and formal sense, and yet may have little force, in that under the institutional principles of adjudication a court should not consistently apply and extend the rule. Nor is the working issue for a deciding court whether a rule announced in a precedent is "binding" in a formal sense. Any such rule is binding in at least the formal sense that if the rule is relevant to the case at hand the deciding court's reasoning should take some account of the rule, if only to overturn it in whole or in part.

Rather, the working issue for the deciding court is whether the rule has force, in the sense that it should be consistently applied and extended. That issue, and therefore the content of the common law, always depends at least in part on whether the rule is justified in the sense that it substantially satisfies the standards of social congruence and systemic consistency. If a rule substantially satisfies those standards the courts should and will apply and extend the rule in a consistent fashion. If a rule substantially fails to satisfy those standards, the courts should not and typically will not apply and extend it in a consistent fashion, but instead will overturn it in whole or in part, as by drawing inconsistent distinctions, radically reconstructing it through a minimalist or result-oriented technique, or overruling it. As a formal matter, such a rule may be deemed a valid and binding rule of the legal system, but it will be so drained of normativity that it will have little or no legal or moral force. If, under the institutional principles of adjudication, the courts should inconsistently distinguish the rule, citizens are under no obligation, legal or moral, to conform to the rule in any respect in which it should be distinguished. If, under those principles, the courts should radically reconstruct the rule, citizens are under no obligation, legal or moral, to conform to the rule in any respect in which it should be reconstructed. If, under those principles, the courts should fully overturn the rule on a retroactive basis, citizens are under no obligation, legal or moral, to conform to the rule in any respect.

The failure of text-based theories to distinguish between whether a rule established in a precedent is valid and binding in a formal sense, and whether it has force, is intimately related to the erroneous conception of such theories that the law can often be determined, even in noncanonical areas, without regard to social propositions. Under text-based theories, a case is "clear" or "regulated" if it is controlled by a doctrinal proposition, established in a past text, that a court is under a duty to apply without regard to the rule's justification. However, whether a deciding court should apply a rule established in a precedent can never be determined simply by inspection of the precedent itself, but always depends at least in part on the justifiability of the rule under applicable social propositions. Thus no common law cases are "regulated," because none are controlled by doctrinal propositions established in past texts, without regard to justification. Cases are "easy" or "clear" only when they fall within a doctrinal rule that is justified by applicable social propositions, so that the standards of doctrinal stability, social congruence, and systemic consistency all point in the same direction.

Indeed, applicable social propositions often figure even in determining just what rule a precedent stands for. Normally, a deciding court will determine that issue by using the announcement technique, which takes the rule as it is stated by the precedent court. However, a deciding court is also institutionally permitted, and indeed may be institutionally required, to consistently distinguish (and thereby reformulate) an announced rule, or to draw inconsistent distinctions or radically reconstruct the rule through the use of minimalist or result-centered techniques. Which technique a court uses to establish the rule of a precedent depends largely on whether the rule substantially satisfies the standard of social congruence.

The Generative Conception of the Common Law

The distinction between whether a rule is formally valid and binding and whether it has substantive force—whether a court should consistently apply and extend it—is tied to an even more fundamental distinction. This is the distinction between the body of doctrinal propositions adopted in past texts, on the one hand, and the content of the common law, on the other. As was shown in the last section, a doctrinal proposition adopted in a binding precedent may be valid and binding in a weak and formal sense and yet not have substantive force as a common law rule, in that it will not be consistently applied and extended. Correspondingly, there may be a common law rule on a matter even in the absence of a doctrinal proposition adopted in a binding precedent. Doctrinal propositions adopted in past texts are a fundamental starting point in determining the content of the common law, but they do not comprise the content of the common law.

What then does the common law consist of? It consists of the rules that would be generated at the present moment by application of the institutional principles of adjudication. I call this the generative conception of the common law. The generative conception, and its contrast with text-based theories, can be illustrated by a sprinkling of hypothetical but fairly realistic cases:

Case I. The issue has never arisen in state A whether a physician is liable for wrongful birth, that is, whether a physician who has been negligent in a manner that foreseeably led to the birth of a healthy but unwanted child is liable to the parents for the expense of the child's birth. Application of the institutional principles of adjudication, however, generates the rule that the physician is liable. Applicable social propositions would not justify exempting physicians from the force of the negligence principle in this kind of case; many other jurisdictions have so held (and no recent case holds to the contrary); and the rule is firmly established in the professional literature. It is then part of the law of state A that a physician is liable for wrongful birth, although that rule has not been adopted in an official text in state A.

Case II. The issue has never arisen in state A whether a judge is liable for the negligent performance of his judicial duties. Application of the institutional principles of adjudication, however, generates the rule that the judge is not liable. Applicable social propositions justify providing judges with immunity against liability for the negligent performance of their judicial duties; many other jurisdictions have so held (and none have held to the contrary); and the immunity is firmly established in the professional literature. It is then part of the law of state A that judges have such an immunity, although that rule has not been adopted in an official text in state A.

Case III. The issue has never arisen in state A whether an acceptance that crosses a revocation is effective on dispatch or on receipt. Application of the institutional principles of adjudication, however, generates the rule that an acceptance that crosses a revocation is effective on dispatch. The courts of many other states have so held; the same position is taken by the *Restatement* and by the commentators; and the rule is justified by applicable social propositions. It is then part of the law of state A that an acceptance that crosses a revocation is effective on dispatch, although that rule has not been adopted in an official text in state A.

Case IV. Many years ago, precedents in state A adopted the rule that a firm offer is revocable. The facts in some of these precedents suggest that the offeree had relied on the offer, although nothing was made of this in the opinions. Application of the institutional principles of adjudication, however, generates an exception to the revocability rule if the offer has been relied upon. After state A adopted its revocability rule, such an exception was widely adopted in many other jurisdictions, all of which had previously adopted the same revocability rule as state A; the exception is justified by applicable social propositions; and it is firmly established in the professional literature, including the *Restatement*. The exception is then the part of the law of state A, although the most salient doctrinal propositions adopted in official state A texts look the other way.

Case V. Many years ago, precedents in state A established the legal-duty rule, that a bargain is unenforceable if one party's performance consists only of an act he had already contracted to perform. It would be inconsistent with that rule to make exceptions where the duty under the prior contract is owed to a third person, or where the bargain consists of a modification of the prior contract that is fair and equitable in light of unanticipated circumstances. Application of the institutional principles of adjudication, however,

would generate both those exceptions. The legal-duty rule substantially fails to satisfy the standards of social congruence and systemic consistency; the two exceptions have been widely adopted
in other jurisdictions that had earlier adopted the legal-duty rule;
and the exceptions are firmly established in the professional literature, including the *Restatement*. These exceptions are then part
of the law of state A, although they are inconsistent with doctrinal
propositions adopted in official state A texts.

These illustrations reflect and explain, as text-based theories do
not, the way that courts talk of and treat the common law. Text-
based theories instruct a court to start with doctrinal propositions
promulgated in past texts by officials of the relevant jurisdiction,
work backward down a chain of authorization to determine whether
the propositions are valid, and if they are, apply them to the cases.
This is not how courts determine the content of the common law.
To determine the content of the common law, courts do not begin
with doctrinal propositions adopted in past texts and work backward
to determine their validity; they begin with a set of institutional
principles and work forward to generate legal rules. These institutional principles instruct the courts that in determining the law
they should take account not only of doctrinal propositions promulgated by officials of the relevant jurisdiction, but also of the
criticism and understanding of those propositions expressed in the
professional discourse, doctrinal propositions established in the
professional literature, and applicable social propositions. The rules
generated by the interplay among those propositions under the institutional principles of adjudication are what courts conceive to be
law, and properly so.

Thus a court in state A asked to impose liability on a physician
whose negligent action had led to the birth of a healthy but unwanted child would hold that the physician had violated his legal
duty to the parents when he acted A court in state A asked to impose
liability on a judge for the negligent performance of his judicial
duties would refuse to do so on the ground that the judge had a
legal immunity when he acted. A court in state A asked to impose
liability on a nonperforming offeror who claimed that his firm offer
was revocable although relied upon, or who claimed that his revocation was effective against a crossing acceptance, would conclude
that the offeror violated his legal duty when he failed to perform.
A court in state A asked to impose liability on a party who refused
to perform a contract modification that was fair and equitable in

light of unanticipated circumstances would conclude that the party violated his legal duty when he refused to perform. Courts will talk of and treat the law this way because it is the generative conception, not text-based theory, that captures the meaning of the common law and determines its content.

The Uncertain Nature of the Common Law

Several fundamental properties of the common law are closely associated with the generative conception. The first is that common law rules are not completely certain. The institutional principles of adjudication make the content of the law depend in part on moral norms, policies, and experiential propositions that have a requisite degree of support. What social propositions have such support, how experiential propositions should mediate among moral norms, policies, and legal rules, how collisions between moral norms and policies with substantial support should be accommodated, whether a doctrine substantially satisfies the standard of social congruence, and the like, are all matters on which certainty is not possible. Since the content of the common law depends in part on such matters, at any moment in time some common law rules are relatively uncertain, some are fairly certain, some are highly certain, and some are almost completely certain, but few if any are completely certain.

This property of the common law, like the generative conception itself, can be verified by observation. Courts do not regard the common law as consisting only of those legal rules that are completely certain, any more than scientists regard the rules of nature as consisting only of those scientific rules that are completely certain. Indeed, if the common law consisted only of those legal rules that are completely certain, there would be virtually no content to the common law.

It might be objected that the law must be certain to make planning reliable. This objection would be incorrect.

First, many people plan on the basis of law implicitly rather than explicitly, because they do not know the law. For these people, planning on the basis of law consists of acting on the implicit belief that if a person conducts himself in a way that society regards as proper, he will be deemed to have acted lawfully, and if a person is injured by conduct that society regards as wrongful, he will have the law's protection. An overemphasis on certainty can make this type of planning less reliable.

Second, even actors who do explicitly plan on the basis of law don't need certainty. If certainty was necessary for planning there would be no planning, because life is uncertain. Any machine may fail, any contracting partner may go bankrupt, any contract may be broken, any day may bring a natural catastrophe. Legal rules that are not certain are consistent with reliable planning, because with few exceptions reliable planning does not depend on certainty, but on a reasonable degree of likelihood and the capacity to estimate probability.[29] Both of these qualities will inhere in a process of reasoning that is replicable, that remains fairly stable, and that employs objective standards. The greater part of the common law, although not certain, is nevertheless sufficiently determinate for planning purposes.

Moreover, to the extent that certainty is needed for planning, what is needed is not certainty of rule, but confidence in result. A lawyer can often predict a result with confidence even if he is uncertain about the legal rule. Usually a lawyer can determine not only that the legal rule is probably rule A, but that the only likely alternative is rule A_1. Frequently the lawyer can conclude that whether the rule is A or A_1 the result in a given case will be the same. For example, assume that C has made an antenuptial agreement with D governing D's property rights on divorce. C asks his lawyer if the agreement will be legally enforceable. The lawyer believes that the law most probably is that the parties to an antenuptial agreement can bargain at arm's length, so that such agreements, if freely arrived at, are enforceable without judicial review of their fairness, and whether or not full disclosure of all material facts has been made, as long as there have been no misrepresentations. Call this rule A. The lawyer also believes, however, that there is some chance that the law permits judicial review of the fairness of such agreements and requires full disclosure. Call this rule A_1. The lawyer satisfies himself that C and D are both sophisticated and wealthy parties, that D was represented by counsel, that the agreement is not unfair, and that C made full disclosure. He can then say with great confidence that the agreement is enforceable, even if he is not certain that the governing rule is rule A rather than rule A_1.[30]

An issue related to certainty is the meaning of the rule of law. That concept was defined by F. A. Hayek to mean that "government in all its actions is bound by rules fixed and announced beforehand—rules which make it possible to foresee with fair certainty how the authority will use its coercive powers in given circumstances and to plan one's individual affairs on the basis of this knowledge."[31] Such a definition, whose elements are not unique to Hayek, suggests that the concept of the rule of law can be satisfied only if law consists of fixed previously existing substantive rules applied on a consistent basis. That is not the case. It has already been shown that planning does not require such rules. Neither does fairness. The fairness aspect of the concept of the rule of law is satisfied, even in the absence of a fixed and previously announced substantive legal rule, by the consistent application of the institutional principles that generate substantive legal rules.

The Comprehensive Nature of the Common Law

Another fundamental property of the common law that is closely associated with the generative conception is that the common law is comprehensive, in that there is a legal answer to every question that takes the form, "What is the law concerning this matter?" Text-based theories of law assume the law is gappy. If the law consisted only of doctrinal propositions adopted in past texts it would indeed have gaps, because the body of such doctrines cannot answer every question in this form. The generative conception, however, permits an answer to be given to every such question, and it is supplemented by an institutional principle that courts should give such an answer; that courts, having capacity under the generative conception to determine the law on every matter, should pass upon the justice under law of any claim that might arise.[32]

Again, this property can be verified by observation. A court asked to decide a novel issue may turn the claimant away with the answer that he has no legal right. It will not, however, turn the claimant away with the answer that it cannot decide whether he has a legal right because there was no law on the issue when the transaction occurred. Nor will a court turn to the respondent and tell him that there was no law on the issue when the transaction occurred, so that he violated no legal duty, but he is nonetheless liable. Similarly, a lawyer asked what is the law on a novel question will give a legal answer. It is true that the answer may be hedged or may be couched as a prediction of what the courts would do, and it might be objected that if the answer is hedged or in predictive form there is no legal rule on that question. Such an objection would be misconceived. Because of the uncertain nature of the common law, together with prudential considerations based on a lawyer's potential liability for wrong advice, almost any answer a lawyer gives under the common law may be in hedged or predictive form, including answers to questions that fall squarely within a doctrinal proposition adopted in a past text.

Factual Criteria and the Moral Obligation of the Courts

Although the dominant strand of positivism has adopted the tenet that courts often have a legislative discretion, that tenet is not integral to positivism. Rather, the central tenet of positivism is that the test for determining the law must turn on factual criteria. In this sense the generative conception is positivistic, since the institutional principles that generate the common law turn on factual criteria, such as social congruence, rather than on critical morality and right policy.

The generative conception of law is, however, inconsistent with the concept, sometimes associated with but also not integral to positivism, that the judge is under no moral obligation to reach his decision by application of the institutional principles of adjudication, however those may be conceived. So Hart: "[I]t is not even true that those [officials] who do accept the system voluntarily, must conceive of themselves as morally bound to do so, though the system will be most stable when they do so. In fact, their allegiance to the system may be based on many different considerations: calculations of long-term interest; disinterested interest in others; an unreflecting inherited or traditional attitude; or the mere wish to do as others do."[33] At least in our society, this concept is incorrect. The judge is morally bound to establish those rules that are generated by the application of the institutional principles of adjudication. This obligation, like the obligation faithfully to employ constitutional and statutory texts, follows from the voluntary assumption and retention of judicial office. That office, like all others, is held in trust. The rules of the trust are the institutional principles of adjudication, which are themselves supported by both social acceptance and independent considerations of fairness and social welfare.

What the Law Is and What It Should Be

Finally, the generative conception sheds light on the long-standing debate over the separability of the questions, what the law is and what the law should be.[34] To the extent that what the law should be turns on critical morality and right policy, the two questions are indeed separable. As positivism has long pointed out, there is no necessary connection between critical morality and right policy, on the one hand, and the content of law, on the other. However, under the institutional principles that govern the way in which the common law is established in our society, there is a necessary connection between the content of the common law and those moral norms, policies, and experiential propositions that play a role in the standards of social congruence and systemic consistency, because those standards figure in determining both what the common law should be and what it is. Because of the dual role those standards play, what the common law is cannot be determined without consideration of what the common law should be.[35]

Notes

1. Introduction

1. *See, e.g.,* J. Bell, *Policy Arguments in Judicial Decisions* (1983); J. Raz, *The Authority of Law* (1979).

2. *See, e.g.,* R. Sartorius, *Individual Conduct and Social Norms* 181–210 (1975); Sartorius, "Social Policy and Judicial Legislation," 8 *Am. Phil. Q.* 151 (1971); Sartorius, "The Justification of the Judicial Decision," 78 *Ethics* 171 (1968).

This view is often associated with the work of Ronald Dworkin, particularly his article, "Hard Cases," 88 *Harv. L. Rev.* 1057 (1975), reprinted in R. Dworkin, *Taking Rights Seriously* 81–130 (1978). *See, e.g.,* K. Kress, "Legal Reasoning and Coherence Theories: Dworkin's Rights Thesis, Retroactivity, and the Linear Order of Decisions," 72 *Calif. L. Rev.* 369 (1984). While Dworkin did once hold this view, he later abandoned it. *See Taking Rights Seriously* 341 (1978). Even "Hard Cases" does not seem to stand for this view, when read closely. *See* Kress, *supra,* at 378 n.53.

3. *See* R. Dworkin, *Law's Empire* 67–68, 119–20, 228–31, 238–39, 248–50, 255–56 (1986); R. Dworkin, *A Matter of Principle* 16, 90 (1985); R. Dworkin, *Taking Rights Seriously* 326, 340–42, 360 (1978); Dworkin, "A Reply by Ronald Dworkin," in *Ronald Dworkin and Contemporary Jurisprudence* 247, 248, 254, 263, 269, 272 (M. Cohen ed. 1983); Dworkin, " 'Natural' Law Revisited," 34 *U. Fla. L. Rev.* 165 (1982).

4. *See* P. Soper, *A Theory of Law* 41 (1984). This obligation, like other moral obligations, is not necessarily unbounded. See the discussion under "Moral Norms" in Chapter 4.

2. The Social Functions of Courts

1. The function of conclusively resolving disputes should be distinguished from the function of conclusively resolving conflict. A court's

resolution of a dispute may not resolve an underlying conflict between the parties that precipitated the dispute.

2. As pointed out in Chapter 1, this book concerns the way in which the common law is established and changed in our society. All references in this book to courts and adjudication should be so understood.

3. *See* M. A. Eisenberg, "Participation, Responsiveness, and the Consultative Process: An Essay for Lon Fuller," 92 *Harv. L. Rev.* 410 (1978).

4. The courts sometimes make decisions even though there is no dispute at the time the court acts, as in uncontested cases involving divorce, incompetency, adoption, or probate. In most such cases, however, there is an actual or potential dispute when the suit is instituted, and it would be inefficient to shunt cases aside to a separate organ when at the last moment it becomes certain the case will be uncontested. Furthermore, it is natural to ask the courts to decide the uncontested cases in these areas because of the expertise they have developed in deciding the contested cases.

5. Claims based on the fault of the respondent without a corresponding injury to the claimant include criminal cases and certain kinds of suits based on unjust enrichment. *See, e.g.*, Brophy v. Cities Service Co., 31 Del. Ch. 241, 70 A.2d 5 (1949).

6. A type of standard whose violation does not give rise to a legally cognizable claim may nevertheless be relevant in applying a type of standard whose violation does give rise to such a claim. For example, whether a portrait satisfies artistic standards may be relevant in a suit by an artist for his commission. Similarly, whether a butler satisfied the standards of etiquette may be relevant in determining whether it was lawful to discharge him before the expiration of his contract.

7. The term *legal rule* is sometimes used to mean all legal standards, and sometimes used to mean only a certain kind of legal standard, such as a standard that is relatively specific. See the discussion under "Reasoning from Principle" in Chapter 6. Except where the text indicates otherwise, I shall use the term to mean all legal standards.

8. This problem is somewhat but not much diminished by such modern institutional mechanisms as expert government agencies with rule-making power and law-revision commissions with power to recommend new laws to the legislature.

9. *Cf.* 2 J. Austin, *Lectures on Jurisprudence* 632 (R. Campbell 3d ed. 1869): "In almost every community, such has been the incapacity, or such the negligence, of the sovereign legislature, that unless the work of legislation had been performed mainly by subordinate judges, it would not have been performed at all, or would have been performed most ineffectually: with regard to a multitude of most important subjects, the society would have lived without law; and with regard to a multitude

of others, the law would have remained in pristine barbarity" (lecture 36).

The courts may perform a variety of less critical functions that are generally consistent with the two paramount functions discussed in the text. For example, the courts may make certain kinds of determinations, particularly those relating to personal status, even in the absence of a dispute. *See supra* note 4.

10. W. Keeton, D. Dobbs, R. Keeton & D. Owen, *Prosser & Keeton on the Law of Torts* § 112 (5th ed. 1984). Today, proof of actual damage may be required even in libel, under the spur of the First Amendment. *See id.*

11. *Compare* Polygram Records, Inc. v. Superior Court, 170 Cal. App. 3d 543, 551 n.9, 216 Cal. Rptr. 252, 257 n.9 (1985), Arno v. Stewart, 245 Cal. App. 2d 955, 961, 54 Cal. Rptr. 392, 396 (1966), *and* Meldrum v. Australian Broadcasting Co., 1932 Vict. L.R. 425, 432 (broadcasting is slander), *with* First Indep. Baptist Church of Arab v. Southerland, 373 So. 2d 647, 649–50 (Ala. 1979), Matherson v. Marchello, 100 A.D.2d 233, 239, 473 N.Y.S.2d 998, 1004 (1984), *and* Shor v. Billingsley, 4 Misc. 2d 857, 158 N.Y.S.2d 476 (1957) (broadcasting is libel). *See also* Sorensen v. Wood, 123 Neb. 348, 355, 243 N.W. 82, 85 *appeal dismissed sub nom.* KFAB Broadcasting Co. v. Sorensen, 290 U.S. 599 (1932); Hartmann v. Winchell, 296 N.Y. 296, 300, 73 N.E.2d 30, 31 (1947) (broadcasting from a written script is libel).

12. A similar problem was raised by the question when and where an acceptance of an offer by telex is effective. Under rules established before development of the telex, an acceptance by mail was effective when and where mailed, but a telephonic acceptance was effective when and where received. In Entores Ld. v. Miles Far East Corp., [1955] 2 Q.B. 327, an agent for the defendant telexed an acceptance from Amsterdam to England. The defendant claimed that the acceptance was effective on dispatch, like a letter, and the contract had therefore been entered into outside England, so that under English law process could not be served outside the jurisdiction. The Court of Appeal held that acceptance by telex should be treated like an acceptance by phone. *Id.* at 334. *See also* Gill and Duffus Landauer Ltd. v. London Export Corp., [1982] 2 Lloyd's Rep. 627 (Q.B. Div'l Ct. 1982); Brinkibon Ltd v. Stahag Stahl und Stahlwarenhandelsgesellschaft, [1982] 1 All E.R. 293 (H.L. 1982). *But see* Norse Petroleum A/S v. LVO Int'l, Inc., 389 A.2d 771 (Del. Super. Ct. 1978); General Time Corp. v. Eye Encounter, Inc., 50 N.C. App. 467, 274 S.E.2d 391 (1981) (sending of acceptance by telex is the final act necessary to make a binding obligation, so that contract was entered into in jurisdiction from which telex was sent).

13. This point is discussed under "Reasoning by Analogy" in Chapter 6.

14. For example, suppose a government official, say an official in a marriage-license or motor-vehicle bureau, regularly decides questions raised by members of the public. Based on bureaucratic practice and the desirab lity of evenhandedness, it may be expected that the official's decisions will be consistent. Therefore, his earlier decisions will have weight when comparable questions arise again. It would not usually be thought, however, that the official is bound by his earlier decisions.

15. See the discussion in Chapter 5 and under "Reasoning from Precedent" in Chapter 6.

16. Hamberger v. Eastman, 106 N.H. 107, 206 A.2d 239 (1964).

17. Rowland v. Christian, 69 Cal. 2d 108, 443 P.2d 561, 70 Cal. Rptr. 97 (1968).

18. See J. Coons, "Approaches to Court Imposed Compromise—The Uses of Doubt and Reason," 58 Nw. U.L. Rev. 750 (1964); M. A. Eisenberg, "Private Ordering through Negotiation: Dispute-Settlement and Rulemaking," 89 Harv. L. Rev. 637, 654-57 (1976).

3. Foundational Principles

1. See Note, "Dworkin's 'Rights Thesis,' " 74 Mich. L. Rev. 1167, 1194–99 (1976). What it means to say that parties are similarly situated for purposes of common law rules is discussed under "Reasoning from Precedent" in Chapter 6.

Another concept entailed by the principle of objectivity is evenhandedness. This concept is discussed under "The Standard of Doctrinal Stability and the Real-World Model of the Common Law" in Chapter 5, and in Chapter 7.

2. Legislators may often or usually be guided by existing social standards. Unlike common law courts, however, legislators do not act improperly in adopting rules that do not reflect existing standards.

3. Legislation may not be entirely free of effects that can be deemed retroactive, because some purely prospective rules may have an impact on previously made investments or ongoing transactions. See L. Kaplow, "An Economic Analysis of Legal Transitions," 99 Harv. L. Rev. 509, 515–16 (1986); M. Graetz, "Legal Transitions: The Case of Retroactivity in Income Tax Revision," 126 U. Pa. L. Rev. 47 (1977). Even if such effects occur, however, they are normally regarded as very different from the effect of a rule imposing liability on the basis of a closed transaction.

4. For important exceptions, see S. Burton, An Introduction to Law and Legal Reasoning (1985); A. Simpson, "The Common Law and Legal Theory," in Oxford Essays in Jurisprudence 77 (2d ser. A. Simpson ed. 1973).

5. In The Concept of Law, H. L. A. Hart drew a distinction between being obliged and being obligated. Hart pointed out that a statement

that a person is obliged to perform an act may be only a statement about the beliefs and motives with which the person does the act. So, for example, a person may believe himself obliged to deliver money to an armed robber out of fear. In contrast, a statement that a person is obligated to perform an act suggests that he should do the act because it is required under some normative rule. H. L. A. Hart, *The Concept of Law* 80–84 (1961). Although this distinction is analytically useful, *obliged* may be and commonly is used in a sense identical to the term *obligated*, and in this book I have used *obliged* in that way, except when referring to Hart's own theories.

4. Social Propositions

1. *See* Angel v. Murray, 113 R.I. 482, 322 A.2d 630 (1974); *Restatement (Second) of Contracts* § 89(a) (1979).

The *Restatements,* prepared by the American Law Institute, state the rules that, in the Institute's view, the courts would follow, giving weight to all the considerations that the courts would deem it right to weigh.

2. *See* Webb v. McGowin, 27 Ala. App. 82, 168 So. 196 (1935); *Restatement (Second) of Contracts* § 86 (1979); M. A. Eisenberg, "The Principles of Consideration," 67 *Cornell L. Rev.* 640, 663–64 (1982).

3. *See, e.g.,* Williams v. Walker-Thomas Furniture Co., 350 F.2d 445 (D.C. Cir. 1965).

4. *See* M. A. Eisenberg, "The Bargain Principle and Its Limits," 95 *Harv. L. Rev.* 741 (1982) (hereafter Eisenberg, "The Bargain Principle").

5. *Cf.* J. Raz, "Legal Rights," 4 *Oxford J. Legal Stud.* 1 (1984).

6. *See* H. Wellington, "Common Law Rules and Constitutional Double Standards: Some Notes on Adjudication," 83 *Yale L.J.* 221, 244 (1973) (hereafter Wellington, "Common Law Rules and Constitutional Double Standards"). Some supplementary points:

(i) In theory, the relevant community for this purpose is the jurisdiction (normally, a state) whose law governs a transaction. In practice, moral norms are usually not so local, and the court will typically look to a wider regional or national community unless it has reason to believe that the norms of the governing jurisdiction are special.

(ii) Joseph Raz argues that although most countries take as a general principle that judges should act only on those values and opinions that have the support of some important segment of the population, the main device controlling the courts' values and ideology is not an institutional principle but the methods of appointing or electing judges. Raz, "Legal Principles and the Limits of Law," 81 *Yale L.J.* 823, 849 & n.47 (1972). This is indeed an important device, but is not a sufficient device, and does not oust the need for an institutional principle. Prospective judges are normally not cross-examined as to their values and ideology, and in any event many judges undoubtedly change their values and ideology over time.

(iii) The principle that when the courts employ moral norms in establishing common law rules they must employ those norms that have substantial social support does not mean that common law courts are obliged to establish the legal rules they believe would have substantial social support or would best represent the will of the people. Common law rules are determined by the interplay of moral norms, policies, experiential propositions, and doctrinal propositions. The requirement of substantial social support applies to norms and policies, but not to experiential propositions or (except very indirectly) to doctrinal propositions. See the discussion under "Experiential Propositions" in this chapter and see generally Chapter 6. Furthermore, moral norms, policies, experiential propositions, and doctrinal propositions will often collide with one another or even with themselves in any given case. In working out a rule that best accommodates colliding elements, a court must exercise its own judgment on such matters as the relevance and importance of each element in the given case, the court's degree of confidence that each element has the requisite support, the extent to which each element is connected to broader social and legal values, the extent to which the colliding elements can be accommodated in a single rule, and the weight placed on doctrinal propositions under the principle of stare decisis. On the last issue see the discussion in Chapter 5 and under "Reasoning from Precedent" in Chapter 6.

(iv) In some cases, the application of a doctrine may by its terms depend in part on the personal morality of one of the parties. This may be true, for example, of doctrines that turn on whether a party acted in good faith.

7. Indeed, it is often in reported cases and in the professional literature that certain kinds of moral issues—for example, the obligations of fiduciaries—are most explicitly confronted and developed.

8. See J. Bell, *Policy Arguments in Judicial Decisions* 190 (1983).

9. See J. Raz, *The Authority of Law* 85–90 (1979).

10. This process need not be overly self-conscious. A judge, as a participant-observer, usually can assume in such cases that his own moral judgments would be widely shared, unless he has reason to believe otherwise. See K. Greenawalt, "Policy, Rights, and Judicial Decision," 11 *Ga. L. Rev.* 991, 1052–53 (1977). A judge may have reason to believe otherwise if he knows that his views are idiosyncratic or if discourse in the narrower or wider arena so suggests.

11. See Eisenberg, "The Bargain Principle," *supra* note 4, at 763–73

12. J. Rawls, *A Theory of Justice* 582 (1971).

13. See J. Feinberg, "Justice, Fairness and Rationality," 81 *Yale L.J* 1004, 1019–20 (1972) (reviewing J. Rawls, *A Theory of Justice*).

Michael Moore has written extensively on the application of coherence morality to legal reasoning. *See* Moore, "Moral Reality," 1982 *Wis. L. Rev.* 1061 (1982).

14. See the discussion under "Responsiveness" in Chapter 3, and under "Reasoning from Precedent" in Chapter 6.

15. See the discussion under "Reasoning from Precedent" in Chapter 6.

Cases where two norms collide may sometimes be distinguishable from cases where evidence from different social sources conflicts. In the latter type of case the court may determine either that the conflicting evidence shows a conflict within the society, and that the issue therefore involves a clash of opposed norms with substantial social support, or that the evidence from one source is more reliable than evidence from others.

16. O. W. Holmes, "Law and the Court," in *Collected Legal Papers* 291, 294–95 (1920).

17. J. Ely, *Democracy and Distrust* 63–69 (1980).

18. *Id.* at 67–68.

19. *See, e.g.,* P. Brest, "The Fundamental Rights Controversy: The Essential Contradictions of Normative Constitutional Scholarship," 90 *Yale L.J.* 1063, 1083 (1981).

20. *See Webster's Third New International Dictionary* 482 (1981); *Random House Dictionary of the English Language* 312 (1966).

21. *See also* H. Wellington, "Common Law Rules and Constitutional Double Standards," *supra* note 6, at 245: "Although the sub-culture problem is real, too much can be made of it. Much of the cleavage that results from diversity manifests itself in interest group politics. Diverse groups can pursue different policies while sharing a basically common morality. More important, the melting pot phenomenon is a real one which the events of the recent past have tended to obscure. The American people have a history and tradition which interact with their common problems to fashion attitudes, values, and aspirations that tend toward a dynamic, but nevertheless relatively cohesive, society, and that make it possible to discern a conventional morality. This morality may impose obligations that sometimes are beyond the capacity of some normal adults; therefore, compliance with its obligations may not be 'a matter of course.' Yet, it is a morality that is at the least *knowable* to socialized persons. This is not to imply that individuals would always agree about the implications of a moral duty or the particular behavior that a moral principle requires. It is merely to insist that normal adults know when particular behavior raises serious moral questions."

Parties who want a dispute to be resolved on the basis of standards other than those that have substantial social support, such as the standards of some subgroup to which they both belong or the standards to which they themselves subscribe, may turn to dispute-settlement institutions of the subgroup, to arbitration, or to mediation.

22. D. Richards, "Rules, Policies and Neutral Principles: The Search for Legitimacy in Common Law and Constitutional Adjudication," 11 *Ga. L. Rev.* 1069, 1091 (1977).

23. Greenawalt, "Policy, Rights, and Judicial Decision," *supra* note 10, at 1051–52.

24. Perhaps in recognition of these difficulties, Greenawalt argues that the adjudicative process "provides some protection against idiosyncratic views, for if a judge sits on an appellate court, his vote alone will not decide an issue, and decisions on the law by lower courts are typically subject to appeal." *Id.* at 1052. This argument is weak in both theory and practice. It is weak in theory because it implicitly licenses appellate judges to adopt institutional principles of adjudication different from those of lower-court judges. It is weak in practice because it is expensive to appeal and because a judge's idiosyncratic morality concerning a given issue can decide a case even in an appellate court if his colleagues are split evenly on other issues. Finally, the argument tends to undercut the basic thesis. How much point is there in licensing a judge to "follow [his convictions] even if he does not think they are shared by most members of the community," if this license is only made tolerable on the ground that the judge's convictions will not prevail if they are not shared?

25. J. Newman, "Between Legal Realism and Neutral Principles: The Legitimacy of Institutional Values," 72 *Calif. L. Rev.* 200, 204 (1984).

26. D. Lyons, *Ethics and the Rule of Law* 100–01 (1984).

27. *Id.* at 85 (1984).

28. *Cf.* R. Dworkin, *Law's Empire* 104–08 (1986); R. Dworkin, *Taking Rights Seriously* 326–27 (1978) ("If the judge decides that the reasons supplied by background moral rights are so strong that he has a moral duty to do what he can to support these rights, then it may be that he must lie, because he cannot be of any help unless he is understood as saying, in his official role, that the legal rights are different from what he believes they are."); Greenawalt, "Policy, Rights, and Judicial Decision," *supra* note 10, at 1050 ("the judge might be morally justified either in resigning his office or [in] subverting the law.").

Another view is that in such a case the judge is under two moral obligations—an obligation not to apply the law in his unavoidable role as a person, and to apply the law in his voluntary assumed office as a judge—and that he should reconcile these obligations by resigning the voluntarily assumed office.

29. Distinguishing between moral norms and policies parallels the discourse of courts and legal commentators, and reflects functional differences in the way different kinds of reasons for conduct tend to figure

in adjudication. The distinction can be drawn for present purposes without taking sides in the debate on whether the rightness of conduct should be measured by the goodness of the state of affairs the conduct aims to achieve.

30. *See Restatement (Second) of Torts* §§ 291–93 (1963 & 1964).

31. *See Restatement (Second) of Torts* §§ 822, 826 (1977).

32. *See Restatement (Second) of Contracts* §§ 350, 351 (1979).

33. *See, e.g.,* Parker v. Twentieth Century-Fox Film Corp., 3 Cal. 3d 176, 184–87 & n.5, 474 P.2d 689, 694–96 & n.5, 89 Cal. Rptr. 737, 742–44 & n.5 (1970) (Sullivan, C.J., dissenting); R. Posner, *Economic Analysis of Law* 114–15 (3d ed. 1986).

34. Other examples of doctrines based on policy include the immunities from tort liability. *See Restatement (Second) of Torts* ch. 45A, Introductory Note, and § 895D comments b & c (1977).

35. *See* M. A. Eisenberg, "The Responsive Model of Contract Law," 36 *Stan. L. Rev.* 1107, 1117–27 (1984).

36. *See* Vaughan v. Menlove, 3 Bingham N.C. 468, 471 (C.P. 1837); W. Keeton, D. Dobbs, R. Keeton & D. Owen, *Prosser & Keeton on the Law of Torts* 177 (5th ed. 1984) (hereinafter *Prosser & Keeton on Torts*); W. Seavey, "Negligence—Subjective or Objective?" 41 *Harv. L. Rev.* 1, 12–13 (1927).

37. *See Restatement (Second) of Contracts* § 73 comment a (1979).

38. *See* Escola v. Coca Cola Bottling Co., 24 Cal. 2d 453, 462–63, 467, 150 P.2d 436, 440–41, 443 (1944) (Traynor, J., concurring); F. Harper, F. James & O. Gray, *The Law of Torts* § 28.7, at 381, § 28.16, at 455 n.5 (2d ed. 1986).

39. *See* Harper, James & Gray, *The Law of Torts, supra* note 38, § 14.13, at 286–88.

40. *See* Coggs v. Bernard, 92 Eng. Rep. 107 (K.B. 1703).

41. *See* N.Y. Penal Law §§ 200.30, 200.35 & Commentary.

42. *See* M. A. Eisenberg, "Donative Promises," 47 *U. Chi. L. Rev.* 1, 3 (1979).

43. *See* Miller v. Miller, 78 Iowa 177, 35 N.W. 464 (1887), *aff'd on rehearing,* 78 Iowa 179, 42 N.W. 641 (1889). *But see* M. Schultz, "Contractual Ordering of Marriage: A New Model for State Policy," 70 *Calif. L. Rev.* 204 (1982).

44. For a comprehensive analysis of policy factors that may enter into judicial rules, see R. Summers, "Two Types of Substantive Reasons: The Core of a Theory of Common-Law Justification," 63 *Cornell L. Rev.* 707 (1978).

45. N.Y. Bus. Corp. Law § 726(e).

46. 45 Okla. Stat. Ann. tit. 45, § 722.

47. *See* Smith v. Brown-Borhek Co., 414 Pa. 325, 333, 200 A.2d 398, 401 (1964).

48. Sherlock v. Stillwater Clinic, 260 N.W.2d 169 (Minn. 1977).

49. *Id.* at 175 & n.10. *See also* Moragne v. States Marine Lines, Inc., 398 U.S. 375, 389–93 (1970) (Harlan, J.) (in allowing suit for wrongful death based on breach of duty under maritime law, the Court stressed numerous statutes indicating a policy in favor of allowing wrongful-death suits).

50. I am indebted to Albert Sacks for this point.

51. D. Lyons, "Justification and Judicial Responsibility," 72 *Calif. L. Rev.* 178, 188 (1984). *See also* G. Hughes, "Rules, Policy and Decision Making," 77 *Yale L.J.* 411, 421–26 (1968).

52. Policies often operate in a negative manner, by inducing a court to refrain from adopting a rule that would otherwise seem desirable, but they also can operate affirmatively. In any event there is little to be served by trying to distinguish between a proposition in the negative form, "We do not adopt rule R because that rule would lead to state of affairs S," and a proposition in the positive form, "We adopt rule not-R so as to achieve state of affairs not-S."

53. R. Dworkin, "Hard Cases," 88 *Harv. L. Rev.* 1057, 1067–68 (1975) (hereafter "Hard Cases"), reprinted in R. Dworkin, *Taking Rights Seriously* 81, 90, 91 (1978) (hereafter *Taking Rights Seriously*). Dworkin there defined an aim as a state of affairs such that it counts in favor of a decision that it is likely to advance or protect that state and counts against a decision that it will retard or endanger that state; a right as an individuated aim; a principle as a proposition that describes a right of an individual or group; and a policy as a proposition that describes a nonindividuated aim, that is, an aim of the community as a whole.

Essentially the same position is taken, although without using the term *rights thesis* and with slightly different argumentation, in R. Dworkin, *Law's Empire* 221–24, 244, 338–39 (1986).

54. "Hard Cases" at 1060, 1063, *Taking Rights Seriously* at 84, 87. Elsewhere in that article Dworkin put the thesis somewhat differently—for example, "The rights thesis, in its descriptive aspect, holds that judicial decisions in hard cases are characteristically generated by principle not policy," and "The rights thesis provides that judges decide hard cases by confirming or denying concrete rights." "Hard Cases" at 1074, 1078, *Taking Rights Seriously* at 96–97, 101.

55. "Hard Cases" at 1061, *Taking Rights Seriously* at 84.

56. "Hard Cases" at 1061–62, *Taking Rights Seriously* at 84-85.

57. For early cases taking policy into account, *see e.g.*, Chesterfield v. Janssen, 26 Eng. Rep. 191, 224 (Ch. 1750); Kellner v. Le Mesurier, 102 Eng. Rep. 883, 885 (K.B. 1803); Fletcher v. Lord Sondes, 130 Eng. Rep. 606, 640–41 (H.L. 1826) (Alexander, C.B.); Egerton v. Brownlow, 10 Eng. Rep. 359, 418 (H.L. 1853) (Pollock, C.B.).

58. *See* Greenawalt, "Policy, Rights, and Judicial Decision," *supra* note 10, at 1004: "[A] legislature simply does not have the time or interest to engage itself in establishing rights for every area of the common law. It leaves certain areas substantially to the development of courts. We may assume that if the legislature got involved in those areas it would pay close attention to what rules would promote the general welfare. Can it be that if it leaves these areas to courts, courts should not pay any attention at all to such considerations?" *See also* K. Greenawalt, "Discretion and Judicial Decision: The Elusive Quest for the Fetters That Bind Judges," 75 *Colum. L. Rev.* 359, 393–94 (1975).

59. D. Regan, "Glosses on Dworkin: Rights, Principles, and Policies," 76 *Mich. L. Rev.* 1213, 1232 (1978) (hereafter Regan, "Glosses on Dworkin").

60. *Id.*

61. Moreover, Dworkin is inconsistent in his opposition to judicial weighting of policies. Dworkin always acknowledged that a court could properly compare the benefits and burdens to the immediate parties. *See* "Hard Cases" at 1075–76, *Taking Rights Seriously* at 98–99, 191–92. As Donald Regan points out, however, concern "about interpersonal comparison of utility. . . . ought to affect all questions or none. Genuine scruples about interpersonal comparisons would make it impossible even to compare benefits and disadvantages to two parties. . . ." Regan, "Glosses on Dworkin," *supra* note 59, at 1250 n.73. Dworkin also acknowledges that a policy could properly prevail over a conflicting principle where a "clear and major" collective interest was involved. This of course requires just the weighting that his elaborated argument from democracy holds to be improper. *See* J. Bell, *Policy Arguments in Judicial Decisions* 210 (1983); Note, "Dworkin's 'Rights Thesis,'" 74 *Mich. L. Rev.* 1174, 1176–77 (1976).

62. "Hard Cases" at 1061, *Taking Rights Seriously* at 84.

63. "Hard Cases" at 1061–62, *Taking Rights Seriously* at 85.

64. *See* Greenawalt, "Policy, Rights, and Judicial Decision," *supra* note 10, at 1005: "[I]t is plausible to suppose that people understand that recognition of their uncertain claims of right will depend on consistency with the general welfare, especially when claims are made in the context of complex social institutions governing all areas of life. . . . If people are aware that their right to do some act may sometimes be contingent on the act's not being inconsistent with the general welfare, it is no more offensive to deny their claim on the basis of the general welfare than on the basis of some arguable principle."

65. "Hard Cases" at 1061, *Taking Rights Seriously* at 84–85.

66. R. Dworkin, *Law's Empire* 67–68, 119–20, 228–31, 238–39, 248–50, 255–56 (1986).

67. See the discussion under "Noninterpretive Elements of the Common Law" in Chapter 7.

A position very different from Dworkin's rights thesis is represented in a recent book by John Bell, *Policy Arguments in Judicial Decision* (1983). Bell's central thesis is as follows:

"[T]he task of the judge in hard cases . . . is of fundamentally the same character as that of the legislator. . . . [W]here settled legal standards fail to produce an answer, the judge may be faced with a number of choices of rules or standards to resolve the case, each of which would not be wildly inconsistent with the existing law. In creating a new rule in such circumstances, the judge has simply to exercise his own judgment on the suitability of the various options, and to decide what is best for society as a whole. . . .

"[W]here judges have a choice between various possible legal results, each of which is compatible with the rest of the law, they choose between them in much the same way as Members of Parliament select the policies which they consider will be most beneficial to the community as a whole." *Id.* at 17, 227. *See also id.* at 244–45.

It will readily be seen that this approach, which Bell appropriately calls the "interstitial legislator" model, *id.* at 17, echoes Greenawalt's position on morality. It is also subject to essentially the same criticisms. First, if courts were free to employ whatever policies they think best, the profession would be unable to replicate the adjudicative process in cases where policy is relevant. Accordingly, in such cases the profession could not reliably determine the law for purposes of planning and dispute-settlement. Second, serious problems of fairness would be raised if liability were imposed on someone who has played by all the prevailing moral and legal rules and acted in conformity with all social policies, as far as either he or a lawyer could determine them, but whose behavior did not further policies the court thinks desirable.

Bell addresses the first of these difficulties by trying to narrowly bound the area in which the courts can properly employ those policies they think best. Just as Greenawalt maintains that the judge can apply his personal morality in marginal cases, so Bell argues that "[o]nly within a limited range of cases and at a relatively low policy level do the judges have any creative work to do." *Id.* at 202. Judges do not "have *carte blanche* to engage in wide-ranging reform or rule-creation. They are primarily concerned with making good minor deficiencies in the existing legal framework, which they must leave intact." *Id.* at 19. However, Bell defines policy arguments as "substantive justifications to which judges appeal when the standards and rules of the legal system do not provide a clear resolution of a dispute"—that is, "hard cases," in which "it is a realistic possibility, given the standards accepted by the legal community, for a judge to argue that no legal solution clearly imposes itself on him from precedent, statute, or other legal standard." *Id.* at 22–23, 25. *See also id.* at 24. At least in the common law, however, few if any cases are controlled purely by doctrinal rules without regard to social propositions. See the discussion in Chapters 6–8, *infra.* Furthermore, social propositions tend to become most salient in just those cases in which the most serious problems are at issue. Under an interstitial-legislator model, therefore, the courts would be free to employ the policies they believe best not only in some cases, but in most or all cases, and not only "at a relatively low policy level" involving "minor deficiencies in the existing legal framework," but in cases of the utmost gravity.

On the fairness issue, Bell argues that parties cannot have built up legitimate expectations in hard cases, because "[t]hese are situations in which there is uncertainty about the law and prediction is already very difficult." *Id.* at 233–34. *See also* J. Raz, *The Authority of Law* 198 (1979); S. Munzer, "Right Answers, Preexisting Rights, and Fairness," 11 *Ga. L. Rev.* 1055, 1061–62 (1977). This argument trades on an ambiguity in the meaning of the term *hard cases.* In common professional parlance, the term means either cases in which the law seems to yield a counterintuitive result or cases in which it is difficult to determine what the result will be. In the parlance Bell seems to adopt, however, the term means a case that cannot be decided purely on the basis of doctrine without reference to social propositions. But common law cases can almost never be decided in this way, and in any event just because there is uncertainty about a case does not mean that it is highly unpredictable. Legitimate expectations may be disappointed when a given decision is highly likely although not completely certain.

68. *See, e.g., Restatement (Second) of Contracts* § 221 illustration 4 (1979): "4. A, a publisher, contracts with B to publish a two-volume work. The contract provides for binding '10,000 copies at .538,' which by usage of the publishing business refers to the number of volumes rather than the number of sets. The usage is part of the contract even though the work is B's first and he does not know of the usage."

See also id. § 222 illustrations 5 & 6: "5. A and B enter into a contract of charter party in which A promises to discharge the vessel 'in 14 days.' Usage in the shipping business may show this means 14 working days. 6. A and B enter into a contract for the purchase and sale of 'No. 1 heavy book paper guaranteed free from ground wood.' Usage in the paper trade may show that this means paper not containing over 3% ground wood."

69. *See, e.g.,* Tropea v. Shell Oil Co., 307 F.2d 757 (2d Cir. 1962); Murphy v. American Barge Line Co., 76 F. Supp. 276 (W.D. Pa. 1948); Roberts v. Indiana Gas & Water Co., 140 Ind. App. 409, 218 N.E.2d 556 (1966); Bailey v. Baker's Air Force Gas Corp., 50 A.D.2d 129, 376

N.Y.S.2d 212 (1975), *appeal denied*, 39 N.Y.S.2d 708, 352 N.E.2d 595, 386 N.Y.S.2d 1025 (1976); *Prosser and Keeton on Torts, supra* note 36, § 33, at 193–96.

70. *See* G. Yale, *Legal Titles to Mining Claims and Water Rights* 58–70 (1867).

71. *See* Swift v. Gifford, 23 F. Cas. 558 (D. Mass. 1872) (No. 13,696); O. W. Holmes, *The Common Law* 212 (1881).

72. *See* Norway Plains v. Boston & Me. R.R., 67 Mass. (1 Gray) 263 (1854).

73. *See* American Law Institute, *Principles of Corporate Governance: Analysis and Recommendations* § 4.01 (Tent. Draft No. 4, 1985).

74. *See, e.g.*, Smith v. Brown-Borhek Co., 414 Pa. 325, 333, 200 A.2d 398, 401 (1964).

75. *See, e.g.*, Joy v. North, 692 F.2d 880, 885–86 (2d Cir. 1982), *cert. denied sub nom.* Citytrust v. Joy, 460 U.S. 1051 (1983).

76. Joy v. North, 692 F.2d at 886.

77. *See* Batsakis v. Demotsis, 226 S.W.2d 673 (Tex. Ct. App. 1949); Eisenberg, "The Bargain Principle," *supra* note 4, at 744–45.

78. *See* Eisenberg, "The Bargain Principle," *supra* note 4, at 746.

79. *See id.* at 745–46.

80. Most propositions of the social sciences are experiential, but some might be better classified as moral norms or policies. A prediction of economics concerning the effects of competition is experiential; a statement that these effects are good is a policy.

5. Standards for the Common Law

1. Applicable social propositions, for this purpose, do not include the institutional principles that govern adjudication, although those principles can be considered social propositions for other purposes insofar as their authority rests on social acceptance.

2. *Webster's Third New International Dictionary* 440 (1981).

3. *Id.* at 440.

4. *See* 1 F. Pollock & F. W. Maitland, *The History of English Law* 441–57 (2d ed. 1898).

5. I assume here and elsewhere in this book that in the subject-matter areas covered by the common law the community's moral norms and policies are not themselves significantly determined by legal rules, although the common law may teach parts of the community the implications of those norms and policies. This assumption is based partly on the fact that most private actors know very little law, and partly on a judgment about the relationship between common law rules and social propositions in our society.

6. What it means to say that the rule of a precedent is binding, and therefore what are the contours of stare decisis, is analyzed in Chapters 6 and 7.

7. *See* M. Golding, *Legal Reasoning* 98 (1984); N. MacCormick, *Legal Reasoning and Legal Theory* 75 (1978).

8. Some cases where the two types of evenhandedness do not converge are discussed under "Noninterpretive Elements of the Common Law" in Chapter 7.

9. Stare decisis also serves the objective of hierarchical administration, since it provides a rough-and-ready technique for higher-court control of lower courts. That objective could also be served, however, by a principle of judicial command under which a higher-court decision was treated as a binding instruction to lower courts, but not as binding on the higher court itself. (By way of comparison, a chief executive might issue orders that his subordinates are bound to follow but that he is free to change or disregard as he believes appropriate.)

For additional factors underlying stare decisis, *see* R. Summers, *Instrumentalism and American Legal Theory* 163–65 (1982).

6. Modes of Legal Reasoning

1. J. Raz, *The Authority of Law* 188 (1979). For important and illuminating discussions of reasoning from precedent, *see* A. Simpson, "The Ratio Decidendi of a Case and the Doctrine of Binding Precedent," in *Oxford Essays in Jurisprudence* 148 (A. G. Guest ed., 1961) (hereafter Simpson, "The Doctrine of Binding Precedent"), and J. Raz, *supra*, at 183–89.

2. J. Raz, *The Authority of Law* 187–88 (1979).

3. For example, the rule that a bargain promise is unenforceable if it is given in exchange for the performance of an act the promisee had already contracted to perform was once rationalized on the technical ground that such a contract involved no legal "detriment," and therefore lacked consideration. It has now been rerationalized as follows: "A claim that the performance of a legal duty furnished consideration for a promise often raises a suspicion that the transaction was gratuitous or mistaken or unconscionable. . . . Because of the likelihood that the promise was obtained by an express or implied threat to withhold performance of a legal duty, the promise does not have the presumptive social utility normally found in a bargain." *Restatement (Second) of Contracts* § 73 comment a (1979). *See also, e.g.*, Kidd v. Thomas A. Edison, Inc., 239 F. 405 (S.D.N.Y.) (L. Hand, J.), *aff'd*, 242 F.2d 923 (2d Cir. 1917).

4. J. Stone, "The Ratio of the Ratio Decidendi," 22 *Mod. L. Rev.* 597 (1959). *See also* A. Simpson, "The Ratio Decidendi of a Case," 20 *Mod.*

L. Rev. 413 (1957), 21 *Mod. L. Rev.* 155 (1958), 22 *Mod. L. Rev.* 453 (1959).

5. A. Goodhart, "Determining the Ratio Decidendi of a Case," 40 *Yale L.J.* 161 (1930). *See also* Goodhart, "The Ratio Decidendi of a Case," 22 *Mod. L. Rev.* 117 (1959).

6. M'Alister (or Donoghue) v. Stevenson, [1932] L.R. App. Cas. 562 (H.L. 1932).

7. Goodhart argued that the level of generality employed by the precedent determined the level of generality intended by the court. Stone showed this approach was unworkable.

A further difficulty in applying Goodhart's theory is that it is often impracticable, in this context, to separate (i) facts in the sense of physical occurrences and (ii) evaluative conclusions that reflect a legal rule. For example, did *Donoghue* concern (i) the liability of a manufacturer for failing to install devices that would prevent dead snails from falling into its bottles, or (ii) the liability of a manufacturer for negligence?

8. *See, e.g.*, Rosenberg v. Lipnick, 377 Mass. 666, 389 N.E.2d 385 (1979); Osborne v. Osborne, 384 Mass. 591, 599, 428 N.E.2d 810, 816 (1981).

9. Prospective overruling is discussed in Chapter 7.

10. Christensen v. Thornby, 192 Minn. 123, 255 N.W. 620 (1934).

11. Sherlock v. Stillwater Clinic, 260 N.W.2d 169 (Minn. 1977).

12. *Christensen*, 192 Minn. at 126, 255 N.W. at 622.

13. *Id.*

14. The court's opening recitation of fact states: "Plaintiff asserts that he approached the defendant . . . and was advised by him that a sterilization operation upon the plaintiff, technically termed vasectomy, would protect his wife against conception and the consequent dangers of which she had been warned. [On] August 1, 1931, the defendant performed the operation upon the plaintiff, and there is no allegation in the complaint that it was not skillfully performed and no claim is now made by the plaintiff that it was not so done. Plaintiff asserts that defendant advised him that the operation had been successful and guaranteed sterility. Plaintiff alleges that sometime following the operation and relying upon the defendant's advice and representations he resumed sexual relations with his wife, and, notwithstanding the operation, his wife became pregnant." *Christensen*, 192 Minn. at 123–24, 255 N.W. at 621.

15. *Sherlock*, 260 N.W.2d at 172. *Sherlock* now represents the majority rule on liability for wrongful birth, although many courts have refused to go as far as *Sherlock* in giving damages for the cost of rearing a child. *See, e.g.*, "Survey of Washington Law: Wrongful Pregnancy," 20 *Gonz. L. Rev.* 613 (1984/85).

16. MacPherson v. Buick Motor Co., 217 N.Y. 382, 111 N.E. 1050 (1916).

17. Thomas v. Winchester, 6 N.Y. 381 (1852).

18. *Id.* at 407–08.

19. *Id.* at 409.

20. Loop v. Litchfield, 42 N.Y. 351 (1870).

21. The court stated: "Poison is a dangerous subject. Gunpowder is the same. A torpedo is a dangerous instrument, as is a spring gun, a loaded rifle or the like. They are instruments and articles in their nature calculated to do injury to mankind, and generally intended to accomplish that purpose. They are essentially, and in their elements, instruments of danger. Not so, however, an iron wheel, a few feet in diameter and a few inches in thickness, although one part may be weaker than another." *Id.* at 359.

22. Losee v. Clute, 51 N.Y. 494 (1873).

23. Devlin v. Smith, 89 N.Y. 470 (1882).

24. *Id.* at 477.

25. Statler v. George A. Ray Manufacturing Co., 195 N.Y. 478, 88 N.E. 1063 (1909).

26. *Statler,* 195 N.Y. at 482, 88 N.E. at 1064–65.

27. *MacPherson,* 217 N.Y. at 389, 111 N.E. at 1053.

28. *Loop v. Litchfield,* said Cardozo, "was the case of a defect in a small balance wheel used on a circular saw. The manufacturer pointed out the defect to the buyer, who wished a cheap article and was ready to assume the risk. The risk can hardly have been an imminent one, for the wheel lasted five years before it broke. In the meanwhile the buyer had made a lease of the machinery. It was held that the manufacturer was not answerable to the lessee." As to *Losee v. Clute,* it "must be confined to its special facts. It was put upon the ground that the risk of injury was too remote. The buyer in that case had not only accepted the boiler, but had tested it. The manufacturer knew that his own test was not the final one. The finality of the test has a bearing on the measure of diligence owing to persons other than the purchaser." *MacPherson,* 217 N.Y. at 386, 111 N.E. at 1052.

29. See on these constraints J. Raz, *The Authority of Law* 183–89 (1979), and Simpson, "The Doctrine of Binding Precedent," *supra* note 1.

30. *Cf.* P. Westen, "The Meaning of Equality in Law, Science, Math, and Morals: A Reply," 81 *Mich. L. Rev.* 604, 640–645 (1983).

31. As pointed out in Chapter 5, occasionally a deep doctrinal distinction may justify a difference in the treatment of two cases even when applicable social propositions do not. In such cases the standard of social congruence may be in tension with the standard of systemic

consistency. For simplicity of exposition, I shall deal in this chapter only with the usual case, in which the standards of social congruence and systemic consistency are aligned. Cases in which those two standards are in tension will be addressed in Chapter 7.

32. *See* J. Angell, *A Treatise on the Law of Carriers* 72 (1849); I. Redfield, *The Law of Carriers* 15–16 (1869).

33. *See* Norway Plains Co. v. Boston & Me. R.R., 67 Mass. (1 Gray) 263 (1854).

34. *See, e.g.*, E. Levi, *An Introduction to Legal Reasoning* 1–27 (1948).

35. D. Dobbs, *Handbook on the Law of Remedies* § 12.25, at 925–26 (1973). As has often been pointed out, use of the term *duty* in this context is questionable, because the employee does not incur liability if he fails to mitigate. *See, e.g.*, McClelland v. Climax Hosiery Mills, 252 N.Y. 347, 358–59, 169 N.E. 605, 609 (1930) (Cardozo, C.J., concurring). However, the nomenclature is well established and has not led to problems in the analysis.

36. Mr. Eddie, Inc. v. Ginsberg, 430 S.W.2d 5 (Tex. Civ. App. 1958).

37. *See Restatement (Second) of Contracts* § 201(1) (1979); M. A. Eisenberg, "The Responsive Model of Contract Law," 36 *Stan. L. Rev.* 1107, 1117–27 (1984).

38. *See* Zetlin v. Hanson Holdings, Inc., 48 N.Y.2d 684, 421 N.Y.S.2d 877, 397 N.E.2d 387 (1979).

39. *See* Gerdes v. Reynolds, 28 N.Y.S.2d 622 (N.Y. Sup. Ct. 1941).

40. *See* Caplan v. Lionel Corp., 20 A.D.2d 301, 246 N.Y.S.2d 913, *aff'd*, 14 N.Y.2d 679, 198 N.E.2d 908, 249 N.Y.S.2d 877 (1964).

41. There are a number of reasons why a person might want to make a legally binding donative promise. For example, he might want to ensure performance by his estate if he dies before having performed the promise, or he might want the satisfaction of having completed an effective disposition, or he might want to protect his present aspirations against defeat by a less worthy future self.

42. *See* Thomas v. Thomas, 114 Eng. Rep. 330 (Q.B. 1842).

43. This issue is considered further in Chapter 7.

44. *Restatement (Second) of Contracts* § 73 (1979).

45. *Id.* at § 73 comment d.

46. *Id.* at §§ 73 comment f, 74.

47. *See* Schwartzreich v. Bauman-Basch, Inc., 231 N.Y. 196, 131 N.E. 887 (1921).

48. *Restatement (Second) of Contracts* § 89 (1979).

49. *See* Cal. Civ. Code §§ 1524, 1541, 1697; Mich. Comp. Laws Ann. § 566.1; N.Y. Gen. Oblig. Law § 5–1103.

50. U.C.C. § 2-209.

51. *See* Goodwin v. Agassiz, 283 Mass. 358, 186 N.E. 659 (1933).

52. *See* Strong v. Repide, 213 U.S. 419, 431 (1909).

53. 17 C.F.R. § 240.10b–5 (1987).

54. See the discussion under "Overruling" in Chapter 7.

55. *See, e.g.,* R. Dworkin, *Taking Rights Seriously* 22–31, 90–91 (1978).

56. For a contrary position, *see* R. Dworkin, *Taking Rights Seriously* 22–28 (1978). *See also* G. Hughes, "Rules, Policy and Decision Making," 77 *Yale L.J.* 411, 419 (1968).

57. The distinction drawn in the text is related to one drawn by Raz— "[r]ules prescribe relatively specific acts; principles prescribe highly unspecific actions." J. Raz, "Legal Principles and the Limits of Law," 81 *Yale L.J.* 823, 838 (1972) (hereafter Raz, "Legal Principles and the Limits of Law").

58. *See* Raz, "Legal Principles and the Limits of Law," *supra* note 57. *But see* R. Dworkin, *Taking Rights Seriously* 22–28, 71–80 (1978).

59. T. Kuhn, *The Structure of Scientific Revolutions* 10, 23, 181–87 (2d ed. 1970).

60. *Restatement [First] of Contracts* § 90 (1932).

61. L. Fuller & W. Perdue, "The Reliance Interest in Contract Damages" (pts. 1 & 2), 46 *Yale L.J.* 52, 373 (1936 & 1937).

62. U.C.C. § 2–302 (1982).

63. Escola v. Coca Cola Bottling Co., 24 Cal. 2d 453, 461, 150 P.2d 436, 440 (1944) (Traynor, J., concurring).

64. *Restatement (Second) of Torts* § 402A (1963 & 1964).

65. *See Restatement (Second) of Contracts* § 87(2) (1979).

66. *See id.* § 139.

67. *See* U.C.C. § 2–302 comment 2 (1982); A. Leff, "Unconscionability and the Code—The Emperor's New Clause," 115 *U. Pa. L. Rev.* 485, 489–95 & n.35 (1967).

68. *See* M. A. Eisenberg, "The Bargain Principle and Its Limits," 95 *Harv. L. Rev.* 741 (1982).

69. *See Restatement (Second) of Contracts* § 153 (1979).

70. *See Restatement [First] of Contracts* § 90 (1932); M. A. Eisenberg, "Donative Promises," 47 *U. Chi. L. Rev.* 1, 18–31 (1979).

71. Raz, "Legal Principles and the Limits of Law," *supra* note 57, at 833.

72. *See* American Law Institute, *Principles of Corporate Governance: Analysis and Recommendations* § 5.02 (Tent. Draft No. 5, 1986).

73. *See id.* § 4.01 (Tent. Draft No. 4, 1985); W. Keeton, D. Dobbs, R. Keeton & D. Owen, *Prosser & Keeton on the Law of Torts* § 132, at 1056–59 (5th ed. 1984).

74. *See Restatement (Second) of Contracts* §§ 350, 351 (1979).

75. *See* J. Raz, *The Authority of Law* 201–06 (1979); L. Becker, "Analogy in Legal Reasoning," 83 *Ethics* 248 (1973). For other important

discussions of reasoning by analogy, see M. Golding, *Legal Reasoning* 44–49, 102–11 (1984); J. Levin, "The Concept of the Judicial Decision," 33 *Case W. Res. L. Rev.* 208, 230–39 (1983).

76. E. Levi, *An Introduction to Legal Reasoning* (1948).

77. MacPherson v. Buick Motor Co., 217 N.Y. 382, 111 N.E. 1050 (1916).

78. M'Alister (or Donoghue) v. Stevenson, [1932] L.R. App. Cas. 562 (H.L. 1932).

79. E. Levi, *An Introduction to Legal Reasoning* 1, 2, 5 (1948).

80. *Id.* at 8–9.

81. Heaven v. Pender, 11 Q.B.D. 503, 506 (1883) (Brett, M.R., concurring).

82. E. Levi, *An Introduction to Legal Reasoning* 16–17 (1948).

83. *Id.* at 17.

84. *Id.* at 27.

85. *See* P. Westen, "On 'Confusing Ideas': Reply," 91 *Yale L.J.* 1153, 1161–64 (1982).

86. Losee v. Clute, 51 N.Y. 494 (1873).

87. Statler v. George A. Ray Manufacturing Co., 195 N.Y. 478, 88 N.E. 1063 (1909).

88. Bennett v. Bennett, 116 N.Y. 584, 23 N.E. 17 (1889).

89. *Bennett,* 116 N.Y. at 590–91, 23 N.E. at 18–19.

90. Oppenheim v. Kridel, 236 N.Y. 156, 140 N.E. 227 (1923).

91. *Oppenheim,* 236 N.Y. at 160, 140 N.E. at 228.

92. *Oppenheim,* 236 N.Y. at 161–62, 168, 140 N.E. at 229, 231.

93. D v. National Society for the Prevention of Cruelty to Children, [1977] 1 All E.R. 589 (H.L.).

94. *Id.* at 595 (Diplock, L.). The other opinions were in substantial accord with that of Lord Diplock. For example, Lord Hailsham stated: "Once . . . it is accepted that information given to the police in the instant case would have been protected, it becomes, in my judgment, manifestly absurd that protection should not be accorded equally to the same information if given by the same informant to the local authority (who would have been under a duty to act on it) or to the appellant society, to whom according to the undisputed evidence, ordinary informants more readily resort. . . .

". . . It may well be that neither the police, the local authority, nor the society can give an absolute guarantee. The informant may in some cases have to give evidence under subpoena. In other cases their identity may come to light in other ways. But the police, the local authority and the society stand on the same footing. The public interest is identical in relation to each. The guarantee of confidentiality has the same and not different values in relation to each. It follows that the society is entitled to succeed on the appeal." *Id.* at 604.

95. *See* B. Boyer, "Promissory Estoppel: Principle from Precedents" (pts. 1 & 2), 50 *Mich. L. Rev.* 639, 873 (1952); W. Shattuck, "Gratuitous Promises—A New Writ?" 35 *Mich. L. Rev.* 908 (1937).

96. The same problem may arise whenever a new rule is established, even if reasoning by analogy is not involved. For example, in Klinicki v. Lundgren, 298 Or. 662, 695 P.2d 906 (1985), the court established the rules of Oregon law governing the taking of a corporate opportunity by a corporate officer. The corporation involved in *Klinicki* was closely held, and the court limited the applicability of the rules it established to such corporations, leaving to another day whether the same rules were applicable to corporations that were publicly held. This approach was prudent if there was a reasonable likelihood that closely and publicly held corporations were distinguishable for these purposes, but questionable if there was not.

97. *Oppenheim*, 236 N.Y. at 166, 140 N.E. at 231.

98. Ploof v. Putnam, 81 Vt. 471, 71 A. 188 (1908).

99. *Ploof*, 81 Vt. at 474–75, 71 A. at 189.

100. *Cf.* J. Gordley, "Legal Reasoning: An Introduction," 72 *Calif. L. Rev.* 138, 147–48 (1984). Similarly, in the *NSPCC* case, Lord Diplock stated: "Your Lordships' sense of values might well be open to reproach if this House were to treat the confidentiality of information given to those who are authorised by statute to institute proceedings for the protection of neglected or ill-treated children as entitled to less favourable treatment in a court of law than information given to the Gaming Board so that gaming may be kept clean." [1977] 1 All E.R. at 595.

101. Of course, the courts may also reason by analogy from rules that are not technically binding, such as cases from other jurisdictions. This form of reasoning by analogy is a special case of reasoning from the professional literature. See the discussion in the next section.

In reasoning from precedent, the court starts with a rule that is applicable on its face. In reasoning by analogy, it does not. As a practical matter, the former type of rule is more likely to be ready to hand than the latter. Finding a rule that is applicable on its face requires only relatively straightforward research skills. Finding rules that are applicable by analogy may require legal imagination as well. Typically, however, any important analogical rules will be readily turned up by a search of secondary sources, like treatises and law review articles, because authors of those sources are likely to have considered the issue.

102. L. Friedman, R. Kagan, B. Cartwright & S. Wheeler, "State Supreme Courts: A Century of Style and Citation," 33 *Stan. L. Rev.* 773, 796–808, 810–16 (1981). The one-fourth figure understates the total citations to nonlocal precedents, because it does not include citations to federal cases or to cases decided by lower or parallel courts in the same jurisdiction. I have excluded citations to federal cases because federal

decisions are characteristically cited by state courts on issues of federal rather than state law. Citations to cases decided by lower or parallel courts in the same jurisdiction are not included because Friedman, Kagan, Cartwright, & Wheeler did not provide data on such citations.

See also B. Canon & L. Baum, "Patterns of Adoption of Tort Law Innovations: An Application of Diffusion Theory to Judicial Doctrines," 75 *Am. Pol. Sci. Rev.* 975 (1981); J. Merryman, "Toward a Theory of Citations: An Empirical Study of the Citation Practice of the California Supreme Court in 1950, 1960, and 1970," 50 *S. Cal. L. Rev.* 381 (1977); J. Merryman, "The Authority of Authority: What the California Supreme Court Cited in 1950," 6 *Stan. L. Rev.* 613 (1954). *See generally* M. Shapiro, "Decentralized Decision-Making in the Law of Torts," in *Political Decision-Making* (S. Ulmer ed. 1970) (hereafter Shapiro, "Decentralized Decision-Making").

103. Shapiro, "Decentralized Decision-Making," *supra* note 102, at 50.

104. Vincent v. Lake Erie Transportation Co., 109 Minn. 456, 124 N.W. 221 (1910).

105. *Vincent*, 109 Minn. at 460, 124 N.W. at 222. The court also employed a third hypothetical, which is less compelling than those set out in the text: "In Depue v. Flateau, 100 Minn. 299, 111 N.W. 1, 8 L.R.A. (N.S.) 485, this court held that where the plaintiff, while lawfully in the defendants' house, became so ill that he was incapable of traveling with safety, the defendants were responsible to him in damages for compelling him to leave the premises. If, however, the owner of the premises had furnished the traveler with proper accommodations and medical attendance, would he have been able to defeat an action brought against him for their reasonable worth?" 109 Minn. at 459, 124 N.W. at 222.

106. Roberson v. Rochester Folding Box Co., 171 N.Y. 538, 64 N.E. 442 (1902).

107. *Roberson*, 171 N.Y. at 544–45, 554–55, 64 N.E. at 443, 447.

7. Overruling and Other Modes of Overturning

1. The primary and secondary literature tracing the rise and fall of the charitable-immunity doctrine is profuse. F. Harper, F. James & O. Gray, *The Law of Torts* §§ 29.16–17 (2d ed. 1986) (hereinafter Harper, James & Gray, *The Law of Torts*), Annotation, "Immunity of nongovernmental charity from liability," 25 A.L.R.2d 29 (1952), Annotation, "Tort immunity of nongovernmental charities—modern status," 25 A.L.R.4th 517 (1983), President and Directors of Georgetown College v. Hughes, 130 F.2d 810 (D.C. Cir. 1942), Collopy v. Newark Eye and

Ear Infirmary, 27 N.J. 29, 141 A.2d 276 (1958), and Bing v. Thunig, 2 N.Y.2d 656, 143 N.E.2d 3, 163 N.Y.S.2d 3 (1957), together provide an excellent description and critique of the doctrine and its exceptions at various stages. The discussion in the text draws on these sources for that purpose.

Descriptions of the history of a doctrine in terms of applicable social propositions must be qualified in two ways. First, courts that establish doctrines may not give all their reasons for doing so, and some reasons must sometimes be reconstructed. Second, it will be recalled that the task of the court in employing social propositions to establish legal rules is not to determine whether the social propositions truly meet the requisite criteria, but to use an appropriate methodology to determine whether the requisite criteria are met, and to respond appropriately to criticism of that determination in the professional and other discourse. Correspondingly, in recounting the history of a doctrine the issue is not what social propositions actually met the requisite criteria at any given time, but what propositions seemed to meet those criteria. It would be tedious to hedge the histories recounted in the text with continual references to these qualifications, but they should be taken as implied.

2. *See, e.g.*, President and Directors of Georgetown College v. Hughes, 130 F.2d 810, 823–24 (D.C. Cir. 1942): "No statistical evidence has been presented to show that the mortality or crippling of charities has been greater in states which impose full or partial liability than where complete or substantially full immunity is given. Nor is there evidence that deterrence of donation has been greater in the former. Charities seem to survive and increase in both, with little apparent heed to whether they are liable for torts or difference in survival capacity.

"Further, if there is danger of dissipation, insurance is now available to guard against it and prudent management will provide the protection. It is highly doubtful that any substantial charity would be destroyed or donation deterred by the cost required to pay the premiums. . . . What is at stake, so far as the charity is concerned, is the cost of reasonable protection, the amount of the insurance premium as an added burden on its finances, not the awarding over in damages of its entire assets."

3. *See, e.g.*, Haynes v. Presbyterian Hosp. Ass'n, 241 Iowa 1269, 1273, 45 N.W.2d 151, 154 (1950); Parker v. Port Huron Hosp., 361 Mich. 1, 24–25, 105 N.W.2d 1, 12–13 (1960).

4. *See, e.g.*, Bing v. Thunig, 2 N.Y.2d 656, 666, 143 N.E.2d 3, 8, 163 N.Y.S.2d 3, 10–11 (1957): "It is not too much to expect that those who serve and minister to members of the public should do so, as do all others, subject to that principle and within the obligation not to injure through carelessness. It is not alone good morals but sound law that individuals and organizations should be just before they are generous,

and there is no reason why that should not apply to charitable hospitals. 'Charity suffereth long and is kind, but in the common law it cannot be careless. When it is, it ceases to be kindness and becomes actionable wrongdoing.' . . . Insistence upon *respondeat superior* and damages for negligent injury serves a two-fold purpose, for it both assures payment of an obligation to the person injured and gives warning that justice and the law demand the exercise of care."

5. *See Bing*, 2 N.Y. 2d at 660–61, 143 N.E.2d at 4-5, 163 N.Y.S.2d at 6.

6. Boeckel v. Orange Memorial Hosp., 108 N.J.L. 453, 158 A. 832 (1932), *aff'd*, 110 N.J.L. 509, 166 A. 146 (1933).

7. Kolb v. Monmouth Memorial Hosp., 116 N.J. 118, 182 A. 822 (1936).

8. Bianchi v. South Park Presbyterian Church, 123 N.J.L. 325, 8 A.2d 567 (1939).

9. Jewell v. St. Peter's Parish, 10 N.J. Super. 229, 76 A.2d 917 (1950).

10. Cullen v. Schmit, 139 Ohio St. 194, 39 N.E.2d 146 (1942).

11. Williams v. First United Church of Christ, 37 Ohio St. 2d 150, 309 N.E.2d 924 (1974).

12. Eads v. Young Women's Christian Ass'n, 325 Mo. 577, 29 S.W.2d 701 (1930).

13. Blatt v. George H. Nettleton Home for Aged Women, 365 Mo. 30, 275 S.W.2d 344 (1955).

14. Similarly, it lacked evenhandedness to differentiate, as the courts did, between the liability of charitable residences, day-care centers, camps, auditoriums, and cemeteries on the one hand, and their commercial counterparts on the other. *Cf.* Thornton v. Franklin Square House, 200 Mass. 465, 86 N.E. 909 (1909) (organization providing housing for working women at market-or-below rates, with unpaid officers and donated furnishings, was charitable); Albritton v. Neighborhood Centers Ass'n for Child Dev., 12 Ohio St. 3d 210, 466 N.E.2d 867 (1984) (nonprofit day-care corporation receiving some government funds was charitable); Fitzer v. Greater Greenville S.C. Young Men's Christian Ass'n, 277 S.C. 1, 282 S.E.2d 230 (1981) (camp operated by YMCA, which plaintiff attended for a fee, may have been either charitable or commercial); Esposito v. Henry H. Stambaugh Auditorium Ass'n, Inc., 49 Ohio L. Abs. 507, 77 N.E.2d 111 (Ohio Ct. App. 1946) (nonprofit corporation which owned and maintained community auditorium, and received donations for it, had charitable immunity in action by a community resident who paid admission to see performers who had rented the auditorium); Felan v. Lucey, 259 S.W.2d 302 (Tex. Civ. App. 1953) (cemetery owned and operated by a church, which sold right of sepulture, had charitable immunity); Lawlor v. Cloverleaf Memorial Park, Inc., 56 N.J. 326, 266 A.2d 569 (1970) (privately promoted non-religious cemetery association did not have charitable immunity).

15. Moragne v. States Marine Lines, Inc., 398 U.S. 375, 403–04 (1970) (quoting H. Hart & A. Sacks, *The Legal Process* 577 (tent. ed. 1958)).

16. President and Directors of Georgetown College v. Hughes, 130 F.2d 810, 817 (D.C. Cir. 1942).

17. *See* J. Appleman, "The Tort Liability of Charitable Institutions," 22 *A.B.A. J.* 48, 55 (1936); Note, "The Insurance Modification of Charitable Institution Immunity from Tort Liability," 43 *Ill. L. Rev.* 248, 250 (1948); Note, "Insurance—Governmental, Charitable, and Intrafamily Immunity from Tort Liability," 33 *Minn. L. Rev.* 634, 650–54 (1949).

Even an institution that did not obtain liability insurance would have saved the premiums it would have paid. The net cost of its reliance would therefore be only the difference between the amount of the judgment and the cost of the premiums it would have paid over the years if it had not relied and had insured.

18. See Note, 43 *Ill. L. Rev.* 248, *supra* note 17, at 250; Note, 33 *Minn. L. Rev.*, *supra* note 17, at 642–43 & n.39.

19. It is also worth noting that insurers go to great lengths to prevent being named as defendants in lawsuits against their insureds. It would be somewhat anomalous to allow insurers to avoid the role of defendant while setting up their reliance as an effective defense.

Another type of reliance sometimes claimed in immunity cases is failure to investigate accidents promptly. *See, e.g.*, Molitor v. Kaneland Community Unit District No. 302, 18 Ill.2d 11, 28–29, 163 N.E.2d 89, 98 (1959), *cert. denied*, 362 U.S. 968 (1960). It's hard to put much stock in this claim. If the charitable institution was insured, the insurance company would have been likely to investigate. Even an uninsured institution would have been likely to investigate, because often it would not be clear at the time of the injury whether an exception to the immunity doctrine applied. Furthermore, it would be morally unjustified for an institution to fail to conduct an investigation to determine whether its personnel and procedures were safe. Although an investigation for that purpose might be less thorough than an investigation for liability purposes, the difference hardly seems sufficient to prevent overruling on the ground of reliance.

20. *See* Harper, James, & Gray, *The Law of Torts, supra* note 1, § 29.17 & n.3; *Restatement (Second) of Torts* § 895D-E (1977).

According to a 1982 Appendix to *Restatement (Second) of Torts* § 895E, of 53 jurisdictions (made up of the 50 states, the District of Columbia, Puerto Rico, and the Virgin Islands), 35 do not provide an immunity for any charitable institutions. Of the remaining 18, 6 have abolished the immunity for charitable hospitals but retained it for other charities, and 8 limit the immunity to charitable trust funds, so that it does not bar suit to the extent that the claim is covered by insurance. In some jurisdictions the doctrine was legislatively abolished rather than judicially overruled. *See* Conn. Gen. Stat. Ann. § 52–557(d); Nev. Rev. Stat. § 41.480; N.C. Gen. Stat. § 1–539.9.

There were a few countercurrents. When the Massachusetts court gave notice that it would overrule the immunity, the legislature responded by abolishing the charitable-immunity rule as such, but placing a $20,000 ceiling on a tort recovery against a charitable institution. See Colby v. Carney Hosp., 356 Mass. 527, 254 N.E.2d 407 (1969); Mass. Gen. Laws Ann. ch. 231, § 85K. When the New Jersey court overruled the charitable-immunity doctrine, the legislature responded by reinstating the immunity (subject to certain exceptions), but permitting recovery against hospitals in an amount not exceeding $10,000. *See* Collopy v. Newark Eye and Ear Infirmary, 27 N.J. 29, 141 A.2d 276 (1958); N.J. Stat. Ann. § 2A:53A-7–11; Comment, "Torts: Charitable Immunity," 10 *Rutgers L.J.* 393 (1985). Finally, several courts declined to overrule the doctrine. *See* Harper, James & Gray, *The Law of Torts, supra* note 1, § 29.17, at 768 & n.30.

21. See the discussion of this doctrine under "Reasoning from Precedent" in Chapter 6.

22. In many cases the ultimate buyer could have sued his vendor on breach of the implied warranty of fitness, and his vendor could then have sued the manufacturer on the same theory, so that even under the old doctrine a manufacturer might ultimately have borne the loss caused by his negligence.

23. Devlin v. Smith, 89 N.Y. 470 (1882).

24. Statler v. George A. Ray Manufacturing Co., 195 N.Y. 478, 88 N.E. 1063 (1909).

25. See the discussion of this rule under "Reasoning from Precedent" in Chapter 6.

26. *See* B. Boyer, "Promissory Estoppel: Principle from Precedents" (pts. 1 & 2), 50 *Mich. L. Rev.* 639, 873 (1952); W. Shattuck, "Gratuitous Promises—A New Writ?" 35 *Mich. L. Rev.* 908 (1937).

27. Of course, markers of any kind are sometimes misplaced, and the ultimate question is not whether the marker of professional criticism is in place but whether the conditions for overruling have been satisfied. Correspondingly, if it is clear that a court does not propose to respond to criticism of a doctrine by overruling, the profession is justified in taking the doctrine as law and rendering opinions on which clients can confidently rely. Even in such cases, however, there may be an issue whether reliance is justified if the client knowingly acts in a manner that violates existing social standards.

28. Tucker v. Howard L. Carmichael & Sons, Inc., 208 Ga. 201, 203–04, 206, 65 S.E.2d 909, 910–11, 912 (1951).

29. Thellusson v. Woodford, 4 Vessey 227, 322, 31 Eng. Rep. 117, 163 (1798–99).

30. *See* Harper, James & Gray, *The Law of Torts, supra* note 1, § 18.3, at 672; W. Keeton, D. Dobbs, R. Keeton, & D. Owen, Prosser & Keeton on the Law of Torts § 55, at 368 (5th ed. 1984); Note, "The Case of the Prenatal Injury," 15 *U. Fla. L. Rev.* 527, 534–35 (1963).

The status of an action on behalf of a nonviable or nonsurviving fetus is less clear. As to the viability issue: "Most of the cases allowing recovery have involved a fetus which was then viable, meaning capable of independent life, if only in an incubator. Many of them have said, by way of dictum, that recovery must be limited to such cases, and others have said that the child, if not viable, must at least be 'quick.' But when actually faced with the issue for decision, most courts have allowed recovery, even though the injury occurred during the early weeks of pregnancy, when the child was neither viable nor quick." Keeton, Dobbs, Keeton & Owen, *supra*, at 368-69. *See also* Harper, James & Gray, *supra*, § 18.3, at 677–78.

As to the survival issue: "Here, of course, the mother may recover for her injury, including the miscarriage, and the only question is whether the estate or survivors of the unborn child may have a separate recovery. To allow the former would recognize an interest in being born alive. And however great the spiritual and moral value of such an interest, its claim to pecuniary compensation is far more tenuous and doubtful than that of the child who lives to bear the seal of defendant's negligence with all the conscious suffering and economic loss it may entail. The interest of the survivors is distinguishable. A number of cases have allowed separate recovery to survivors where the child is not born alive, although there remains considerable support for the view that the question of live birth is the fairest and most practical place to draw the line." Harper, James & Gray, *supra*, § 18.3, at 679–81. *See also* Keeton, Dobbs, Keeton & Owen, *supra*, § 55, at 369–70.

The present state of the law on injury to a fetus brings out that whether a doctrine has become jagged for purposes of overruling must sometimes be determined not only by the state of the case-law but by its direction. For example, an exception for fetuses who were injured before they were viable might be viewed as inconsistent with the new rule. That would not make the new rule jagged for overruling purposes, because the direction of the case-law was not to adopt the new rule and then create the exception, but to provisionally state the new rule at less than its fullest level of generality. See the discussion under "Reasoning by Analogy" in Chapter 6, and "The Drawing of Inconsistent Distinctions" in this chapter.

31. The absence of significant criticism in the professional literature does not prove that a deciding court would be wrong to overrule: per-

haps the doctrine is new or there has been a new change in the social propositions on which the doctrine rests.

32. See the discussion under "Reasoning from Precedent" in Chapter 6, and "The Drawing of Inconsistent Distinctions" in this chapter.

33. A special problem may arise where the validity of a transaction can be subject to challenge long after the transaction occurs. In such cases a doctrine may have become jagged or criticized, or moral norms and policies may have changed, after a transaction occurred but while it is still open to judicial review. This problem is not unique to overruling. It can occur even in the case of an incremental change—for example, through a loosening of the rigor with which a tort plaintiff must prove causation, or with which a contract plaintiff must prove that his damages were reasonably foreseeable.

There are two administrative reasons for not tailoring institutional principles to reflect this problem. First, the problem is likely to occur only infrequently: moral norms are usually very durable, policies that are not durable normally should not be taken into account, jaggedness should lead to overruling only when it has become established, and the statute of limitations will usually preclude suit on transactions that have occurred substantially before suit is brought. Second, it is probably too difficult for the courts to decide on a case-by-case basis whether material and relevant changes in jaggedness or social propositions have in fact occurred between the time of the transaction and the time of the challenge.

34. Norcross v. James, 140 Mass. 188, 2 N.E. 946 (1885).

35. Shade v. M. O'Keefe, Inc., 260 Mass. 180, 156 N.E. 867 (1927).

36. Shell Oil Co. v. Henry Ouellette & Sons Co., 352 Mass. 725, 227 N.E.2d 509 (1967).

37. *Ouellette,* 352 Mass. at 730, 227 N.E.2d at 512.

38. *Ouellette,* 352 Mass. at 730–31, 227 N.E.2d at 512–13.

39. Gulf Oil Corp. v. Fall River Housing Authority, 364 Mass. 492, 306 N.E.2d 257 (1974).

40. Whitinsville Plaza, Inc. v. Kotseas, 378 Mass. 85, 390 N.E.2d 243 (1979).

41. *Whitinsville Plaza,* 378 Mass. at 98, 390 N.E.2d at 250. On the technique I call signaling, see K. Llewellyn, *The Common Law Tradition: Deciding Appeals* 299–309 (1960); P. Mishkin & C. Morris, *On Laws in Courts* 297–303 (1965).

42. *See, e.g.,* Javins v. First Nat'l Realty Corp., 428 F.2d 1071 (D.C. Cir.) (implied warranty of habitability), *cert. denied,* 400 U.S. 925 (1970); Sommer v. Kridel, 74 N.J. 446, 378 A.2d 767 (1977) (duty to mitigate). The implied warranty of habitability is not identical to the implied warranty of merchantability, but the differences can by and large be justified by functional differences in the underlying subject matter.

43. An issue closely related to overruling is whether a lower court should follow a higher-court precedent in cases where it believes the higher court would overrule the precedent if given the opportunity. The practice of declining to follow precedents in such cases is usually referred to as "anticipatory overruling." I shall use that terminology here, although it is somewhat imprecise because a lower court cannot formally overrule an upper court's decision.

The propriety of anticipatory overruling has been most extensively discussed in connection with decisions by lower federal courts. *See, e.g.*, M. Kniffin, "Overruling Supreme Court Precedents: Anticipatory Action by United States Courts of Appeals," 51 *Fordham L. Rev.* 53 (1982). The issue is particularly salient in the federal-court system, in which the Supreme Court reviews very few cases because of its limited resources, and for most purposes the Courts of Appeals are therefore courts of last resort. It is easy to see why the practice of anticipatory overruling should be adopted in such a regime. Suppose that *Jones v. Smith* is up for decision in a Court of Appeals. Under *Brown v. Green*, a Supreme Court decision, Jones would prevail. However, the Court of Appeals rightly believes that if *Jones v. Smith* reached the Supreme Court, that Court would overrule or otherwise overturn *Brown v. Green* and hold for Smith. If the Court of Appeals nevertheless held for Jones, the chances of Supreme Court review would be slim, because the Court takes up so few cases. Under these circumstances, following *Brown v. Green* would be unjust to Smith and would delay, perhaps for a very long period, the announcement of the proper legal rule. Accordingly, both fairness and institutional considerations suggest that in determining whether a case should be anticipatorily overruled, the lower federal courts should replicate the reasoning the Supreme Court uses to determine whether a case should be actually overruled. The same analysis is applicable to any state-court system in which, because of limited resources, the highest court refuses to review a number of cases.

Suppose that in a given state the highest court reviews substantially all the cases that litigants want to appeal. It is still desirable that lower courts should replicate higher-court reasoning. The practical effect of not adopting the practice of anticipatory overruling is to force appeals and delay announcement of the new rule. Appeals are costly to both the litigants and the courts, and it is socially desirable that a new and better rule be officially announced as early as possible.

44. Stephen Munzer has argued that if a rule is reasonably knowable when a transaction occurred, "there is nothing 'retroactive' about applying it to events occurring after the rule has come into existence as part of a legal system." Munzer, "Retroactive Law," 6 *J. Legal Stud.* 373, 377 (1977) (discussing H. Wellington's analysis in "Common Law Rules and Constitutional Double Standards: Some Notes on Adjudi-

cation," 83 *Yale L.J.* 221, 257–58 (1973)). There is force to this argument—indeed, it identifies the reason why application of the newly formulated rule is fair—but it seems more accurate to say that a newly formulated rule has elements of both retroactivity and nonretroactivity.

45. *See, e.g.,* Goller v. White, 20 Wis. 2d 402, 122 N.W.2d 193 (1963).

There is a great deal of literature on prospective overruling, but much of it deals with overruling the interpretation of a constitutional or statutory provision. Prospective overruling in this context often involves special considerations, particularly where the provision relates to civil or criminal procedure or to the substantive criminal law. On prospective overruling in the common law, see P. Mishkin & C. Morris, *On Laws in Courts* 293–317 (1965).

46. *See, e.g.,* Williams v. City of Detroit, 364 Mich. 231, 111 N.W.2d 1 (1961).

47. Spanel v. Mounds View School District No. 621, 264 Minn. 279, 118 N.W.2d 795 (1962).

48. Molitor v. Kaneland Community Unit District No. 302, 18 Ill. 2d 11, 26–27, 163 N.E.2d 89, 97 (1959).

49. *Molitor,* 24 Ill. 2d 467, 182 N.E.2d 145 (1962).

50. Li v. Yellow Cab Co., 13 Cal. 3d 804, 532 P.2d 1226, 119 Cal. Rptr. 858 (1975).

51. Tucker v. Budoian, 376 Mass. 907, 384 N.E.2d 1195 (1978).

52. Whitney v. City of Worcester, 373 Mass. 208, 210, 366 N.E.2d 1210, 1212 (1977).

53. *Whitney,* 373 Mass. at 210–12, 366 N.E.2d at 1212–13. The court added that if the legislature did not act, the overruling would be retroactive to the date of a prior opinion in which overruling had been signaled. "While there was widespread and justifiable reliance on the immunity doctrine prior to our decision in *Morash & Sons v. Commonwealth,* 363 Mass. 612 (1973), we think that subsequent to that opinion further reliance was misplaced. Accordingly, if the doctrine is to be changed by future action of this court, it is our intention to abrogate the principle as to all injuries which occurred since the publication of *Morash* on May 13, 1973." 373 Mass. at 225, 366 N.E.2d at 1219–20.

54. L. Kaplow, "An Economic Analysis of Legal Transitions," 99 *Harv. L. Rev.* 509, 599–600, 615 (1986).

55. A number of the cases that utilize prospective overruling seem relatively unsophisticated in determining whether there was justifiable reliance on the old rule. For example, Spanel v. Mounds View School District No. 621, 264 Minn. 279, 118 N.W.2d 795 (Minn. 1962), invoked reliance as a ground for prospectivity while justifying overruling in part on the ground that "the handwriting has long been on the courtroom wall." 264 Minn. at 285, 118 N.W.2d at 799. In some of these cases,

however, prospective overruling could have been supported on the alternative ground that overruling would probably be legislatively overturned. *Spanel* itself falls in this category. *See* 264 Minn. at 292–93, 118 N.W.2d at 804–05.

56. MacPherson v. Buick Motor Co., 217 N.Y. 382, 111 N.E. 1050 (1916).

57. Sherlock v. Stillwater Clinic, 260 N.W.2d 169 (Minn. 1977).

58. *See* Loop v. Litchfield, 42 N.Y. 351 (1870); Losee v. Clute, 51 N.Y. 494 (1873).

59. Letter from Peter Westen to the author, February 1, 1987.

60. *See* R. Davis, "A Re-examination of the Doctrine of MacPherson v. Buick and Its Application and Extension in the State of New York," 24 *Fordham L. Rev.* 204 (1955).

61. *See, e.g.,* Briggs v. Miller, 176 Wis. 321, 186 N.W. 163 (1922).

62. *See, e.g.,* Feinberg v. Pfeiffer Co., 322 S.W.2d 163 (Mo. Ct. App. 1959).

63. *See, e.g.,* Dickinson v. Dodds, 2 Ch. D. 463 (C.A. 1876).

64. *See, e.g.,* Drennan v. Star Paving Co., 51 Cal. 2d 409, 333 P.2d 757 (1958).

65. See the discussion under "Reasoning from Precedent" and "Reasoning from Principle" in Chapter 6.

66. *See, e.g.,* Kirksey v. Kirksey, 8 Ala. 131 (1845).

67. *See, e.g.,* James Baird Co. v. Gimbel Bros., Inc., 64 F.2d 344 (2d Cir. 1933).

68. *See, e.g.,* Sardo v. Fidelity & Deposit Co., 100 N.J. Eq. 332, 134 A. 774 (1926).

69. R. Dworkin, *Law's Empire* 225, 226, 240 (1986).

70. *Id.* at 217.

71. *Id.* at 96–97, 164–65.

72. *Id.* at 218. The only exception Dworkin admits is that in some cases the judge might decide for moral reasons to depart from the law. *Id.* at 218–19.

73. See the discussion under "Reasoning by Analogy" in Chapter 6.

74. Of course, this doesn't mean that courts simply "find" or "discover" the law. Judgment is required to determine such matters as what moral norms and policies have the requisite social support, how these norms and policies are mediated by experiential propositions, how to fashion social standards into efficacious legal rules, how to elaborate doctrinal rules so as to make them applicable to specific cases, how to deal with cases where norms, policies, and doctrines collide, and so forth.

75. *See* R. Dworkin, *Law's Empire* 67–68, 119–20, 228–31, 238–39, 244, 248–50, 255–57 (1986). Fit can be relevant under the convictions thesis even after the threshold-fit test is passed, because the judge's

substantive convictions may require him to consider the extent as well as the fact of fit. Conversely, the judge's notions of what constitutes fit will depend partly on his substantive convictions. *See id.* at 231, 236–37, 246–50, 257.

76. *See, e.g.,* R. Sartorius, *Individual Conduct and Social Norms* 181–210 (1975); Sartorius, "Social Policy and Judicial Legislation," 8 *Am. Phil. Q.* 151 (1971); Sartorius, "The Justification of the Judicial Decision," 78 *Ethics* 171 (1968).

77. *See* R. Dworkin, *Taking Rights Seriously* 341 (1978).

78. R. Dworkin, *Law's Empire* 238–50 (1986).

79. See the discussion under "Reasoning from Precedent" in Chapter 6.

80. McLoughlin v. O'Brian, [1983] 1 App. Cas. 410 (H.L. (E.) 1982).

81. R. Dworkin, *Law's Empire* 238–50 (1986).

82. Dworkin recognizes that as a matter of conviction the judge may decide to refer to social morality, but he need do so only if and to the extent his convictions require. *See id.* at 249–50.

Of course, under the convictions thesis, or any other theory that makes the judge's personal morality relevant, the judge should not employ his own convictions because they are his own convictions, but because he believes they are the convictions the best morality would require. From the perspective of the institutional principles of adjudication, however, this distinction is not significant, because almost everyone thinks his own moral convictions are the convictions that the best morality would require, and thinks the method by which he arrives at his convictions is the best method for arriving at moral convictions.

83. See the discussion under "Reasoning from Principle" in Chapter 6.

84. R. Dworkin, *Law's Empire* 95, 151, 410 (1986).

8. The Theory of the Common Law

1. H. L. A. Hart, *The Concept of Law* 78–79 (1961).

2. *Id.* at 92. Hart sometimes formulates the distinction between primary and secondary rules in other terms. *See* C. Tapper, "Powers and Secondary Rules of Change," in *Oxford Essays in Jurisprudence* 242 (2d ser. A. Simpson ed. 1973).

3. H. L. A. Hart, *The Concept of Law* 92 (1961).

4. *Id.*

5. *Id.* at 100. Two other types of secondary rules are rules of change and rules of adjudication. A rule of change empowers an official to introduce new primary rules and to eliminate old ones. *Id.* at 93. A rule of adjudication empowers an official to determine authoritatively whether a primary rule has been broken. *Id.* at 94.

6. *See id.* at 123–24; Hart, "Problems of Philosophy of Law," 6 *Encyclopedia of Philosophy* 264, 270–71 (1967).

7. Even under a binary analysis of adjudication, like that of Hart, a rule adopted in a past text may by its terms require the employment of social propositions for its application. This would be true, for example, of a rule whose application turned on trade usage. Social propositions would not be relevant, however, in establishing the content of the rule itself.

8. H. L. A. Hart, *The Concept of Law* 124 (1961) (emphasis in original).

9. *Id.* at 132.

10. *Id.*

11. J. Raz, *The Authority of Law* 43–45 (1979).

12. *Id.* at 43, 105.

13. *Id.* at 172.

14. *Id.* at 71, 181.

15. *Id.* at 90, 96.

16. *Id.* at 48–50.

17. *Id.* at 182.

18. *Id.* at 96.

19. *Id.* at 193.

20. *Id.* at 181–82.

21. *Id.* at 48–50.

22. *Id.* at 59, 96, 113.

23. *Id.* at 197.

24. *Id.* at 200–201. Raz recognizes that in practice adjudication is seldom if ever as mechanical as his binary model suggests it often should be, but he argues that this is not because the model is inaccurate, but because regulated cases can be more complex than unregulated cases, because regulated cases tend to shade into unregulated cases, and because the reasoning used to justify lawmaking in unregulated cases is often similar to the reasoning used to justify law-application in regulated cases. *Id.* at 182, 206–09.

25. *See* on this issue, J. Raz, "Authority, Law and Morality," 68 *The Monist* 295 (1985).

26. J. Raz, *The Authority of Law* 87 (1979).

27. *Id.* at 51–52.

28. *Id.*

29. *See generally* Joint Committee of the Real Property Law Section of the State Bar of California and the Real Property Section of the Los Angeles County Bar Association, "Legal Opinions in California Real Estate Transactions," 42 *Bus. Law.* 1139, 1151–53 (1987); Vagts, "Legal Opinions in Quantitative Terms: The Lawyer as Haruspex or Bookie?" 34 *Bus. Law.* 421 (1979).

30. *Cf.* Rosenberg v. Lipnick, 337 Mass. 666, 389 N.E.2d 385 (1979).

31. F. A. Hayek, *The Road to Serfdom* 72 (1944).

32. *Cf.* H. Hart & A. Sacks, *The Legal Process* 396–98 (tent. ed. 1958). Of course, constitutions and statutes are not comprehensive. However, since the common law applies when neither constitution nor statute governs, if the common law is comprehensive so is the law.

33. H. L. A. Hart, *The Concept of Law* 198 (1961). *See also* H. L. A. Hart, *Essays on Bentham* 153–61, 262–68 (1982). Raz takes a different position, which is criticized by Hart. *See* J. Raz, *The Authority of Law* 153–57 (1979). *See generally* P. Soper, *A Theory of Law* (1984); Soper, "Metaphors and Models of Law: The Judge as Priest," 75 *Mich. L. Rev.* 1196, 1205–09 (1977).

34. *See* H. L. A. Hart, "Positivism and the Separation of Law and Morals," 71 *Harv. L. Rev.* 593 (1958).

35. Although this book is concerned with the common law, the generative conception might be extended, with suitable modifications, to statutory and constitutional law. Those bodies of law differ from the common law in that they are rooted in canonical texts, which the courts cannot properly reformulate. However, the application of a canonical text to a given case is frequently far from self-evident, and establishing the full meaning of such a text often requires the application of institutional principles of interpretation. *See, e.g.,* B. Barry, "Courts and Constitutions" (book review), *Times Literary Supp.,* Oct. 25, 1985, at 1195, 1196. The term *interpretation* suggests a process that focuses on the text, its context, its authorship, and its objectives, but in reality establishing the full meaning of a canonical text may also involve application of the standard of systemic consistency, the standard of doctrinal stability, and a standard of congruence with relevant social propositions (which in the case of canonical texts may include moral norms and policies embraced or subsumed in the text, even though they lack social support). It is, for example, not uncommon for a court to prefer a given reading of a statutory or constitutional text because that reading is given by a precedent, or because it makes the text more congruent with some relevant moral norm or policy, or more consistent with the body of the law, than would its alternatives. This is nicely illustrated by a trilogy of Supreme Court cases under the Securities Acts. In Schreiber v. Burlington Northern, Inc., 427 U.S. 1 (1985), the Court, in establishing the meaning of Section 14(e) of the Securities Exchange Act of 1934, gave weight to a precedent interpreting another section of the act that used similar language. In Blue Chip Stamps v. Manor Drug Stores, 421 U.S. 723 (1975), the Court, in establishing the meaning of Section 10(b) of the 1934 Act and Rule 10b-5, gave weight to "what may be described as policy considerations"—in particular, a concern with vexatious litigation that might be spawned by an alternative reading. 421 U.S. at 737. In Ernst & Ernst v. Hochfelder, 425 U.S. 185 (1976),

the Court, in establishing the meaning of Section 10(b) and Rule 10b-5, gave weight to the Securities Act of 1933, on the ground that "[t]he 1933 and 1934 Acts constitute interrelated components of the federal regulatory scheme governing transactions in securities." 425 U.S. at 206.

Therefore, although courts must faithfully employ constitutional and statutory texts in cases to which they are applicable, it might be said that constitutional and statutory law is not comprised solely of those texts, but consists of the rules that would be generated at the present moment by the application to those texts of the governing principles of interpretation (including the standard of doctrinal stability, the standard of systemic consistency, and a standard of congruence with relevant social propositions). Under this analysis, the content of all law in our society, not merely the common law, would be determined by the generative conception; that is, the law would consist of the rules that would be generated at the present moment by application of the institutional principles that determine how courts establish the common law and the full meaning of canonical texts.

Index